STUDY PLANNER

CHAPTER 01 문장의 형식	학습일	
UNIT 01	월	일
UNIT 02	월	일
UNIT 03	월	일
Review Test	월	일

CHAPTER 02 to부정사	학습일	
UNIT 04	월	일
UNIT 05	월	일
Review Test	월	일

CHAPTER 03 동명사	학습일	
UNIT 06	월	일
UNIT 07	월	일
Review Test	월	일

CHAPTER 04 현재완료	학습일	
UNIT 08	월	일
UNIT 09	월	일
Review Test	월	일

CHAPTER 05 조동사	학습일	
UNIT 10	월	일
UNIT 11	월	일
UNIT 12	월	일
Review Test	월	일

CHAPTER 06 명사, 부정대명사	학습일	
UNIT 13	월	일
UNIT 14	월	일
Review Test	월	일

CHAPTER 07 수동태	학습일	
UNIT 15	월	일
UNIT 16	월	일
UNIT 17	월	일
Review Test	월	일

CHAPTER 08 관계사	학습일	
UNIT 18	월	일
UNIT 19	월	일
UNIT 20	월	일
Review Test	월	일

CHAPTER 09 비교 구문	학습일	
UNIT 21	월	일
UNIT 22	월	일
Review Test	월	일

CHAPTER 10 형용사, 부사, 분사	학습일	
UNIT 23	월	일
UNIT 24	월	일
Review Test	월	일

CHAPTER 11 접속사	학습일	
UNIT 25	월	일
UNIT 26	월	일
Review Test	월	일

CHAPTER 12 의문문	학습일	
UNIT 27	월	일
UNIT 28	월	일
Review Test	월	일

CHAPTER 13 가정법	학습일	
UNIT 29	월	일
UNIT 30	월	일
Review Test	월	일

SCORECARD

CHAPTER 01 **문장의 형식**	점수	PASS
UNIT 01	/ 35점	30점
UNIT 02	/ 35점	30점
UNIT 03	/ 35점	30점
Review Test	/ 80점	68점

CHAPTER 02 **to부정사**	점수	PASS
UNIT 04	/ 30점	26점
UNIT 05	/ 30점	26점
Review Test	/ 60점	51점

CHAPTER 03 **동명사**	점수	PASS
UNIT 06	/ 30점	26점
UNIT 07	/ 30점	26점
Review Test	/ 60점	51점

CHAPTER 04 **현재완료**	점수	PASS
UNIT 08	/ 30점	26점
UNIT 09	/ 35점	30점
Review Test	/ 60점	51점

CHAPTER 05 **조동사**	점수	PASS
UNIT 10	/ 30점	26점
UNIT 11	/ 30점	26점
UNIT 12	/ 30점	26점
Review Test	/ 70점	60점

CHAPTER 06 **명사, 부정대명사**	점수	PASS
UNIT 13	/ 35점	30점
UNIT 14	/ 25점	22점
Review Test	/ 60점	51점

CHAPTER 07 **수동태**	점수	PASS
UNIT 15	/ 35점	30점
UNIT 16	/ 30점	26점
UNIT 17	/ 30점	26점
Review Test	/ 80점	68점

CHAPTER 08 **관계사**	점수	PASS
UNIT 18	/ 35점	30점
UNIT 19	/ 35점	30점
UNIT 20	/ 30점	26점
Review Test	/ 80점	68점

CHAPTER 09 **비교 구문**	점수	PASS
UNIT 21	/ 30점	26점
UNIT 22	/ 30점	26점
Review Test	/ 70점	60점

CHAPTER 10 **형용사, 부사, 분사**	점수	PASS
UNIT 23	/ 30점	26점
UNIT 24	/ 35점	30점
Review Test	/ 70점	60점

CHAPTER 11 **접속사**	점수	PASS
UNIT 25	/ 35점	30점
UNIT 26	/ 35점	30점
Review Test	/ 70점	60점

CHAPTER 12 **의문문**	점수	PASS
UNIT 27	/ 30점	26점
UNIT 28	/ 35점	30점
Review Test	/ 60점	51점

CHAPTER 13 **가정법**	점수	PASS
UNIT 29	/ 35점	30점
UNIT 30	/ 30점	26점
Review Test	/ 70점	60점

내신공략 중학영문법

개념이해책

2

내신공략 중학영문법의 구성 및 특징

시리즈 구성

내신공략 중학영문법 시리즈는 중학교 영어 교과과정의 문법 사항을 3레벨로 나누어 수록하고 있으며, 각각의 레벨은 **개념이해책**과 **문제풀이책**으로 구성됩니다. 두 책을 병행하여 학습하는 것이 가장 이상적인 학습법이지만, 교사와 학생의 필요에 따라 둘 중 하나만을 독립적으로도 사용할 수 있도록 구성했습니다.

개념이해책은 문법 개념에 대한 핵심적인 설명과 필수 연습문제로 이루어져 있습니다.

문제풀이책은 각 문법 개념에 대해 총 3단계의 테스트를 통해 체계적으로 문제를 풀어볼 수 있도록 구성되어 있습니다.

특징

❶ 최신 내신 출제 경향 100% 반영

- 신유형과 고난도 서술형 문제 비중 강화

  점점 어려워지는 내신 문제의 최신 경향을 철저히 분석 • 반영하여 고난도 서술형과 신유형 문제의 비중을 더욱 높였습니다. 이 책으로 학습한 학생들은 어떤 유형의 문제에도 대처할 수 있습니다.

- 영어 지시문 문제 제시

  영어로 문제가 출제되는 최신 경향을 반영하여, 일부 문제를 영어 지시문으로 제시했습니다. 문제풀이책의 Level 3 Test는 모두 영어 지시문으로만 제시됩니다.

- 독해 지문 어법 문제 수록(문제풀이책)

  독해 지문에서 어법 문제가 출제되는 내신 문제 스타일에 익숙해지도록, 독해 지문과 함께 다양한 어법 문제를 풀어볼 수 있습니다.

❷ 개념이해책과 문제풀이책의 연계 학습

문법 개념 설명과 필수 문제로 구성된 개념이해책으로 문법 개념을 학습한 후, 다양한 문제를 3단계로 풀어보는 문제풀이책으로 복습하며 확실한 학습 효과를 거둘 수 있습니다.

❸ 성취도 평가와 수준별 맞춤형 학습 제안

문제를 풀어보고 나서 점수 기준에 따라 학생의 성취도를 평가할 수 있습니다. 개념이해책에서 Let's Check It Out과 Ready for Exams 점수를 합산한 결과에 따라 문제풀이책의 어느 레벨부터 학습하면 되는지 가이드가 제시됩니다. Review Test에서는 일정 점수 이상을 받아야 다음 챕터로 넘어갈 수 있습니다.

❹ 추가 학습을 위한 다양한 학습자료 제공

다양하게 수업에 활용할 수 있는 교사용 자료가 제공됩니다. 다락원 홈페이지(www.darakwon.co.kr)에서 무료로 다운받으실 수 있습니다.

개념이해책과 문제풀이책 연계 학습법

개념이해책으로 문법 개념 학습

문제풀이책으로 문법 개념을 복습

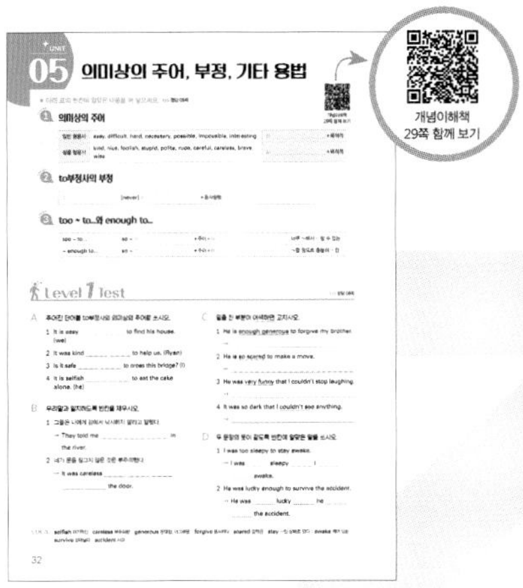

QR코드를 찍으면 개념이해책 문법 설명이 보여요!

개념이해책 Let's Check It Out과 Ready for Exams 풀고 점수 합산

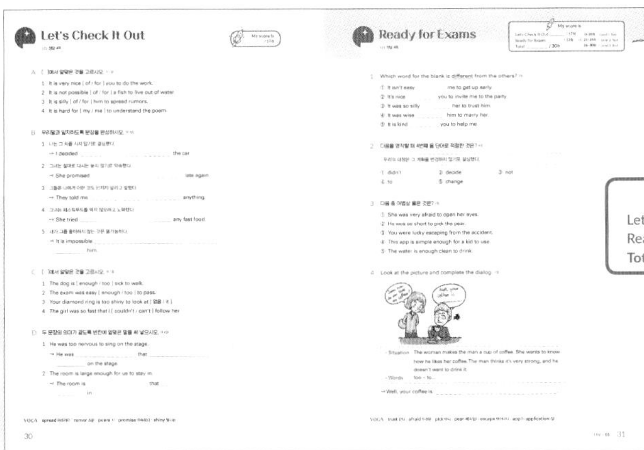

My score is

Let's Check It Out _______ / 18점		0~20점	→ Level 1 Test
Ready for Exams _______ / 12점	➡	21~25점	→ Level 2 Test
Total _______ / 30점		26~30점	→ Level 3 Test

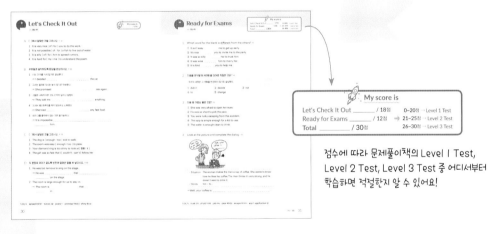

점수에 따라 문제풀이책의 Level 1 Test, Level 2 Test, Level 3 Test 중 어디서부터 학습하면 적절한지 알 수 있어요!

챕터 내용을 모두 학습한 후 Review Test 풀기

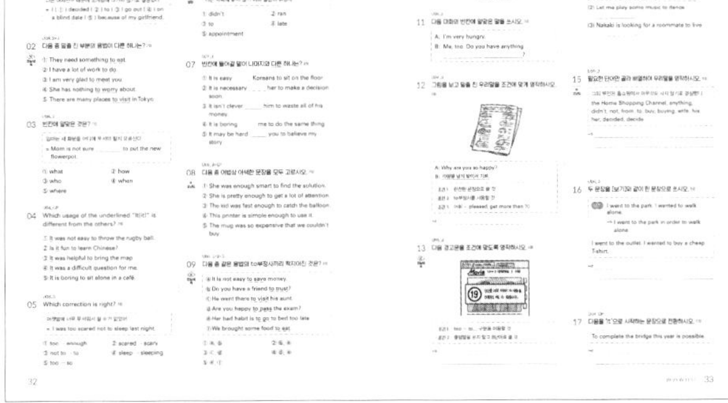

My score is
/ 60점
51점 이상 PASS!!

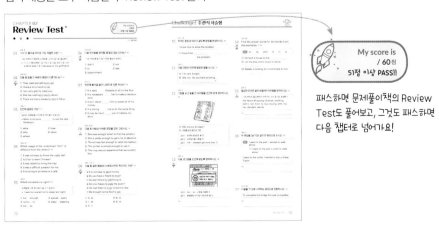

패스하면 문제풀이책의 Review Test도 풀어보고, 그것도 패스하면 다음 챕터로 넘어가요!

개념이해책의 구성

문법 개념 설명

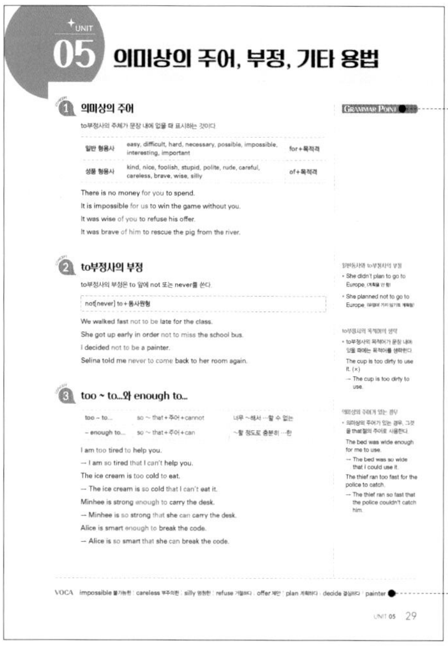

문법 항목에 대한 핵심 내용이 개념(Concept)별로 간결하게 정리되어 있습니다. 표와 도식을 통해 내용을 한눈에 파악하기 쉽습니다.

Grammar Point

학생들이 잘 모르는 중요한 내용을 꼼꼼하게 짚고 넘어갈 수 있습니다.

VOCA

예문에 쓰인 주요 단어가 정리되어 편리하며, 문법과 단어 공부를 같이 할 수 있습니다.

Let's Check It Out

Ready for Exams

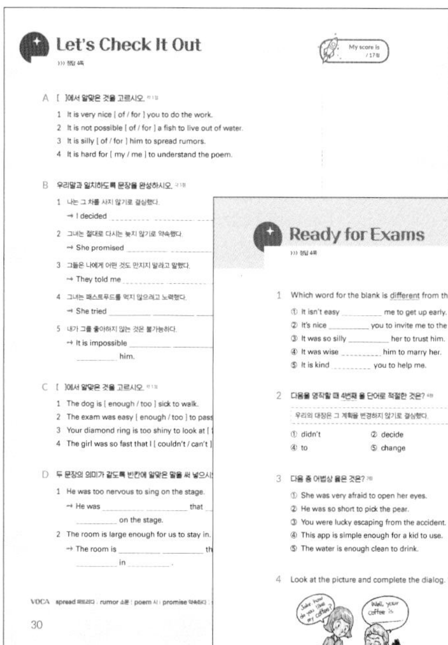

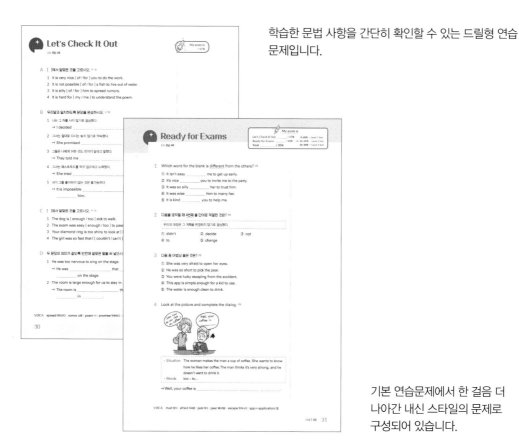

학습한 문법 사항을 간단히 확인할 수 있는 드릴형 연습 문제입니다.

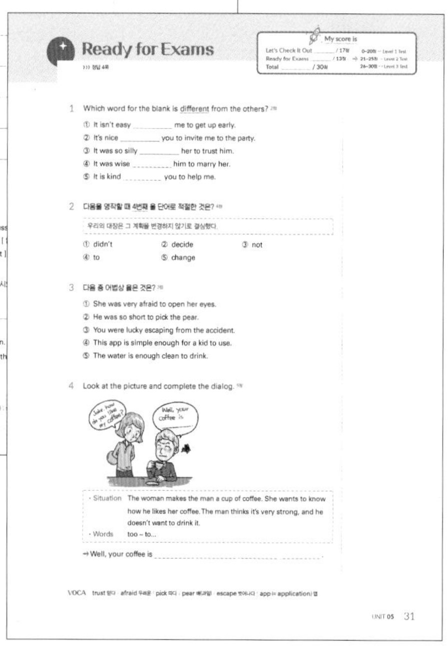

기본 연습문제에서 한 걸음 더 나아간 내신 스타일의 문제로 구성되어 있습니다.

Review Test

챕터 학습이 끝나면 내신 시험 유형의 문제를 풀어보며 배운 내용을 정리합니다. 챕터 내 여러 유닛의 내용을 통합적으로 구성한 문제를 통해 응용력과 실전 감각을 키울 수 있습니다.

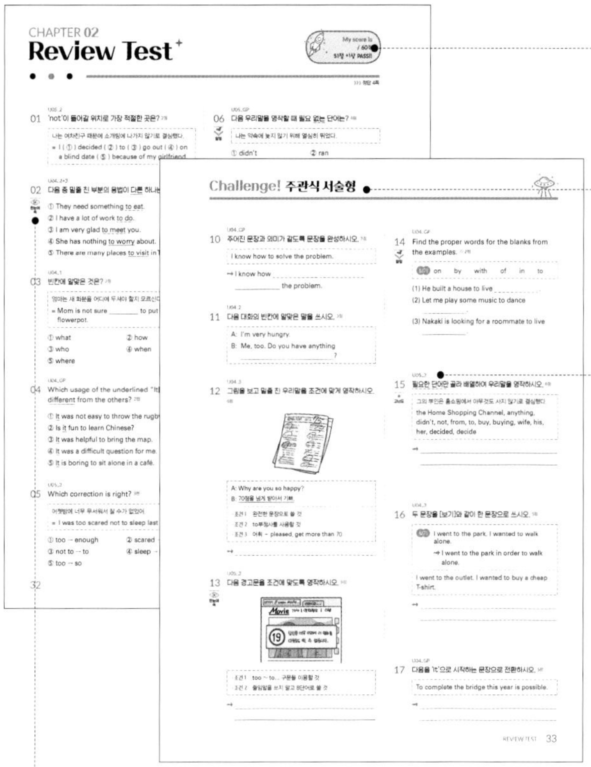

My score is

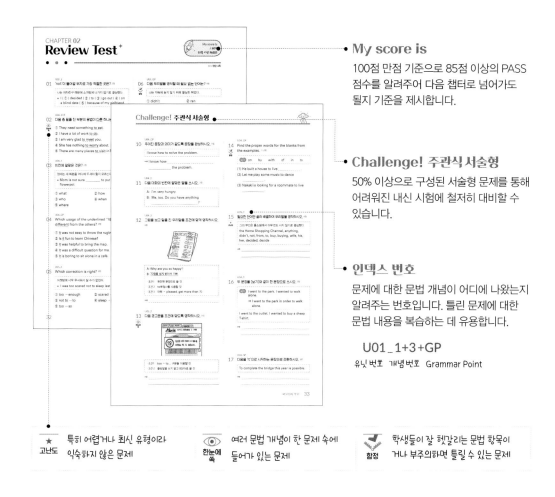

100점 만점 기준으로 85점 이상의 PASS 점수를 알려주어 다음 챕터로 넘어가도 될지 기준을 제시합니다.

Challenge! 주관식 서술형

50% 이상으로 구성된 서술형 문제를 통해 어려워진 내신 시험에 철저히 대비할 수 있습니다.

인덱스 번호

문제에 대한 문법 개념이 어디에 나왔는지 알려주는 번호입니다. 틀린 문제에 대한 문법 내용을 복습하는 데 유용합니다.

U01_1+3+GP

유닛 번호 개념 번호 Grammar Point

★ 고난도: 특히 어렵거나 최신 유형이라 익숙하지 않은 문제	한눈에 쏙: 여러 문법 개념이 한 문제 속에 들어가 있는 문제	함정: 학생들이 잘 헷갈리는 문법 항목이거나 부주의하면 틀릴 수 있는 문제

시험 직전에 챙겨 보는 비법 노트

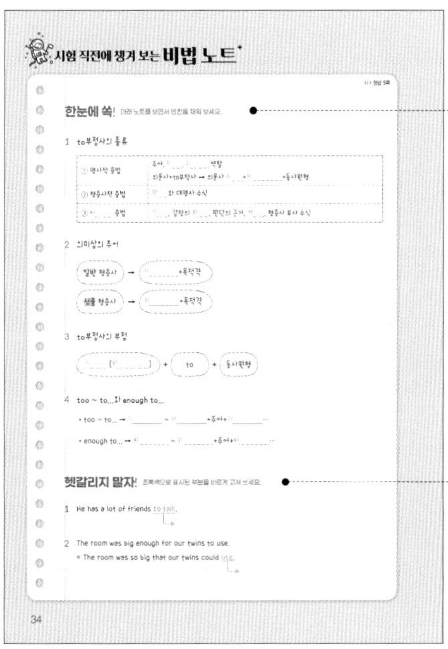

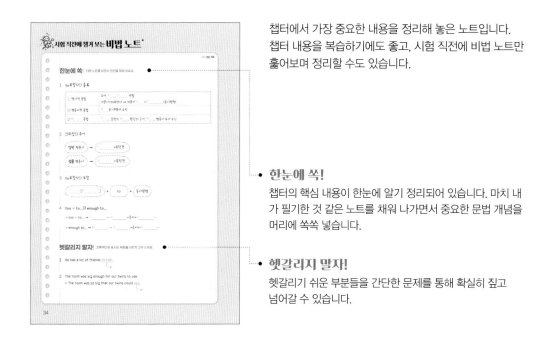

챕터에서 가장 중요한 내용을 정리해 놓은 노트입니다. 챕터 내용을 복습하기에도 좋고, 시험 직전에 비법 노트만 훑어보며 정리할 수도 있습니다.

한눈에 쏙!

챕터의 핵심 내용이 한눈에 알기 정리되어 있습니다. 마치 내가 필기한 것 같은 노트를 채워 나가면서 중요한 문법 개념을 머리에 쏙쏙 넣습니다.

헷갈리지 말자!

헷갈리기 쉬운 부분들을 간단한 문제를 통해 확실히 짚고 넘어갈 수 있습니다.

차례

꼼꼼한 개념 정리와 바로 적용 가능한 예제들, 그리고 깔끔한 단원 정리 리뷰 문제들까지, 학생들은 물론이고 가르치는 선생님의 마음까지 꿰뚫은 너의 이름은, 내공 중학영문법! 5년째 제 특강 교재로 pick 중입니다.

잠실 이은재 어학원 강사 **김한나**

이 책을 만난 초등학교 때부터 실질적인 대학 입시에 치중하였던 고교 시절 내내 가장 많이 열어본 영어 과목의 교재이다. 어려운 문법 용어로 힘들어하고 탄탄한 구조와 내용에 목말라했을 때 나를 극복하게 하고 탄탄한 기본기를 유지하게 해줄 수 있는 독보적인 능력을 가진 교본이었다.

분당 대진고 졸업 고려대학교(본캠) 20학번 **김주현**

최근 실제 시험 유형을 상세히 검토 분석한 정성이 돋보이는 교재이다. 문법 개념을 스스로 말로 풀어 정리할 수 있게 하여 기본기를 정확히 다질 수 있게 해준 부분이 특히 인상적이다.

경기도 일산 원장 **강선혜**

처음 나왔을 때부터 몇 년째 내 수업 메인 교재로 쓰고 있는 대한민국 최고의 문법책.👍👍 재치 있는 예문과 삽화도 좋지만 문법의 기본 개념을 깊게 생각해 볼 수 있는 문제들은 타의 추종을 불허한다. 문제풀이책의 학생들을 위한 개념 리뷰 페이지에서도 학생들에 대한 배려가 묻어 나온다.

대치동 강사 **최성실(레이첼)**

내공은 다른 문법책처럼 문제만 쓸데없이 많지 않고, 꼭 필요한 개념과 개념 복습을 위한 빈칸이 마련되어 있어서 내가 이해했는지 체크하고 구조를 한 번 더 정리할 수 있었다.

도곡중 1학년 **최준혁**

내공 중학영문법은 제목만 보면 중등을 위한 교재 같지만 초등 고학년부터 고2 기초반까지 다양하게 쓸 수 있으며, 무엇보다도 톡톡 튀는 예문과 문제풀이책 구성이 좋아서 학생과 선생님 모두에게 유익한 책입니다. 실제 영어를 포기했던 중3(현 고1)의 기초를 잡으며 내신 준비를 완벽하게 해줄 수 있었던 교재입니다.

청주 리드인 잉글리쉬 원장 최서린

내공 중학영문법… 처음 보는 책이라 어색하고 문제풀이책은 개념이해책을 다 이해하지 못하면 풀 수 없어서 처음엔 공부하기 힘들었는데 점점 아는 것이 늘어나고 숙제 양도 익숙해지니 문제 풀기가 재밌어지고 처음으로 최고의 영어 점수를 맞고 나니 자신감이 생기게 되었습니다.

청주 율량중 3학년 김태연

한국에서 중2까지 신영주 선생님이랑 영어 공부하고 미국으로 유학 갔을 때 처음으로 간절히 생각 났던 책이다. 다시 한국에 있는 선생님께 미국으로 책을 보내 달라고 했다. 미국에서도 이렇게 쉽게 잘 정리되어 있는 책은 없었다. 이 책으로 배운 내용들은 오랫동안 기억에 남을 정도로 쉽고 확실하다.

Chaminade College Preparatory School sophomore 황인산

개념이해책으로 개념을 익히고 간단한 점검을 한 뒤, 문제풀이책의 난이도별 문제들로 그 개념을 탄탄히 정리할 수 있었다. 익혀야 하는 개념은 자주 문제에서 접할 수 있어 금방 암기하였고 간단한 개념은 생각해서 논리적으로 풀어내는 문제를 통하여 더 확실히 감을 잡을 수 있었다. 문제들이 실제로 중학교 내신에서 자주 출제되는 유형들이라서 시험 전에 몇 번 더 펼쳐보며 참고하기 좋았다.

늘푸른중학교 김혜준

교재 속의 문제들은 무의미한 단순 반복 연습을 하게 하는 것이 아니라 원리를 터득하고 문제에 따라 적합하게 반응하고 사고하게 만들어 주는 교재임에 틀림없다. 오랜 기간 동안 영어 교육의 길을 함께 걸어온 교육자로서 내공 중학영문법은 문법적 정확성을 높여 궁극적으로 의사소통의 유창성까지 길러줄 것이다.

블레싱 아카데미 원장 이봉주

CHAPTER 01

문장의 형식

UNIT 01

1형식, 2형식, 3형식

CONCEPT 1 1형식

주어와 동사만으로 문장이 성립하는 형식을 말하며, 대개 부사(구)와 함께 쓰인다.

주어+동사+(부사/부사구)	He runs (fast).
There/Here+동사+주어+(부사/부사구)	There is a festival (at my school).

I went (to school by electric kickboard today).

There were many cars (on the road).

CONCEPT 2 2형식

주어와 동사, 그리고 주어를 설명하는 주격 보어로 이루어진 문장을 말한다.

주어+be동사+주격 보어(형용사/명사)	He is handsome. He is a teacher.
주어+감각동사+주격 보어(형용사)	It may sound strange.
주어+상태동사+주격 보어(형용사)	The city became famous.

My parents are generous.

They are diplomats.

It doesn't look so right.

The leaves turn red and yellow in autumn.

CONCEPT 3 3형식

주어, 동사, 목적어로 이루어진 문장을 말한다. 목적어로는 명사류(명사, 대명사, to부정사, 동명사 등)가 온다.

주어+동사+목적어(명사)	She loved the book.
주어+동사+목적어(대명사)	I honestly didn't understand that.
주어+동사+목적어(to부정사구)	We want to watch TV.
주어+동사+목적어(동명사구)	They enjoyed talking to each other.

We didn't expect it.

Mary decided to marry Phillip.

They finished arguing.

GRAMMAR POINT

8품사와 문장 성분

- 8품사: 명사, 대명사, 동사, 부사, 형용사, 접속사, 감탄사, 전치사
- 문장 성분: 주어, 동사, 목적어, 보어, 수식어

부사(구)

- 부사(구)는 문장의 필수 성분이 아니다. 보충 설명하기 위한 말이므로 없어도 문장이 성립된다.

감각동사와 상태동사

- 감각동사: look, sound, smell, taste, feel+형용사
- 상태동사: get, become, grow, turn, go+형용사
- 감각동사+like+명사: 감각동사 뒤에 명사가 올 경우, 동사 뒤에 전치사 like를 써야 한다.

  He looks like a model.
  (그는 모델처럼 보인다.)

타동사구

- '동사+부사'로 이루어진 타동사구도 목적어를 취할 수 있다.

  turn on(~을 켜다), turn off(~을 끄다), take out(~을 꺼내다), pick up(~을 집어 올리다), put on(~을 입다), take off(~을 벗다), put out(불을 끄다), put off(~을 미루다)

  She picked up the trash.
  (그녀는 쓰레기를 집었다.)

동사+to부정사/동명사

- to부정사만 목적어로 취하는 동사

  want, wish, hope, expect, plan, promise, decide, would like
- 동명사만 목적어로 취하는 동사

  enjoy, mind, give up, finish, practice, stop, keep, quit, dislike
- to부정사와 동명사 둘 다 목적어로 취하는 동사

  like, hate, begin, start, continue

VOCA festival 축제 | electric kickboard 전동 킥보드 | generous 관대한 | diplomat 외교관 | autumn 가을 | honestly 솔직히, 정직하게 | argue 논쟁하다 | promise 약속하다 | decide 결심하다, 결정하다 | mind 싫어하다, 꺼리다 | practice 연습하다 | quit 그만두다

Let's Check It Out

››› 정답 2쪽

My score is
/ 20점

A 다음 문장에 주어(S), 동사(V), 보어(C)를 표시하시오. (보어는 있는 경우에만 표시할 것) 각 1점

1 There goes a nice car.

2 The turtle walks slowly.

3 There were a lot of children at the park.

4 It is getting dark.

5 Earth moves around the sun.

B [ ]에서 알맞은 것을 고르시오. 각 1점

1 This food tastes [good / well].
2 She moved [quick / quickly] to the door.
3 He read the book [quiet / quietly].
4 Here [comes the bus / the bus comes].
5 I felt [terrible / terribly] about the accident.
6 The apples in the basket taste [sour / sourly].
7 She can solve the problem [easy / easily].
8 His little brother looks [lovely / nicely].

C 다음 문장에서 목적어를 찾아 밑줄을 치시오. 각 1점

1 She put the phone on the table.

2 Mina explained the meanings of the words.

3 We enjoyed taking pictures.

D 어법상 어색한 부분이 있으면 바르게 고치시오. 각 1점

1 The pasta tasted delicious.

______________ → ______________

2 He wanted making a model plane.

______________ → ______________

3 Susan continued solving the questions.

______________ → ______________

4 She looked at him sad.

______________ → ______________

VOCA around ~ 주위에 | terrible 끔찍한 | accident 사고 | meaning 의미 | word 단어 | take a picture 사진을 찍다

Ready for Exams

››› 정답 2쪽

My score is		
Let's Check It Out ________ / 20점		0~24점 → Level 1 Test
Ready for Exams ________ / 15점		25~29점 → Level 2 Test
Total ________ / 35점		30~35점 → Level 3 Test

1 밑줄 친 ①~⑤ 중에서 어법상 어색한 것은? 2점

① The cake ② in the box ③ smells ④ very ⑤ sweetly.

2 다음 문장들에 대해 잘못 설명한 학생은? 3점

ⓐ They lived happily.
ⓑ Mike laughed a lot.
ⓒ There my day goes.
ⓓ The game was really boring.
ⓔ That doesn't sound well to me.

① 민희: ⓐ와 ⓑ는 1형식 문장이다.
② 보라: ⓒ는 There 다음에 동사 goes가 바로 와야 한다.
③ 기리: ⓓ에서 boring은 주어를 설명하는 보어이다.
④ 재우: ⓔ에서 well은 good이 되어야 알맞다.
⑤ 별이: 틀린 문장은 ⓐ와 ⓒ이다.

3 Which is grammatically incorrect? 2점

① I feel sorry for the cat.
② She looks healthy.
③ It sounds a funny story.
④ He wants to be a singer.
⑤ Do you mind opening the door?

4 다음 우리말을 조건에 맞게 영작하시오. 4점

그는 매우 무례하게 웃었다.

· 조건 1 laugh, rude, very를 활용하되 필요하면 단어를 변형할 것
· 조건 2 4단어로 쓸 것

→ ______________________________

5 Find the error and correct it by changing one word. 4점

Sam is a shopkeeper. He sells things good. Lots of customers visit Sam's store.

______________ → ______________

VOCA boring 지루한 | rude 무례한 | shopkeeper 가게 주인 | sell 팔다 | customer 손님

UNIT
02 4형식, 5형식

CONCEPT
1 4형식

주어, 동사, 간접 목적어(사람), 직접 목적어(사물)로 이루어진 문장을 말한다.

주어	동사	간접 목적어	직접 목적어
I	gave	him	a present.
She	made	me	a cake.
We	asked	her	a question.

4형식 문장을 3형식으로 전환할 경우에는 직접 목적어(사물)를 앞에 쓰고, 전치사를 쓴 후에 간접 목적어(사람)를 쓴다.

주어	동사	직접 목적어	전치사	간접 목적어
I	gave	a present	to	him.
She	made	a cake	for	me.
We	asked	a question	of	her.

Could you lend me your phone? (4형식)

→ Could you lend your phone to me? (3형식)

He couldn't buy me the piano. (4형식)

→ He couldn't buy the piano for me. (3형식)

CONCEPT
2 5형식

주어, 동사, 목적어, 목적격 보어로 이루어진 문장을 말한다.

주어	동사	목적어	목적격 보어
Mom	calls	me	a pig. (명사)
I	found	this story	interesting. (형용사)
The news	made	us	happy. (형용사)
You	should keep	your room	clean. (형용사)

My grandparents called me a prince.

Did you find the city beautiful?

We may not make the plan perfect.

Should I keep my laptop plugged in all the time?

GRAMMAR POINT

4형식 문장에서 대명사 사용

- 4형식 문장에서 직접 목적어 자리에 대명사를 쓸 수 없다.

Show me it. (×)
→ Show it to me. (○)
→ Show me the ticket. (○)

4형식 → 3형식 전환

- 4형식에서 3형식으로 문장을 전환할 때 동사에 따라 전치사를 달리 쓴다.

① to를 사용하는 동사: give, bring, lend, send, sell, show, teach, write, hand

② for를 사용하는 동사: make, buy, cook, get, find

③ of를 사용하는 동사: ask

5형식 동사

- 목적격 보어로 명사, 형용사, 분사 등을 쓸 수 있는 5형식 동사: call, keep, name, make, find, get

We found James funny.
(우리는 James가 재미있다고 생각했다.)

4형식과 5형식의 구분

- 5형식에서 목적어와 목적격 보어의 관계는 주어-동사의 관계이다.

She gave me a book.
(me ≠ a book)
→ 4형식 (그녀는 나에게 책을 주었다.)

My friends call me a bookworm.
(me = a bookworm)
→ 5형식 (나의 친구들은 나를 책벌레라고 부른다.)

목적격 보어의 품사

- 목적격 보어도 주격 보어처럼 명사 또는 형용사를 사용한다. 부사는 될 수 없다.

His efforts made him ~~successfully~~. (→ successful)
(그의 노력이 그를 성공하게 만들었다.)

VOCA present 선물 | lend 빌려주다 | hand 건네주다 | inquire 묻다 | laptop 노트북 컴퓨터 | plugged in 전원이 연결되어 있는 | bookworm 책벌레 | effort 노력 | successful 성공한

Let's Check It Out

››› 정답 2쪽

My score is
/ 19점

A 다음 문장이 4형식이면 간접 목적어(IO)와 직접 목적어 (DO)를, 5형식이면 목적어(O)와 목적격 보어(OC)를 표시하시오. 각 1점

1 You should keep yourself warm.

2 I will get you something to eat.

3 Will you pass me the salt?

4 We found the movie boring.

B 우리말과 같은 뜻이 되도록 괄호 안의 말을 빈칸에 바르게 배열하시오. 각 1점

1 그는 내게 약간의 돈을 빌려주었다. (lent, some money, me)

→ He ______________________________.

2 내가 너에게 초대장을 보낼게. (send, to, you, an invitation)

→ I'll ______________________________.

3 아빠는 나에게 노트북을 사주지 않으셨다. (for, me, a laptop, didn't, buy)

→ My dad ______________________________.

4 그녀를 슬프게 하지 마. (her, make, sad)

→ Don't ______________________________.

5 선생님은 그 질문이 어렵다고 생각했다. (hard, found, the question)

→ The teacher ______________________________.

C 다음 4형식 문장을 3형식으로 바꾸어 쓰시오. 각 2점

1 He sold me his tablet PC.

→ He sold ______________________________.

2 May I ask you something?

→ May I ______________________________?

3 He bought his fiancée a ring.

→ He bought ______________________________.

4 Let me get you something.

→ Let me ______________________________.

5 Sam made us some pizza.

→ Sam made ______________________________.

VOCA invitation 초대장 | tablet PC 태블릿 컴퓨터 | fiancée 약혼녀

Ready for Exams

››› 정답 2쪽

My score is

Let's Check It Out _______	/ 19점	0~24점 → Level 1 Test
Ready for Exams _______	/ 16점	25~29점 → Level 2 Test
Total _______	/ 35점	30~35점 → Level 3 Test

1 Which word is proper for the blank? 2점

She asked strange questions ______________ me.

① on ② to ③ by
④ of ⑤ for

2 다음 중 어법상 어색한 문장으로만 묶인 것은? 3점

ⓐ He made a hammock to the children.
ⓑ I showed my picture to her.
ⓒ He sold his bike to me.
ⓓ My sister told to me a secret.
ⓔ Your speech made us happily.

① ⓐ, ⓒ ② ⓐ, ⓒ, ⓔ ③ ⓐ, ⓓ, ⓔ
④ ⓒ, ⓓ ⑤ ⓒ, ⓓ, ⓔ

3 빈칸에 들어갈 전치사가 다른 하나는? 2점

① He gave a little time __________ me.
② I will buy a souvenir __________ him.
③ She sent a letter __________ him.
④ Show your pictures __________ me.
⑤ Grandma told a story __________ me.

4 Find the error and correct it. 4점

수지는 자신의 머리를 예쁘게 만들었다.
= Susie made her hair prettily.

______________________ → ______________________

5 Translate the sentence according to the conditions. 5점

나는 그가 친절하다고 생각했다.

· 조건 1 어휘 – find, friendly
· 조건 2 4단어로 쓸 것

→ ____

VOCA hammock 해먹(나무에 달아 매는 그물·천 등으로 된 침대) | speech 연설 | souvenir 기념품

UNIT 03

5형식

CONCEPT 1 목직격 보어로 to부징사가 오는 경우

5형식 문장의 목적격 보어로 to부정사가 오는 경우 「주어+동사(want, ask, tell, advise, would like 등)+목적어+목적격 보어(to부정사)」의 어순을 취한다.

주어	동사	목적어	목적격 보어(to부정사)
I	want	you	to come back.
Mom	asked	me	to lock the door.
She	told	him	to stop the game.
The doctor	advised	me	to rest.

CONCEPT 2 목적격 보어로 동사원형이 오는 경우

사역동사(make, let, have)나 지각동사(see, watch, hear, listen to, feel)가 사용된 문장에서는 목적격 보어로 동사원형이 온다. 「주어+사역동사/지각동사+목적어+목적격 보어(동사원형)」의 어순으로 쓴다.

주어	동사	목적어	목적격 보어(동사원형)
Our teacher	made	us	study hard.
Mom	had	me	do the dishes.
She	saw	him	play the game.
I	heard	the monsters	scream loudly.

CONCEPT 3 준사역동사

help는 형식상, get은 의미상 사역동사와 유사하여 준사역동사라고 한다. help는 「주어+help+목적어+(to)+동사원형」의 형태로, get은 「주어+get+목적어+to+동사원형」의 형태로 쓴다.

주어+help+목적어+(to)+동사원형	I helped him (to) repair the car.
주어+get+목적어+to+동사원형	I will get her to water the plants.

CONCEPT 4 목적격 보어가 과거분사인 경우

지각동사나 사역동사의 목적어와 목적격 보어가 수동의 관계일 때는 목적격 보어로 과거분사가 사용된다.

주어+지각동사/사역동사+목적어+과거분사	She heard her name called.
	I had the box carried by some boys.

GRAMMAR POINT

지각동사 구문에서 현재분사 사용

- 지각동사가 사용된 문장에서 동작을 강조하여 목적격 보어로 현재분사(-ing)를 쓸 수도 있다.

I saw him playing the game.
(나는 그가 게임을 하고 있는 것을 봤다.)

I heard some dogs barking.
(나는 개 몇 마리가 짖는 것을 들었다.)

VOCA lock 잠그다 | advise 충고하다 | rest 쉬다 | monster 괴물 | scream 비명을 지르다 | loudly 크게 | repair 수리하다 | water 물을 주다 | plant 식물

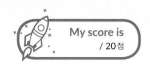

Let's Check It Out

››› 정답 2쪽

My score is / 20점

A 다음 문장에서 목적격 보어를 찾아 밑줄을 치시오. 각 1점

1 I found the rumor false.

2 We named the girl Nancy.

3 She wanted me to become a judge.

4 They let me use their hair dryer.

5 He helped the old lady carry the luggage.

B [ ]에서 알맞은 것을 고르시오. 각 1점

1 He asked her [come / to come] here.
2 Let me [to help / help] you.
3 Your mom told me [to say / say] hi to you.
4 We heard the girl [scream / to scream].
5 My brother got me [put up / to put up] the tent.

C 괄호 안에 주어진 단어를 빈칸에 알맞은 형태로 쓰시오. 각 1점

1 He didn't tell me ________________ the trash can. (empty)
2 Will you help me ________________ for the information? (search)
3 How would you like the package ________________? (send)
4 Don't ask him ________________ anything illegal. (do)
5 I can't get him ________________ up his mind. (make)

D 밑줄 친 부분이 어법상 어색하면 바르게 고치시오. 각 1점

1 Did he want her bring his clothes? → ________________
2 It made me realizing the power of love. → ________________
3 I advise you to meet her. → ________________
4 Did you hear your name to call? → ________________
5 She had her son set the alarm. → ________________

VOCA rumor 소문 | false 잘못된 | judge 판사 | hair dryer 드라이어 | luggage 짐 | say hi to ~에게 안부 전하다 | put up 세우다, 치다 | empty 비우다 | trash can 쓰레기통 | search 찾다 | package 소포, 택배 | illegal 불법의 | realize 깨닫다 | set the alarm 알람을 맞추다

Ready for Exams

››› 정답 3쪽

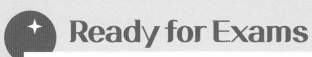

My score is
Let's Check It Out ________ / 20점
Ready for Exams ________ / 15점
Total ________ / 35점

0~24점 → Level 1 Test
25~29점 → Level 2 Test
30~35점 → Level 3 Test

1 How many sentences are incorrect? 3점

ⓐ My aunt told us to be quiet.
ⓑ Jack helped me climbing up a tree.
ⓒ Kim asked us to help her.
ⓓ He made her feel stupid.
ⓔ I saw some students bothering your sister.
ⓕ Let me to help you.

① zero ② one ③ two
④ three ⑤ four

2 다음 중 빈칸에 들어갈 수 없는 것은? 3점

She ________________ him to go to the concert.

① helped ② got ③ wanted
④ made ⑤ advised

3 Write the common word for the blanks. 4점

• He told me ________________ get back.
• He didn't show his feelings ________________ us.

→ ________________

4 Look at the picture and complete the sentence by using the given words. 5점

→ She made her child ________________ the empty plastic bottle. (throw away)

VOCA bother 괴롭히다 | throw away 버리다

CHAPTER 01

Review Test

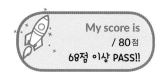

My score is / 80점
68점 이상 PASS!!

››› 정답 3쪽

U01_GP

01 다음 중 성격이 다른 하나는? 2점

함정

① lovely ② safely
③ daily ④ friendly
⑤ lively

U01_1+2+GP

02 Choose the grammatically incorrect sentences. 3점

한눈에 쏙

ⓐ That building looks safely.
ⓑ Did she look familiar?
ⓒ Her voice sounds sharply.
ⓓ His face turned pale.
ⓔ The machine doesn't work good.

① ⓐ, ⓑ, ⓒ ② ⓐ, ⓒ, ⓔ
③ ⓒ ④ ⓓ, ⓔ
⑤ ⓐ, ⓔ

U01_2+3

03 밑줄 친 부분의 쓰임이 나머지 넷과 다른 것은? 2점

① John likes music.
② She cleaned her car.
③ I saw a box of chocolate on the shelf.
④ She didn't wash the dish.
⑤ My cousin became a soldier.

U01_2+GP

04 다음 빈칸에 알맞지 않은 것은? 2점

That dress is really pretty, and it looks ________ on you.

① good ② great
③ well ④ nice
⑤ beautiful

U02_1+GP

05 Which words are correct for the blanks? 2점

• Leo gave some brilliant answers ________ me in the interview.
• Mom cooked ham and eggs ________ herself.

① to – to ② to – for
③ for – for ④ to – of
⑤ of – to

U01_1+3

06 다음 중 문장의 형식이 나머지 넷과 다른 것은? 2점

함정

① I learn Spanish at school.
② He explained how to use it.
③ They enjoyed having the party on Saturday.
④ He traveled during summer vacation.
⑤ I will start to save my money.

U02_1+GP+U03_1

07 Which word is common for the blanks? 2점

• Brian will teach English conversation ________ us this year.
• They didn't expect ________ succeed so well.

① for ② to
③ of ④ in
⑤ at

U03_2+GP

08 다음 중 어법상 어색한 것은? 2점

한눈에 쏙

① She helped me to cover the hole.
② He watched the kid ran to the park.
③ Her mother expected us to be more patient.
④ I had the wall painted green.
⑤ Thanks for letting me know where I can get it.

U01_3+GP

09 다음 중 어법상 어색한 것을 모두 고르시오. 2점

함정

① I want some ice cream.

② She didn't want eating pork cutlet.

③ We finished to play soccer.

④ They continued shopping.

⑤ She loves swimming.

U03_1

10 Which word is NOT proper for the blank? 2점

한눈에 쏙

I ________ my sister cry a lot.

① advised ② heard

③ watched ④ made

⑤ listened to

U01_2+GP

11 다음 빈칸에 들어갈 말로 알맞지 않은 것은? 2점

This movie looks ________.

① artistic ② fantasy

③ romantic ④ peaceful

⑤ dramatic

U02_2

12 Choose the sentence that has the same meaning as the one in the box. 2점

I found that he was smart.

① I found he smart.

② I found his smart.

③ I found him smart.

④ I found that he smart.

⑤ I found that him be smart.

U01_3

13 다음 주어진 단어들을 배열해서 문장을 만들 때 6번째로 오는 단어는? 4점

downloaded / I / a / useful / very / application / on / my smartphone

① downloaded ② very

③ a ④ application

⑤ useful

U02_1+GP+U01_3+GP

14 빈칸에 알맞은 표현을 순서대로 나열한 것은? 2점

한눈에 쏙

• He asked some personal questions ________ Ms. Shin.
• We promised ________ tomorrow.

① of – meeting ② of – to meet

③ to – meeting ④ for – meeting

⑤ to – to meet

U03_4

15 단어들을 조합하여 완전한 문장을 만들 수 없는 것은? 4점

★ 고난도

① give / a / present / you / ? / did / him

② the / doctor / rest / advised / . / me / to

③ help / we / will / to / her / us / . / get

④ he / name / heard / call / his / . / someone

⑤ my / dad / box / . / had / the / carry / me / by

U02_1+3+U03_1+GP

16 밑줄 친 부분의 역할이 같은 것끼리 묶인 것은? 3점

ⓐ He sent her flowers.
ⓑ I made him happy.
ⓒ Mr. Lee taught us English last year.
ⓓ Grace helped me to finish the project.
ⓔ We saw Tony sleeping in class.

① ⓐ, ⓑ ② ⓐ, ⓓ

③ ⓑ, ⓒ, ⓓ ④ ⓑ, ⓓ, ⓔ

⑤ ⓒ, ⓓ, ⓔ

U01_1

17 우리말과 같은 뜻이 되도록 문장을 완성하시오. 3점

여기 다른 예들이 있다.

→ ____________ ____________ other examples.

U01_1+2+GP

18 Find TWO errors and correct them. 4점

Yesterday, it rained heavy. Everything looked differently in the rain.

____________ → ____________

____________ → ____________

U01_2+GP

19 그림을 보고 조건에 맞게 B가 할 말을 쓰시오. 4점

A: How does the bird look? B: ____________________
·조건 1 완전한 문장으로 쓸 것 ·조건 2 어휘 angry를 활용할 것 ·조건 3 대명사를 사용해 3단어로 쓸 것

→ ________________________________

U02_1+GP

20 Write the correct words for the blanks. 각 2점

(1) He cooked lobster ____________ us.

(2) He asked a question ____________ my dad.

U03_4

21 함정 다음 우리말과 같은 뜻이 되도록 필요한 단어만 골라 배열하시오. 4점

그는 그 컴퓨터가 수리되도록 했다. he, had, fixed, to, the computer, fix

→ ________________________________

U03_1

22 다음 우리말을 주어진 조건에 맞게 영작하시오. 6점

그 사서는 나에게 토요일까지 그 책을 반납하라고 말했다.
·조건 1 어휘 – librarian, tell, return, by Saturday ·조건 2 10단어로 쓸 것

→ ________________________________

____

U02_1+GP

23 Change the sentence to have the same meaning as the one in the box. 4점

He will make me a unique bag.

→ ________________________________ me.

U01_2+U02_2

24 한눈에 쏙 Write the common word for the blanks. 3점

• It's fall now. The weather is ________. • I'm thirsty. Give me something ________. • His car looks ________. I want to drive it. • It was very hot, but the wind made us ________.

→ ____________

U03_2

25 주어진 단어를 빈칸에 알맞은 형태로 써서 문장을 완성하시오. 4점

The fireworks made him ____________ his family. (miss)

U03_2+GP

26 두 문장을 [보기]처럼 한 문장으로 고쳐 쓰시오. 6점

보기 I heard him. He spoke Chinese. → I heard him speak Chinese.
He felt something. It came close to him.

→ ________________________________

››› 정답 4쪽

한눈에 쏙! 아래 노트를 보면서 빈칸을 채워 보세요.

1 2형식

명사류(ⓝ, 1) ________, 2) ________)

S(주어) + V(동사) + 3)

① be동사	ⓐ(형용사), ⓝ(명사)
② 감각동사 4)l___, 5)so___, 6)sm___, taste, feel)	ⓐ ⓐⓓ(부사)
③ 상태동사 7)g__, 8)b_____, 9)g___, 10)t___, go)	ⓐ

2 5형식

S + V + O(목적어) + OC(목적격 보어)

① 1)c___, 2)k___, 3)m___, 4)f___	ⓝ, ⓐ
② 5)w___, 6)a__, tell, advise	to+Ⓡ(= to부정사)
③ 사역동사 7)m___, 8)l__, have	Ⓡ(동사원형), p.p.(과거분사) 수동
④ 지각동사 9)s__, watch, 10)h___	Ⓡ, p.p., -ing(현재분사) 수동 동작 강조
⑤ 준사역동사 11)h___	to+Ⓡ, Ⓡ

헷갈리지 말자! 초록색으로 표시된 부분을 바르게 고쳐 쓰세요.

1 It may sound strangely.

→

2 I heard the monsters to scream loudly.

→

CHAPTER 02

to부정사

명사적, 형용사적, 부사적 용법

CONCEPT 1 명사적 용법

to부정사가 문장 안에서 명사처럼 주어, 보어, 목적어의 역할을 한다.

역할	뜻	예문
주어	~하는 것은	To finish the work now is necessary.
보어	~하는 것이다	His job was to repair toy cars.
목적어	~하는 것을	I want to ride my bicycle.

「의문사+to부정사」는 '~해야 할지'의 의미이다.

what to do	무엇을 해야 할지	how to use	어떻게 사용해야 할지
which to wear	어느 것을 입어야 할지	where to go	어디로 가야 할지
when to stop	언제 멈춰야 할지	who(m) to pick	누구를 뽑아야 할지

CONCEPT 2 형용사적 용법

to부정사가 형용사처럼 앞의 명사 또는 대명사를 수식하는 역할을 한다.

역할	뜻	예문
명사 수식	~하는, ~할	He's not a person to tell lies. 그는 거짓말할 사람이 아니다.
대명사 수식		I have something important to tell you. 나는 너에게 말할 중요한 어떤 것이 있다.

CONCEPT 3 부사적 용법

to부정사가 문장 안에서 부사처럼 동사, 형용사, 부사를 수식하는 역할을 한다.

역할	뜻	예문
목적	~하기 위해	The children ran to catch the rabbit. 그 아이들은 토끼를 잡기 위해 달렸다.
감정의 원인	~해서	We were very surprised to hear that. 우리는 그것을 들어서 매우 놀랐어요.
판단의 근거	~하다니	Your son must be crazy to say that. 당신 아들이 그렇게 말하다니 미쳤음에 틀림없습니다.
결과	~해서 (결국) …하다	The boy grew up to be a race car driver. 그 소년은 자라서 카레이서가 되었다.
형용사·부사 수식	~하기에	Your handwriting is hard to read. 너의 손글씨는 읽기 어렵다.

가주어-진주어 구문

- to부정사구 주어가 길 경우 간결성을 위해 뒤로 보내고 형식적으로 가주어 it을 앞에 쓴다.

To have your own opinion is important.
→ It is important to have your own opinion.

의문사+to부정사

- 「의문사+to부정사」는 「의문사+주어+should+동사원형」으로 바꿔 쓸 수 있다.

He didn't know what to do.
→ He didn't know what he should do.

They couldn't decide which house to sell.
→ They couldn't decide which house they should sell.

(대)명사 + to부정사 + 전치사

- to부정사의 목적어에 전치사가 필요하면 써야 한다.

She doesn't have a friend to talk with. (← talk with a friend)

전치사에 따른 다양한 의미

- She needs something to write. (쓸 거리)
- She needs something to write on. (쓸 종이)
- She needs something to write with. (쓸 도구)

in order to[so as to]

- in order to[so as to]는 '목적(~하기 위해)'을 나타내는 부사적 용법의 to부정사와 같은 의미로 사용된다.

He uses the Internet in order to do his homework.

VOCA necessary 필요한 | own 자신만의 | opinion 의견 | person 사람 | crazy 미친 | race car driver 카레이서 | handwriting 필체, 손글씨

Let's Check It Out

››› 정답 4쪽

My score is / 19점

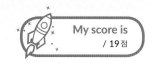

A 밑줄 친 to부정사의 의미를 [보기]에서 고르시오. 각 1점

보기		
ⓐ ~하기 위해	ⓑ ~해서 (결국) …하다	ⓒ ~하기에
ⓓ ~하는, ~할	ⓔ ~하는 것	ⓕ ~해서

1 Your topic is difficult to understand. → ____________

2 She was disappointed to fail the test. → ____________

3 The poor boy grew up to be a CEO. → ____________

4 She hurried to the station to catch the train. → ____________

5 Would you like something to drink? → ____________

B 밑줄 친 to부정사의 용법을 쓰시오. (명사/형용사/부사) 각 1점

1 His dream is to become a K-pop star. → ____________

2 She didn't know where to go. → ____________

3 He went to the store to see the clerk. → ____________

4 They had no place to sleep in. → ____________

5 I was so happy to see you again. → ____________

C 다음 문장에서 to부정사가 어떤 역할을 하는지 [보기]에서 골라 쓰시오. 각 1점

보기		
ⓐ 목적	ⓑ 감정의 원인	ⓒ 판단의 근거
ⓓ 형용사 수식	ⓔ 결과	

1 I was surprised to meet him there. → ____________

2 Korean is hard to learn. → ____________

3 She must be a fool to love me. → ____________

4 The king lived to be 100 years old. → ____________

5 She came early to get a good seat. → ____________

D to부정사를 이용하여 문장을 완성하시오. 각 2점

1 He has a camping car, and he'll live in the car.

→ He has a camping car ________ ________ ________.

2 I went to the café because I needed to meet my friend.

→ I went to the café ________ ________ ________ ________

________ ________.

VOCA topic 주제 | disappointed 실망한 | CEO (= chief executive officer) 최고 경영자 | hurry 서둘러 가다 | clerk 점원

Ready for Exams

››› 정답 4쪽

My score is

Let's Check It Out _______ / 19점
Ready for Exams _______ / 11점
Total _________ / 30점

0~20점 → Level 1 Test
21~25점 → Level 2 Test
26~30점 → Level 3 Test

1 다음 밑줄 친 부분 중 나머지 넷과 쓰임이 다른 하나는? 2점

① She met Jay to borrow some money.
② He got up early to catch the airplane.
③ Andrew practiced hard to be a famous b-boy.
④ Today's homework is to watch a documentary.
⑤ She does yoga every day to lose weight.

2 Which usage of the underlined "It[it]" is different from the others? 2점

① It is really hard to park this truck.
② Is it easy to read that English book?
③ It is important to keep the air clean.
④ It is not that dangerous to children.
⑤ It is not okay to give out my personal information.

3 밑줄 친 to부정사의 용법이 같은 것끼리 짝지어진 것은? 3점

ⓐ Is it fun to go camping?
ⓑ She was so happy to win the race.
ⓒ I have something to tell you.
ⓓ We didn't know where to go.
ⓔ The boy grew up to be an entertainer.
ⓕ I need a friend to talk with.

① ⓐ, ⓑ　② ⓑ, ⓒ　③ ⓒ, ⓕ
④ ⓓ, ⓕ　⑤ ⓒ, ⓔ

4 Read the situation and complete the question. 4점

You're talking on the phone. The other person tells you her address. You want to write it down. You have a piece of paper, but you don't have a pen. In this situation, what would you say to your friend next to you?

→ Do you have anything __________ __________ __________?

VOCA borrow 빌리다 | documentary 다큐멘터리 | lose weight 살을 빼다 | give out ~을 내주다 | personal information 개인 정보 | entertainer 연예인 | next to ~ 옆에 | situation 상황

UNIT

05 의미상의 주어, 부정, 기타 용법

CONCEPT

1 의미상의 주어

to부정사의 주체가 문장 내에 없을 때 표시하는 것이다.

일반 형용사	easy, difficult, hard, necessary, possible, impossible, interesting, important	for+목적격
성품 형용사	kind, nice, foolish, stupid, polite, rude, careful, careless, brave, wise, silly	of+목적격

There is no money for you to spend.

It is impossible for us to win the game without you.

It was wise of you to refuse his offer.

It was brave of him to rescue the pig from the river.

CONCEPT

2 to부정사의 부정

to부정사의 부정은 to 앞에 not 또는 never를 쓴다.

not[never] to+동사원형

We walked fast not to be late for the class.

She got up early in order not to miss the school bus.

I decided not to be a painter.

Selina told me never to come back to her room again.

CONCEPT

3 too ~ to...와 enough to...

too ~ to...	so ~ that+주어+cannot	너무 ~해서 …할 수 없는
~ enough to...	so ~ that+주어+can	~할 정도로 충분히 …한

I am too tired to help you.

→ I am so tired that I can't help you.

The ice cream is too cold to eat.

→ The ice cream is so cold that I can't eat it.

Minhee is strong enough to carry the desk.

→ Minhee is so strong that she can carry the desk.

Alice is smart enough to break the code.

→ Alice is so smart that she can break the code.

GRAMMAR POINT

일반동사와 to부정사의 부정

- She didn't plan to go to Europe. (계획을 안 함)
- She planned not to go to Europe. (유럽에 가지 않기로 계획함)

to부정사의 목적어의 생략

- to부정사의 목적어가 문장 내에 있을 때에는 목적어를 생략한다.

The cup is too dirty to use it. (×)

→ The cup is too dirty to use.

의미상의 주어가 있는 경우

- 의미상의 주어가 있는 경우, 그것을 that절의 주어로 사용한다.

The bed was wide enough for me to use.

→ The bed was so wide that I could use it.

The thief ran too fast for the police to catch.

→ The thief ran so fast that the police couldn't catch him.

VOCA impossible 불가능한 | careless 부주의한 | silly 멍청한 | refuse 거절하다 | offer 제안 | plan 계획하다 | decide 결심하다 | painter 화가

Let's Check It Out

››› 정답 4쪽

My score is / 17점

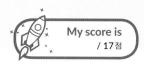

A [ ]에서 알맞은 것을 고르시오. 각 1점

1 It is very nice [of / for] you to do the work.
2 It is not possible [of / for] a fish to live out of water.
3 It is silly [of / for] him to spread rumors.
4 It is hard for [my / me] to understand the poem.

B 우리말과 일치하도록 문장을 완성하시오. 각 1점

1 나는 그 차를 사지 않기로 결심했다.
→ I decided ___________ ___________ ___________ the car.

2 그녀는 절대로 다시는 늦지 않기로 약속했다.
→ She promised ___________ ___________ ___________ late again.

3 그들은 나에게 어떤 것도 만지지 말라고 말했다.
→ They told me ___________ ___________ ___________ anything.

4 그녀는 패스트푸드를 먹지 않으려고 노력했다.
→ She tried ___________ ___________ ___________ any fast food.

5 내가 그를 좋아하지 않는 것은 불가능하다.
→ It is impossible ___________ ___________ ___________ ___________ ___________ him.

C [ ]에서 알맞은 것을 고르시오. 각 1점

1 The dog is [enough / too] sick to walk.
2 The exam was easy [enough / too] to pass.
3 Your diamond ring is too shiny to look at [없음 / it].
4 The girl was so fast that I [couldn't / can't] follow her.

D 두 문장의 의미가 같도록 빈칸에 알맞은 말을 써 넣으시오. 각 2점

1 He was too nervous to sing on the stage.
→ He was ___________ ___________ that ___________ ___________ ___________ on the stage.

2 The room is large enough for us to stay in.
→ The room is ___________ ___________ that ___________ ___________ ___________ in ___________.

VOCA spread 퍼뜨리다 | rumor 소문 | poem 시 | promise 약속하다 | shiny 빛나는

Ready for Exams

››› 정답 4쪽

My score is

Let's Check It Out ______ / 17점		0~20점 → Level 1 Test
Ready for Exams ______ / 13점	→	21~25점 → Level 2 Test
Total ______ / 30점		26~30점 → Level 3 Test

1 Which word for the blank is different from the others? 2점

① It isn't easy __________ me to get up early.
② It's nice __________ you to invite me to the party.
③ It was so silly __________ her to trust him.
④ It was wise __________ him to marry her.
⑤ It is kind __________ you to help me.

2 다음을 영작할 때 4번째 올 단어로 적절한 것은? 4점

우리의 대장은 그 계획을 변경하지 않기로 결심했다.

① didn't ② decide ③ not
④ to ⑤ change

3 다음 중 어법상 옳은 것은? 2점

① She was very afraid to open her eyes.
② He was so short to pick the pear.
③ You were lucky escaping from the accident.
④ This app is simple enough for a kid to use.
⑤ The water is enough clean to drink.

4 Look at the picture and complete the dialog. 5점

• Situation	The woman makes the man a cup of coffee. She wants to know how he likes her coffee. The man thinks it's very strong, and he doesn't want to drink it.
• Words	too ~ to...

→ Well, your coffee is __________ __________ __________ __________.

VOCA trust 믿다 | afraid 두려운 | pick 따다 | pear 배(과일) | escape 벗어나다 | app (= application) 앱

CHAPTER 02

Review Test

My score is / 60점
51점 이상 PASS!!

››› 정답 4쪽

U05_2

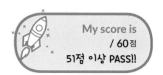

01 'not'이 들어갈 위치로 가장 적절한 곳은? 2점

> 나는 여자친구 때문에 소개팅에 나가지 않기로 결심했다.
> = I (①) decided (②) to (③) go out (④) on a blind date (⑤) because of my girlfriend.

U04_2+3

02 다음 중 밑줄 친 부분의 용법이 다른 하나는? 2점

한눈에 쏙

① They need something to eat.
② I have a lot of work to do.
③ I am very glad to meet you.
④ She has nothing to worry about.
⑤ There are many places to visit in Tokyo.

U04_1

03 빈칸에 알맞은 것은? 2점

> 엄마는 새 화분을 어디에 두어야 할지 모르신다.
> = Mom is not sure ________ to put the new flowerpot.

① what ② how
③ who ④ when
⑤ where

U04_GP

04 Which usage of the underlined "It[it]" is different from the others? 2점

① It was not easy to throw the rugby ball.
② Is it fun to learn Chinese?
③ It was helpful to bring the map.
④ It was a difficult question for me.
⑤ It is boring to sit alone in a café.

U05_3

05 Which correction is right? 3점

> 어젯밤에 너무 무서워서 잘 수가 없었어.
> = I was too scared not to sleep last night.

① too → enough ② scared → scary
③ not to → to ④ sleep → sleeping
⑤ too → so

U05_GP

06 다음 우리말을 영작할 때 필요 없는 단어는? 4점

함정

> 나는 약속에 늦지 않기 위해 열심히 뛰었다.

① didn't ② ran
③ to ④ late
⑤ appointment

U05_1

07 빈칸에 들어갈 말이 나머지와 다른 하나는? 2점

① It is easy ______ Koreans to sit on the floor.
② It is necessary ______ her to make a decision soon.
③ It isn't clever ______ him to waste all of his money.
④ It is boring ______ me to do the same thing.
⑤ It may be hard ______ you to believe my story.

U05_3+GP

08 다음 중 어법상 어색한 문장을 모두 고르시오. 3점

★ 고난도

① She was enough smart to find the solution.
② She is pretty enough to get a lot of attention.
③ The kid was fast enough to catch the balloon.
④ This printer is simple enough to use it.
⑤ The mug was so expensive that we couldn't buy.

U04_1+2+3

09 다음 중 같은 용법의 to부정사끼리 짝지어진 것은? 2점

한눈에 쏙

> ⓐ It is not easy to save money.
> ⓑ Do you have a friend to trust?
> ⓒ He went there to visit his aunt.
> ⓓ Are you happy to pass the exam?
> ⓔ Her bad habit is to go to bed too late.
> ⓕ We brought some food to eat.

① ⓐ, ⓑ ② ⓑ, ⓔ
③ ⓒ, ⓓ ④ ⓓ, ⓔ
⑤ ⓔ, ⓕ

Challenge! 주관식 서술형

U04_GP

10 주어진 문장과 의미가 같도록 문장을 완성하시오. 3점

I know how to solve the problem.

→ I know how ________ ________ ________ the problem.

U04_2

11 다음 대화의 빈칸에 알맞은 말을 쓰시오. 3점

A: I'm very hungry.
B: Me, too. Do you have anything ________ ________?

U04_3

12 그림을 보고 밑줄 친 우리말을 조건에 맞게 영작하시오. 6점

A: Why are you so happy?
B: 70점을 넘게 받아서 기뻐.

· 조건 1 완전한 문장으로 쓸 것
· 조건 2 to부정사를 사용할 것
· 조건 3 어휘 – pleased, get more than 70

→ ____________________

U05_3

13 다음 경고문을 조건에 맞도록 영작하시오. 6점

한눈에 쏙

· 조건 1 too ~ to... 구문을 이용할 것
· 조건 2 줄임말을 쓰지 말고 8단어로 쓸 것

→ ____________________
____

U04_GP

14 Find the proper words for the blanks from the examples. 각 2점

함정

보기 on by with of in to

(1) He built a house to live ________.
(2) Let me play some music to dance ________.
(3) Nakaki is looking for a roommate to live ________.

U05_2

15 필요한 단어만 골라 배열하여 우리말을 영작하시오. 6점

고난도

그의 부인은 홈쇼핑에서 아무것도 사지 않기로 결심했다.
the Home Shopping Channel, anything, didn't, not, from, to, buy, buying, wife, his, her, decided, decide

→ ____________________
____

U04_3

16 두 문장을 [보기]와 같이 한 문장으로 쓰시오. 5점

보기 I went to the park. I wanted to walk alone.
→ I went to the park in order to walk alone.

I went to the outlet. I wanted to buy a cheap T-shirt.

→ ____________________
____

U04_GP

17 다음을 'It'으로 시작하는 문장으로 전환하시오. 5점

To complete the bridge this year is possible.

→ ____________________
____

시험 직전에 챙겨 보는 비법 노트

››› 정답 5쪽

한눈에 쏙! 아래 노트를 보면서 빈칸을 채워 보세요.

1 to부정사의 종류

① 명사적 용법	주어, 1) __, 2) ___ 역할 의문사+to부정사 → 의문사 3) __+4) ______ +동사원형
② 형용사적 용법	5) __와 대명사 수식
③ 6) ___ 용법	7) __, 감정의 8) __, 판단의 근거, 9) __, 형용사·부사 수식

2 의미상의 주어

일반 형용사 → 1) ______ +목적격

성품 형용사 → 2) ______ +목적격

3 to부정사의 부정

1) ___ [2) _____] + to + 동사원형

4 too ~ to...와 enough to...

- too ~ to... → 1) ______ ~ 2) ______ +주어+3) ______ ...
- enough to... → 4) ______ ~ 5) ______ +주어+6) ______ ...

헷갈리지 말자! 초록색으로 표시된 부분을 바르게 고쳐 쓰세요.

1 He has a lot of friends to talk.
→

2 The room was big enough for our twins to use.
= The room was so big that our twins could use.
→

CHAPTER 03

동명사

UNIT 06 동명사의 쓰임, 동명사와 to부정사

UNIT 07 동명사와 현재분사, 관용적 표현

UNIT

06 동명사의 쓰임, 동명사와 to부정사

CONCEPT 1

동명사의 역할

동사에 -ing를 붙인 형태로 명사 역할을 하는 것을 말한다. '~하는 것, ~하기'로 해석된다.

역할	예문
주어	Saving money is good for your future.
보어	Her hobby is collecting old toys.
동사의 목적어	He enjoys traveling alone.
전치사의 목적어	Are you poor at singing?

CONCEPT 2

동명사와 to부정사

A 동명사를 목적어로 취하는 동사와 to부정사를 목적어로 취하는 동사

enjoy, mind, dislike, stop, quit, avoid, practice, finish, imagine, deny, keep (on), give up	+ 동명사
want, plan, hope, promise, expect, wish, decide, would like, need	+ to부정사

Jenny enjoys jogging in the morning.

He doesn't want to be a lawyer.

B 목적어로 둘 다 쓸 수 있는 동사

like, begin, start, continue, love, hate	+ to부정사 또는 동명사

She likes riding (= to ride) her motorcycle.

C 뒤에 오는 말의 형태에 따라 의미가 달라지는 경우

forget/remember	+ 동명사	~한 것을 잊다/기억하다
	+ to부정사	~할 것을 잊다/기억하다
try	+ 동명사	시험 삼아 ~해보다
	+ to부정사	~하려고 노력하다
stop	+ 동명사	~하는 것을 그만두다
	+ to부정사	~하기 위해 멈추다

GRAMMAR POINT

-ing형 만들기

- 동사의 -ing형 만드는 법은 〈내공 중학영문법 1 개념이해책〉 p. 48 참조.

동명사 주어

- 동명사 주어는 단수 취급한다.

Cleaning all the tables ~~were~~ (→ was) not easy at all.

dislike + 동명사

- dislike는 동명사만 목적어로 취한다.

I disliked ~~to stay~~ (→ staying) away from home.

would like + to부정사

- would like는 to부정사만 목적어로 취한다.
- What would you like ~~having~~ (→ to have) for lunch?

의미가 달라지는 경우

- forget/remember + 동명사/to부정사

How can you forget visiting the resort with me?
(너는 어떻게 나랑 그 리조트에 갔던 걸 잊을 수 있니?)

I will remember to lock all of the doors.
(문을 모두 잠글 것을 기억할게요.)

- try + 동명사/to부정사

Why don't you just try calling this number?
(이 번호에 시험 삼아 걸어보지 그래?)

I tried to call you, but the line was busy.
(너에게 전화하려고 했는데 통화 중이었어.)

- stop + 동명사/to부정사

Stop talking. The teacher is coming.
(그만 얘기해. 선생님이 오고 계셔.)

They stopped to watch the parade.
(그들은 퍼레이드를 보기 위해 멈췄다.)

VOCA save 저축하다 | collect 수집하다 | be poor at ~을 못하다 | dislike 싫어하다 | deny 부인하다 | lawyer 변호사 | lock 잠그다 | parade 행렬, 퍼레이드

Let's Check It Out

››› 정답 5쪽

My score is / 16점

A 밑줄 친 부분의 역할을 [보기]에서 고르시오. 각 1점

보기 ⓐ 주어 ⓑ 보어 ⓒ 동사의 목적어 ⓓ 전치사의 목적어

1 Making good friends is important. → ____________
2 Thank you for helping me. → ____________
3 Max enjoyed playing the drums. → ____________
4 Her hobby is collecting fashion accessories. → ____________
5 She continued calling me last night. → ____________

B 주어진 단어를 빈칸에 알맞은 형태로 쓰시오. 각 1점

1 ________ money is not easy. (make)
2 I am interested in ________ the river. (protect)
3 She practiced ________ the guitar. (play)

C 밑줄 친 부분이 어색하면 고치시오. 각 1점

1 She really hated meeting the trainer. → ____________
2 I am really sorry for to bother you. → ____________
3 They didn't mind to give me another chance. → ____________
4 Would you like to introduce yourself? → ____________
5 Where do you plan going during vacation? → ____________

D [ ]에서 알맞은 것을 고르시오. 각 1점

1 I tried [to keep / keeping] my eyes open, but I fell asleep.
2 Don't worry. I'll remember [to turn / turning] off the machine.
3 She stopped [to learn / learning] yoga and started Pilates.

VOCA accessory 액세서리, 장신구 | protect 보호하다 | introduce 소개하다 | fall asleep 잠이 들다 | Pilates 필라테스

Ready for Exams

››› 정답 5쪽

My score is

Let's Check It Out ______ / 16점		0~20점 → Level 1 Test
Ready for Exams ______ / 14점	→	21~25점 → Level 2 Test
Total ______ / 30점		26~30점 → Level 3 Test

1 밑줄 친 부분의 역할이 [보기]와 같은 것은? 2점

보기 Eating healthy food is important.

① He kept sending messages to her.
② We like watching late-night movies.
③ The little baby finally stopped crying.
④ Teaching children is not easy at all.
⑤ His hobby is playing basketball.

2 다음 문장들에서 어법상 어색한 부분을 모두 찾은 학생은? 3점

ⓐ I love going to the movies.
ⓑ Let's keep moving forward.
ⓒ Why do you practice to jump?
ⓓ She dislikes to have parties on Sundays.

① 수영: ⓐ going ⓒ practice
② 진영: ⓑ moving ⓓ to have
③ 치용: ⓐ going ⓑ moving
④ 지선: ⓒ to jump ⓓ to have
⑤ 영선: ⓑ moving ⓒ to jump

3 Find the sentence that has an error and correct it. 4점

ⓐ Can you finish to cook the pizza soon?
ⓑ People hate to change their minds.

(　　) ____________ → ____________

4 다음 빈칸에 들어갈 말을 조건에 맞게 완성하시오. 5점

A: Don't you remember the man over there?
B: Who? The guy in the red cap?
A: Right. We saw him at the station a few hours ago.
B: Oh, now I ____________ ____________ him there.

· 조건 대화에서 언급된 단어를 활용할 것

VOCA healthy 건강에 좋은 | forward 앞으로 | change one's mind 마음을 바꾸다

UNIT 07

동명사와 현재분사, 관용적 표현

CONCEPT 1

동명사와 현재분사

동명사와 현재분사는 「동사원형+-ing」로 같은 형태이지만 아래와 같이 역할과 의미가 다르다.

	동명사	현재분사
형태	동사원형+-ing	동사원형+-ing
기능	명사(주어, 목적어, 보어)	형용사, 진행형
표현	용도, 목적	동작, 상태
의미	~하는 것, ~하기	~하고 있는, ~하는

Miki is swimming in the pool. (현재분사)

She wants to buy a house with a swimming pool. (동명사)

The sleeping baby looks so peaceful. (현재분사)

The child wants to sleep in a sleeping bag. (동명사)

CONCEPT 2

동명사의 관용적 표현

	뜻	예문
go+-ing	~하러 가다	She goes hiking on weekends.
be busy+-ing	~하느라 바쁘다	I'm busy doing the dishes.
be tired of+-ing	~에 싫증이 나다	He's tired of living in an apartment.
be worth+-ing	~할 가치가 있다	It is worth talking with the doctor.
feel like+-ing	~하고 싶다	She felt like going shopping again.
How[What] about+-ing ~?	~하는 게 어때?	How about going to the concert tonight?
spend[waste] 시간[돈]+-ing	~하느라 시간[돈]을 쓰다[낭비하다]	She spent about 30 minutes waiting for me.
look forward to+-ing	~하기를 고대하다	She is looking forward to seeing the rainbow bridge.
have difficulty [a hard time]+-ing	~하는 데 어려움을 겪다	We had difficulty persuading him. I had a hard time leaving the town.

GRAMMAR POINT

be + -ing의 구분

- He is watching the birds in the tree. (현재분사)
- His hobby is / watching the birds in the trees. (동명사)

dancing room과 dancing boy

- a dancing room
  방이 춤춘다 (×) → 동명사
- a dancing boy
  소년이 춤춘다 (○) → 현재분사

go + -ing의 여러 가지 표현

- go fishing 낚시하러 가다
- go camping 캠핑하러 가다
- go swimming 수영하러 가다
- go bowling 볼링을 하러 가다
- go hiking 가벼운 등산을 가다
- go shopping 쇼핑을 하러 가다
- go skating 스케이트 타러 가다
- go hunting 사냥을 하러 가다
- go skiing 스키를 타러 가다

VOCA peaceful 평화로운 | sleeping bag 침낭 | do the dishes 설거지를 하다 | persuade 설득하다 | leave 떠나다

Let's Check It Out

››› 정답 5쪽

My score is / 20점

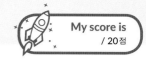

A 밑줄 친 단어를 어법에 맞게 고쳐 쓰시오. 각 1점

1 We were sitting in the wait room. → ______________
2 The cry boy is my cousin. → ______________
3 She bought a run machine. → ______________
4 Can you get a shop cart? → ______________
5 I love your smile face. → ______________

B 밑줄 친 부분이 동명사인지 현재분사인지 구분하시오. 각 1점

1 The girl liked reading books. → ______________
2 Her father is watching a fashion show. → ______________
3 The thief was jumping over the fence. → ______________
4 Are you afraid of telling the truth? → ______________
5 One of my friends hates spending his money. → ______________

C 밑줄 친 부분의 쓰임이 [보기]와 같으면 S, 다르면 D를 쓰시오. 각 1점

보기	I didn't bring my sleeping bag.

1 I am drinking grapefruit juice. → ______________
2 The man's hobby is driving cars. → ______________
3 Sleeping outside in a tent is fun. → ______________
4 The boring movie made me sleepy. → ______________
5 They enjoyed watching the stars. → ______________

D 밑줄 친 부분이 어색하면 고치시오. 각 1점

1 We went to skating last night. → ______________
2 She was busy chatting on the phone. → ______________
3 Don't waste money to buy useless things. → ______________
4 We had difficulty to follow you. → ______________
5 What about rent a car? → ______________

VOCA fence 울타리 | tell the truth 사실을 말하다 | grapefruit 자몽 | chat 수다 떨다 | useless 쓸모없는 | rent (돈을 주고) 빌리다, 대여하다

Ready for Exams

››› 정답 6쪽

My score is

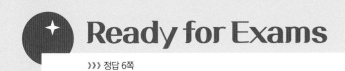

Let's Check It Out ______ / 20점		0~20점 → Level 1 Test
Ready for Exams ______ / 10점	➜	21~25점 → Level 2 Test
Total ______ / 30점		26~30점 → Level 3 Test

1 다음 중 밑줄 친 단어의 쓰임이 같은 것끼리 짝지어진 것은? 2점

ⓐ a sleeping baby	ⓑ a living room	ⓒ a washing machine
ⓓ a dancing girl	ⓔ a smoking room	ⓕ a frying pan

① ⓐ, ⓒ　② ⓑ, ⓒ, ⓓ　③ ⓐ, ⓓ, ⓔ
④ ⓒ, ⓓ, ⓔ, ⓕ　⑤ ⓑ, ⓒ, ⓔ, ⓕ

2 Which of the underlined words is used differently than the others? 2점

① Swimming is my favorite sport.
② Do you mind passing me the salt?
③ Was she dancing on the stage?
④ Thank you for helping me.
⑤ Haruto is good at speaking English.

3 다음 중 어법상 어색한 것은? 2점

① She went bowling this morning.
② I didn't feel like to go there alone.
③ How about giving him a big hand?
④ He was busy finding his password.
⑤ We look forward to seeing you again.

4 다음은 동명사와 현재분사에 대해 필기한 내용에 대한 대화이다. 규민이의 설명에서 잘못된 것을 찾아 고치시오. 4점

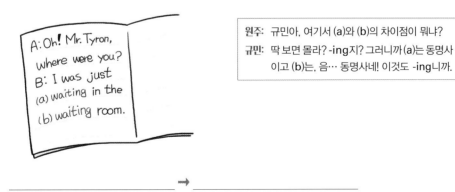

A: Oh! Mr. Tyron,
where were you?
B: I was just
(a) waiting in the
(b) waiting room.

원주: 규민아, 여기서 (a)와 (b)의 차이점이 뭐냐?
규민: 딱 보면 몰라? -ing지? 그러니까 (a)는 동명사이고 (b)는, 음… 동명사네! 이것도 -ing니까.

__________________ ➜ __________________

VOCA give A a big hand A에게 큰 박수를 치다 | password 비밀번호

CHAPTER 03

Review Test

My score is
/ 60점
51점 이상 PASS!!

››› 정답 6쪽

U06_1

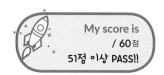

01 다음 빈칸에 알맞은 것은? (답 2개) 2점

________ too much is bad for your health.

① Work　② Have
③ Walk　④ Sleeping
⑤ To eat

U06_2

02 다음 빈칸에 알맞은 것끼리 짝지어진 것은? 2점

• They want ________ him a present. • Did she enjoy ________ the song?

① to give – singing　② giving – singing
③ to give – to sing　④ giving – to sing
⑤ gave – sings

U06_2

03 짝지어진 두 문장의 의미가 다른 것은? 2점

한눈에 쏙

① It started to snow.
= It started snowing.
② She likes to collect pink socks.
= She likes collecting pink socks.
③ I hate swimming in the river.
= I hate to swim in the river.
④ They began to search for a boat.
=They began searching for a boat.
⑤ He tried to enter the password.
= He tried entering the password.

U06_1

04 다음 빈칸에 들어갈 말을 바르게 쓰지 못한 학생은? 2점

She left without ________.

① 중권: any money
② 주연: saying a word
③ 진우: to tell me why
④ 하랑: paying the bill
⑤ 초현: anything but water

U07_1

05 밑줄 친 부분의 쓰임이 다른 하나는? 2점

한눈에 쏙

① Do you like swimming?
② I'm interested in swimming.
③ He's not very good at swimming.
④ Her sisters are swimming in the pool.
⑤ My favorite hobby is swimming.

U06_GP

06 다음 중 밑줄 친 부분이 어법상 어색한 것은? 2점

함정

① We practiced jumping high.
② I would like meeting you soon.
③ She likes eating out every night.
④ He planned to join the fitness center.
⑤ My brother promised to buy me a doll.

U06_2

07 Which is suitable for the blank? 2점

I remember ________ them somewhere before.

① meet　② to meet
③ meeting　④ met
⑤ to meeting

U07_2

08 다음을 영작할 때 쓸 수 없는 단어는? 3점

함정

나는 영춘권(Wing Chun)을 숙달하는 데 어려움을 겪지 않았다.

① did　② have
③ difficulty　④ mastering
⑤ to

U06_2+GP

09 다음 중 어법상 어색한 것은? (답 2개) 3점

★ 고난도

① He dislikes to chat online.
② She denied stealing my bike.
③ I wish to speak to the manager.
④ He quit playing computer games.
⑤ Do you really need going there?

U06_1

10 다음 빈칸에 공통으로 들어갈 단어를 쓰시오. 3점

- Are you good at ________ care of pets?
- My sister is interested in ________ pictures of bridges.

→ ____________

U06_1

11 Find the sentence that has an error and correct it. 4점

ⓐ Watch the stars was fun.
ⓑ Thank you for listening to my story.

(   ) ____________ → ____________

U06_2

12 다음 영작에서 어법상 어색한 부분을 찾아 고치시오. 4점

그는 춤추기를 멈추고 노래를 부르기 시작했다.
= He stopped to dance and started to sing.

____________ → ____________

U06_1+GP

13 다음 두 문장이 의미가 통하도록 빈칸에 알맞은 말을 각 1단어로 쓰시오. 4점

Eat a lot of vegetables. They're good for your health.

→ ________ a lot of vegetables
________ good for your health.

U06_2

14 빈칸에 들어갈 수 있는 단어들의 첫 글자를 이용하여 주어진 단어를 완성하시오. 5점
★ 고난도

The old man ________ watching a black-and-white film.

ⓐ started　ⓑ avoided　ⓒ would like
ⓓ minds　ⓔ wished　ⓕ enjoyed

→ □w□□o□e

U06_2

15 할머니께서 게임 사이트에 접속하시다가 아래와 같은 경고 문구를 받았다. 이 상황에서 할머니께 해드릴 수 있는 말을 주어진 단어를 이용하여 완성하시오. 5점

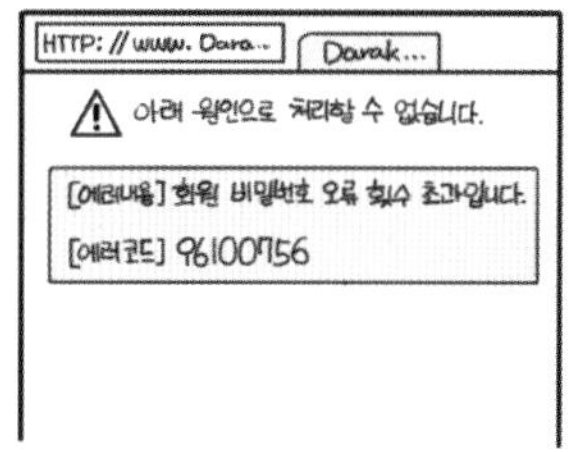

	What's wrong with this stupid computer?
	Grandma, you ________ ________ the ________ password. (keep, wrong, enter)

U06_2

16 다음 우리말을 영작하시오. 6점

Edward는 그 치킨을 먹은 것을 부인했다.

→ ____________

U07_2

17 다음 주어진 단어들을 바르게 배열하시오. 5점

had, hard, house, time, we, a, the, cleaning

→ ____________

U06_2

18 우리말을 같은 의미의 영어 문장과 짝지으시오. 4점

(가) 난 집에 걸어 온 것이 기억 안 나.
(나) 그녀는 똑바로 걸으려고 애썼다.

ⓐ I don't remember walking home.
ⓑ I don't remember to walk home.
ⓒ She tried to walk straight.
ⓓ She tried walking straight.

(가) ________　(나) ________

시험 직전에 챙겨 보는 비법 노트

》》 정답 6쪽

한눈에 쏙! 아래 노트를 보면서 빈칸을 채워 보세요.

1 동명사의 역할

주어 | 1)__ | 동사의 2)___ | 전치사의 3)___

2 동명사 vs. to부정사

① 동명사를 목적어로 취하는 동사	1)e____, 2)m___, 3)d_______*, 4)q___, 5)a____, 6)f_____ 등
② to부정사를 목적어로 취하는 동사	7)w___, 8)p___, 9)h___, 10)p_______, 11)e_____, 12)d_____ 등
③ 둘 다 목적어로 취하는 동사	13)li__**, 14)b____, 15)s____, 16)c_______, 17)lo__, 18)h___ 등
④ 의미가 달라지는 동사	19)t__, 20)r________, 21)s___, 22)f_____

*3)d_______는 동명사만! **13)li__는 동명사와 to부정사 둘 다!

3 동명사 vs. 현재분사

동명사 → 용도, 1)__ — 명사

현재분사 → 2)__, 상태 — 형용사, 3)___

헷갈리지 말자! 초록색으로 표시된 부분을 바르게 고쳐 쓰세요.

1 Putting together all the figures were not easy.

→

2 I won't forget closing all the windows because it may rain this afternoon.

→

3 ⓐ My mother is watching Netflix. ⓑ Her hobby is watching Netflix.

위 두 문장에서 ⓐ의 watching은 동명사, ⓑ의 watching은 현재분사이다.

→ →

CHAPTER 04

현재완료

UNIT 08

현재완료의 의미와 용법

CONCEPT 1 현재완료의 의미

과거에 시작된 동작이나 상태가 현재까지 영향을 미치는 시제를 말한다.

기본 형태: have+과거분사(p.p.)

The cat began to live in the attic. (과거)

The cat still lives in the attic. (현재)

→The cat has lived in the attic. (현재완료)

CONCEPT 2 현재완료 부정문과 의문문

부정문	have/has+not/never+p.p.
의문문	Have/Has+주어+p.p. ~? – Yes, 주어+have/has. / No, 주어+haven't/hasn't.

The bus has not left yet.

Have we met before? –Yes, we have. / No, we haven't.

How have you been? – I've been so-so.

CONCEPT 3 현재완료의 용법

	의미	함께 자주 쓰이는 표현
완료	막 ~했다	just, already, yet
경험	~한 적이 있다	ever, never, before, once, twice
계속	~해 오고 있다	for, since, how long
결과	~해버렸다(그래서 지금은 …하다)	go, come, leave, lose, buy

She has just gotten up. (완료)

I have cheated on a test once. (경험)

They've lived here for three years. (계속)

He has lost his pet dog. (결과)

GRAMMAR POINT

동사 변화표

- 주요 불규칙 동사 변화표는 p. 157 참조.

완료와 결과의 구분

- just, already, yet이 있으면 완료 용법으로 봐도 된다.

She has just come home. (완료)

She has come home. (결과 또는 완료)

for와 since

- 'for+기간', 'since+과거 시점'으로 쓰며, since 다음에는 '주어+동사'도 올 수 있다.

We have kept the secret for over 5,000 years.

The ghost has bothered me since last Halloween.

The man has lived there since he was 10.

already와 yet

- already는 '벌써'라는 의미이고, yet은 의문문에서는 '벌써', 부정문에서는 '아직'이라는 의미이다.
- already는 주로 have와 p.p. 사이에 위치하고, yet은 주로 문장 끝에 온다.

I have already finished my diet.

She hasn't ridden on the subway yet.

Have you visited Gyeongbok Palace yet?

VOCA attic 다락 | so-so 그저 그런 | cheat 부정 행위를 하다 | bother 괴롭히다

Let's Check It Out

››› 정답 6쪽

My score is
/ 18점

A [ ]에서 알맞은 것을 고르시오. 각 1점

1 Woobin has [catched / caught] a catfish.

2 The children [have / has] left their home.

3 She [didn't / hasn't] done her homework yet.

4 [Have / Has] you hugged your mommy?

5 They have stayed here [for / since] five days.

B 주어진 단어들을 이용하여 현재완료 문장을 완성하시오. 각 1점

1 (just, make, a mistake)

→ She ______________________.

2 (eat, lunch, already)

→ We ______________________.

3 (lose, for a week)

→ The team ______________________.

4 (not, throw, the ball, yet)

→ He ______________________.

5 (you, fix)

→ ______________________ the kitchen door?

C [보기]처럼 문장을 전환할 때 빈칸에 알맞은 말을 쓰시오. 각 2점

보기 He was sick last week, and he is still sick.
→ He has been sick since last week.

1 I lost your bag, and I don't have it now.

→ I ________ ________ your bag.

2 I saw the movie yesterday, and I saw it today.

→ I ________ ________ the movie twice.

3 I began to draw her face, and I just finished it.

→ I ________ just ________ ________ her face.

4 He moved here two years ago. He still lives here.

→ He ________ ________ ________ ________ two years.

VOCA catfish 메기 | hug 껴안다 | throw 던지다 | fix 고치다 | move 이사하다

Ready for Exams

››› 정답 7쪽

My score is

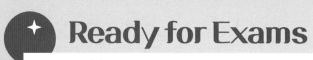

Let's Check It Out ______ / 18점		0~20점 → Level 1 Test
Ready for Exams ______ / 12점	→	21~25점 → Level 2 Test
Total ______ / 30점		26~30점 → Level 3 Test

1 Which is suitable for the blank? 2점

Harang ______________ sick since last Friday. She is in the hospital now.

① is ② have been ③ has been
④ were ⑤ been

2 다음 대화의 빈칸에 알맞은 것으로 짝지어진 것은? 3점

A: ______________ a UFO?
B: ______________. I saw one a few years ago.

① Did you see – Yes, I do
② Did you saw – Yes, I did
③ Have you saw – No, I didn't
④ Have you seen – Yes, I have
⑤ Have you seen – No, I haven't

3 다음 중 같은 현재완료 용법끼리 바르게 짝지은 학생은? 3점

ⓐ The poor girl has lost her way.
ⓑ They have already sold the mansion.
ⓒ I've never seen a koala before.
ⓓ Have you finished the email yet?
ⓔ We have baked pizza since 1971.
ⓕ Have you ever visited the museum?

① 가민: ⓐ, ⓔ ② 단아: ⓑ, ⓒ ③ 별이: ⓓ, ⓕ
④ 하늘: ⓑ, ⓓ ⑤ 유준: ⓐ, ⓕ

4 현재완료 시제를 사용해서 그림의 상황을 묘사하는 문장을 완성하시오. 4점

→ The picture ______________________ from the wall. (fall down)

VOCA mansion 대저택 | museum 박물관 | fall down 떨어지다

UNIT 09

주의해야 할 현재완료

CONCEPT 1

주의해야 할 현재완료

A 현재완료와 함께 쓸 수 없는 어구

과거 시점 표현	yesterday, last, ago, then, just now, in+연도
특정한 때	what time, when

She ~~has worked~~ at the bank last year. (→ worked)

~~Have they stayed~~ at the hotel in 2018? (→ Did they stay)

When ~~have you cooked~~ the fish? (→ did you cook)

What time ~~has the plumber visited~~ your house? (→ did the plumber visit)

B have been to와 have gone to

have been to	경험	~에 가본 적이 있다
have gone to	결과	~에 가버렸다

They have been to Madagascar.

(They are not in Madagascar; they are here now.)

They have gone to Madagascar.

(They are in Madagascar, so they are not here now.)

CONCEPT 2

과거와 현재완료

과거	특정한 과거에 발생	현재의 정보를 알 수 없음
현재완료	불확실한 과거에 발생	현재의 정보도 알 수 있음

The school nurse was sick yesterday. (지금은 아픈지 모름)

The school nurse has been sick since yesterday. (지금도 아픔)

GRAMMAR POINT

since + 과거 부사

- 'since+과거 부사'는 현재완료와 함께 쓸 수 있다.

  She has been at home <u>since yesterday</u>.

in과 since

- She had nose surgery in 2014. (과거)
- We haven't seen the player since 2014. (현재완료)

완료 용법의 have been to

- have been to는 완료 용법으로도 쓰인다.

  A: Where have you been? (어디 있었어?)

  B: I've just been to the market. (시장에 막 갔다 왔어.)

have gone to

- have gone to와 1·2인칭은 특수한 경우를 제외하고는 함께 잘 쓰이지 않는다.

  I have gone to the market. (×)

  You have gone to Europe. (×)

VOCA plumber 배관공 | Madagascar 마다가스카르(나라 이름) | school nurse 보건 선생님 | surgery 수술

Let's Check It Out

››› 정답 7쪽

My score is
/ 20점

A [ ]에서 알맞은 것을 고르시오. 각 1점

1 Leslie [visited / has visited] Korea last year.
2 He [stayed / has stayed] here since last week.
3 Mr. Simpson got married [in / since] 2008.
4 [How long / When] have you practiced skiing?
5 What time [did he go / has he gone] to the festival?

B [ ]에서 알맞은 것을 고르시오. 각 1점

1 I have never [been / gone] to North Korea.
2 Where is Yoon? Has he [been / gone] to work?
3 Tina has [been / gone] to Japan, so I can't see her now.
4 A: Have you ever [been / gone] to Florida?
B: Yes, I have. I [was / have been] there last month.

C 밑줄 친 부분을 어법에 맞게 고치시오. 각 1점

1 We have moved to Mok-dong six years ago. → ______________
2 My father bought this car since 2018. → ______________
3 We were on vacation since yesterday. → ______________
4 Everybody has gone fishing last night. → ______________
5 When have you met her? → ______________

D 우리말과 일치하도록 빈칸을 채우시오. 각 2점

1 난 오늘 아침부터 아무것도 안 먹었어.
→ I __________ __________ anything __________ this morning.

2 그녀는 2020년도에 이 핸드폰을 샀다.
→ She __________ this cell phone __________ 2020.

3 이틀 전부터 몸에 열이 나요.
→ I __________ __________ a fever __________ two days ago.

VOCA get married 결혼하다 | festival 축제 | on vacation 휴가 중인 | fever 열

Ready for Exams

››› 정답 7쪽

My score is

Let's Check It Out ______ / 20점		0~24점 → Level 1 Test
Ready for Exams ______ / 15점	➡	25~29점 → Level 2 Test
Total ______ / 35점		30~35점 → Level 3 Test

1 다음 빈칸에 알맞은 것으로 짝지어진 것은? 2점

• Ashley ________________ a boyfriend, but now she's single.
• Have you ever ________________ to Turkey?

① has – went ② had – been ③ had – gone
④ has had – been ⑤ has had – gone

2 다음 문장을 바르게 분석한 학생은? 4점

ⓐ He has lost the item last night.
ⓑ Amy has already finished her homework.

① 태연: ⓐ는 '계속'을 나타내는 현재완료야.
② 연주: ⓐ에서 has lost를 loses로 바꿔야 해.
③ 주민: ⓐ에서 last night이 있으니까 과거로 써야 해.
④ 민철: ⓑ에서 already는 현재완료에만 쓸 수 있어.
⑤ 철희: ⓑ는 현재완료 용법 중 '결과' 용법이야.

3 다음 그림을 보고 문장을 완성하시오. 4점

→ Sarah ________________ Phuket.

4 Correct the error and rewrite the sentence. 5점

When has she returned home?

→ ________________________________

VOCA single 혼자인 | Phuket 푸켓(태국의 휴양지) | return 돌아오다

CHAPTER 04

Review Test

My score is / 60점
51점 이상 PASS!!

››› 정답 7쪽

U08_2

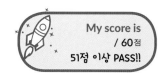

01 다음을 부정문으로 바르게 고친 것은? 2점

I have drunk the juice.

① I didn't have drunk the juice.
② I can't have drunk the juice.
③ I am not have drunk the juice.
④ I have not drunk the juice.
⑤ I have drunk not the juice.

U08_1+3

02 다음 두 문장을 한 문장으로 나타낼 때 빈칸에 알맞은 것은? 2점

She lost her phone. She doesn't have it now. →She ________ her phone.

① has
② has lost
③ has lose
④ is losing
⑤ was losing

U08_3+U09_GP

03 밑줄 친 부분이 어법상 어색한 것은? (답 2개) 3점

★ 고난도

① Have you done the dishes yet?
② Has your dog ever eaten French fries?
③ I have never gone to Mt. Geumgang.
④ He has just taken a bath.
⑤ My daughter has became a class leader.

U08_3+U09_1

04 다음 빈칸에 들어갈 말이 바르게 짝지어진 것은? 2점

함정

• He has ________ left for Siberia. • He left for Siberia ________.

① just – just
② just – just now
③ yet – already
④ already – just
⑤ just now – just

U08_3

05 밑줄 친 부분의 쓰임이 나머지 넷과 다른 것은? 2점

한눈에 쏙

① I have just eaten dinner.
② He has already taken notes.
③ We haven't decided what to do yet.
④ Have you found the solution yet?
⑤ I have been to London twice.

U08_3+GP

06 다음 영작에 대해 바르게 설명한 학생은? 3점

한눈에 쏙

Sarawut은 2019년부터 나에게 무술을 가르쳐 왔다. = Sarawut has taught me martial arts for 2019.

① 희경: 현재완료는 'have+p.p.'니까 has를 have로 써야 해.
② 경민: '나에게'니까 me를 to me로 써야 해.
③ 광민: teach의 과거분사는 teached니까 taught를 teached로 고쳐야 해.
④ 선혜: 2019년은 과거니까 taught만 써야 해.
⑤ 해천: 과거 시점이 있으니까 for를 since로 써야 해.

U08_3

07 다음 문장과 현재완료의 쓰임이 같은 것은? 2점

보기 I have lived in Daegu for two years.

① I have told my password to her twice.
② Mrs. Bronson has gone to Mt. Jiri.
③ My dogs have been sick since Sunday.
④ Have you ever been to Koreatown?
⑤ I haven't finished my science homework yet.

U09_1

08 How many sentences are incorrect? 3점

★ 고난도

ⓐ What time has he gone home? ⓑ He hasn't come home last night. ⓒ The boy has lost his tricycle. ⓓ I took a picture of you just now. ⓔ The man has been there since yesterday.

① one
② two
③ three
④ four
⑤ five

U08_2

09 주어진 단어를 넣어 문장을 다시 쓰시오. 4점

They have had a merry Christmas. (never)

→ ______________________________

U08_2

10 대화에 나온 단어를 이용하여 질문을 완성하시오. 4점

A: ________ ________ ________ his songs? B: No, I haven't, but I heard he's a good singer.

U08_1+3

11 Complete the translation by using the given word. 3점

저는 3주 동안 입원해 있는 중이에요. (be)

→ I ____________ ____________ in the hospital for three weeks.

U08_GP+U09_1

12 대화의 빈칸에 들어갈 말을 [보기]에서 골라 쓰시오. 6점

함정

보기 just now already yet just almost
A: I heard about the musical ____________. Have you bought a ticket ____________? B: We're too late. They've ____________ sold all the tickets.

U08_3

13 우리말과 일치하도록 조건에 맞게 영작하시오. 5점

난 전에 이렇게 작은 강아지를 한 번도 본 적이 없어.
·어휘 never, see, such, tiny, before, puppy ·조건 1 주어진 어휘를 모두 사용하되 필요 시 어형을 변화시킬 것 ·조건 2 주어진 단어를 포함하여 9단어로 쓸 것

→ ______________________________

____

U08_1+GP

14 다음 두 문장을 한 문장으로 나타낼 때 빈칸에 알맞은 말을 쓰시오. 5점

Yunho started playing golf in 2018. He still plays it.

→ Yunho ______________________ 2018.

U08_1+GP

15 주어진 단어들 중에서 필요한 것만 골라 활용하여 우리말을 영작하시오. 5점

Carmen은 2일 동안 다이어트를 하고 있다. was, been, on a diet, for, since, has, two days

→ ______________________________

U09_1

16 다음 두 문장 중 어법상 어색한 것을 찾아 고치시오. 4점

ⓐ He has visited Hong Kong five years ago. ⓑ My dad has gotten a new job.

( ) ____________ → ____________

U08_2+GP

17 다음 대화에 나타난 상황을 한 문장으로 요약할 때 빈칸에 알맞은 말을 쓰시오. 5점

★ 고난도

Vicky: I have a terrible headache.
Doctor: Okay, take off your hat, and I'll examine you.
Vicky: I can't get it off, Doc. It's too tight.
Doctor: How long have you worn the hat?
Vicky: I don't know... since last Halloween?
Doctor: I believe I've discovered the cause of your problem.

*examine: 진찰하다

→ The problem is that Vicky ____________ ____________ her hat ____________ too long.

시험 직전에 챙겨 보는 비법 노트

>>> 정답 8쪽

한눈에 쏙! 아래 노트를 보면서 빈칸을 채워 보세요.

1 현재완료의 의미와 용법

- 의미: 1)__의 동작이나 상태가 2)__까지 영향을 미치는 시제
- 용법: 3)__, 4)__, 5)__, 6)__

2 현재완료 부정문

have/has + 1)_____[2)_____] + p.p.

3 현재완료 의문문

1)_____/2)_____ + 주어 + p.p. ~?

4 주의 사항

- 현재완료 + 과거를 나타내는 1)___ (X)
- have 2)____ to: 경험(~에 가본 적이 있다)
  have 3)____ to: 결과(~에 가버렸다)

헷갈리지 말자! 초록색으로 표시된 부분을 바르게 고쳐 쓰세요.

1 The ghost has followed us since the whole week.

→

2 Have they left the hotel yesterday?

→

3 We have gone to the theater.

→

CHAPTER 05

조동사

UNIT 10

can, may, will

CONCEPT 1 조동사

조동사란 동사를 도와 허락, 가능, 충고, 부탁, 의무 등의 뜻을 갖게 하는 말로 조동사의 뒤에는 동사원형이 온다. 조동사의 의문문은 「조동사+주어+동사원형 ~?」이고, 응답은 「Yes, 주어+조동사.」 또는 「No, 주어+조동사+not.」으로 한다.

CONCEPT 2 can

조동사	의미	긍정	부정
can, could	형태	can+동사원형	cannot[can't]+동사원형
	능력, 가능	~할 수 있다 (= be able to) I can play the cello.	~할 수 없다 (= be not able to) He can't speak Thai.
	허락	~해도 된다 (= may) You can take a break.	~하면 안 된다 (= may not) You cannot park here.

CONCEPT 3 may

조동사	의미	긍정	부정
may, might	형태	may+동사원형	may not+동사원형
	약한 추측	~일지도 모른다 He may be late for the meeting.	~이 아닐지도 모른다 It may not snow tomorrow.
	허락	~해도 된다 (= can) May I ask a question?	~하면 안 된다 (= cannot) You may not take any pictures without permission.

CONCEPT 4 will

조동사	의미	긍정	부정
will, would	형태	will+동사원형	will not[won't]+동사원형
	미래	~할 것이다 (= be going to) Will you participate in the elections? (= Are you going to participate in the elections?)	~하지 않을 것이다 (= be not going to) I won't do that again. (= I'm not going to do that again.)

GRAMMAR POINT

추측의 의미를 갖는 cannot

- cannot[can't]은 '~일 리가 없다'라는 부정적인 추측의 의미로도 사용된다.

It can't be true.
(그건 사실일 리가 없어.)

조동사 could의 두 가지 뜻

- can의 과거형: ~할 수 있었다

He could run fast.

- 공손한 의미(주로 의문문)

Could you give me a ride? (요청)

be able to의 활용

- 미래: ~할 수 있을 것이다

She will be able to enter Harvard.
→ will can (×)

- 완료: ~해 올 수 있었다/없었다

I haven't been able to sleep for 3 days.

조동사 might의 두 가지 뜻

- may의 과거형

He said he might come tomorrow.

- 약한 추측

He might[may] be in the classroom.

will과 be going to 비교

- will: '요청, 의지'의 의미를 나타낼 수 있다.

Will you come to my house? (요청)
I will do it. (의지)

- be going to: '예정'의 의미를 나타낸다.

I am going to meet him. (예정된 미래)

조동사 would의 두 가지 뜻

- will의 과거형

He said he would be here.

- 공손한 의미

Would you like to come to my house? (초대)

VOCA Thai 태국어; 태국인 | take a break 휴식을 취하다 | park 주차하다 | take a picture 사진을 찍다 | permission 허락 | participate in ~에 참여하다 | election 선거

Let's Check It Out

››› 정답 8쪽

My score is / 18점

A 우리말과 같은 뜻이 되도록 [ ]에서 알맞은 것을 고르시오. 각 1점

1 미나는 스페인어를 말할 수 있다.
→ Mina [can / will] speak Spanish.

2 서둘러. 거기서 약간의 음식을 얻을지도 몰라.
→ Hurry up. You [will / may] get some food there.

3 내가 먼저 가도 될까요?
→ [Will / May] I go first?

4 우리는 내년에 16살이 될 거야.
→ We [can / will] be sixteen next year.

B 두 문장의 뜻이 같도록 빈칸에 알맞은 말을 쓰시오. 각 2점

1 She could get into the foreign language high school.
→ She ________ ________ ________ get into the foreign language high school.

2 Will you take care of it?
→ ________ ________ ________ ________ take care of it?

3 We aren't going to volunteer at the school bazaar this year.
→ We ________ volunteer at the school bazaar this year.

C 우리말과 같은 뜻이 되도록 괄호 안의 말을 배열하시오. 각 2점

1 Edward가 아플 리가 없다. (sick, be, can't)
→ Edward ________________________.

2 그는 오늘 저녁에 돌아올 것이다. (back, be, will)
→ He ________________________ tonight.

3 그는 그녀의 충고를 따르지 않을 것이다. (not, to, going, he's, follow)
→ ________________________ her advice.

4 나는 일출을 볼 수 있을 것이다. (see, be, able, will, to)
→ I ________________________ the sunrise.

VOCA get into 들어가다 | foreign language high school 외국어고등학교 | take care of 돌보다 | volunteer 자원봉사하다 | bazaar 바자회 | sunrise 일출

Ready for Exams

››› 정답 8쪽

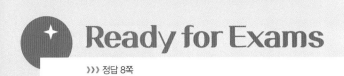

My score is		
Let's Check It Out ______ / 18점		0~20점 → Level 1 Test
Ready for Exams ______ / 12점	➡	21~25점 → Level 2 Test
Total ______ / 30점		26~30점 → Level 3 Test

1 다음 대화의 빈칸에 알맞은 것은? 2점

A: Can I borrow your science notebook?
B: ______________. I already lent it to Minsu.

① Yes, I can ② Yes, you can ③ Yes, you can't
④ No, you can't ⑤ No, I can't

2 How many sentences are grammatically <u>incorrect</u>? 2점

ⓐ She couldn't be able to catch the ball.
ⓑ He won't come here soon.
ⓒ She said she will ignore it.
ⓓ He might interested in your plan.
ⓔ It can't be true.

① zero ② one ③ two
④ three ⑤ four

3 빈칸에 공통으로 들어갈 알맞은 말은? 2점

• ______________ you do me a favor?
• I ______________ visit a museum next week.

① Will[will] ② Would[would] ③ Could[could]
④ May[may] ⑤ Do[do]

4 우리말과 같은 뜻이 되도록 빈칸에 알맞은 말을 쓰시오. 3점

너는 그의 억양을 흉내 낼 수 있니?

→ ______________ you ______________ ______________ imitate his accent?

5 Complete the sentence according to the conditions. 3점

• Condition 1 대답에 알맞은 질문을 영작할 것
• Condition 2 what을 활용할 것

A: ______________________________ with the rest of the cake?
B: I am going to get a refund.

VOCA borrow 빌리다 | lend 빌려주다 | ignore 무시하다 | favor 호의, 관심 | imitate 흉내 내다 | accent 억양 | get a refund 환불을 받다

UNIT 11

must, have to, should, ought to

CONCEPT 1 must, have to

조동사	의미	긍정	부정
must, have to	의무	must+동사원형: ~해야 한다 (= have/has to) You must[have to] follow the rules. Must I come early? = Do I have to come early? - Yes, you must. (의무) = Yes, you do. - No, you don't have to. (불필요)	don't/doesn't have to+ 동사원형: ~할 필요가 없다 (= don't/doesn't need to+동사원형 = need not+동사원형) You don't have to lock the door. must not[mustn't]+동사원형: ~해서는 안 된다 (= may not) They must not make any noise.
must	강한 추측 (확신)	must+동사원형: ~임에 틀림없다 He must be sleepy.	cannot[can't]+동사원형: ~일 리가 없다 He cannot be a liar.

CONCEPT 2 should, ought to

조동사	의미	긍정	부정
should, ought to	충고, 조언	should+동사원형: ~해야 한다 (= ought to) You should drink lots of water. = You ought to drink lots of water. You ought to be kinder to kids. = You should be kinder to kids.	should not[shouldn't]+동사원형: ~해서는 안 된다 (= ought not to) You should not be rude to adults. = You ought not to be rude to adults. You ought not to tell lies. = You should not tell lies.

GRAMMAR POINT

두 개의 조동사 사용

- 조동사는 두 개를 나란히 쓰지 못하므로 둘 중 하나의 조동사를 동사구로 바꾸어야 한다.

  David will can get a good grade. (×)

  David will be able to get a good grade. (○)

must의 사용

- must가 추측을 나타낼 경우는 have to나 has to로 바꿔 쓸 수 없다.
- must는 긍정이고 의무일 때에만 have to로 바꾸어 쓸 수 있다.

must(의무)의 과거 표현

- must가 과거의 의무를 나타낼 때 'had to+동사원형'을 쓴다.
- 과거 표현의 부정은 'didn't have to+동사원형'을 쓴다.

  You had to call me.

  You didn't have to call me.

must와 should

- must: 개인적, 강제적

  You must finish your homework.

- should: 도덕적 의무, 충고 (must보다 약한 의미)

  You should help the old.

VOCA follow 따르다 | rule 규칙 | lock 잠그다 | make noise 시끄럽게 하다 | liar 거짓말쟁이 | rude 무례한 | the old (= old people) 노인들

Let's Check It Out

››› 정답 8쪽

My score is
/ 19점

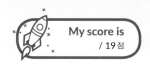

A [ ]에서 알맞은 것을 고르시오. 각 1점

1 We [must / have] to finish the project by the due date.
2 You [should / ought] to be kind to customers.
3 The boy must be [lie / lying] to you.
4 Did you [must / have to] quit the game?
5 You [must not / don't have to] cross the street when the light is red.

B 우리말과 같은 뜻이 되도록 빈칸에 알맞은 말을 쓰시오. 각 2점

1 너는 병원에 갈 필요가 없다.
→ You ________ ________ ________ go to the hospital.

2 우리는 식사를 직접 요리해야만 했다.
→ We ________ ________ cook our own meals.

3 우리는 집에 머물러 있어야 하나요?
→ ________ we ________ ________ stay at home?

4 오늘이 나의 행운의 날임에 틀림없어.
→ Today ________ ________ my lucky day.

5 그런 일들은 허용되어서는 안 된다.
→ Such things ________ ________ ________ be allowed.

C 두 문장의 뜻이 같도록 빈칸에 알맞은 말을 쓰시오. 각 1점

1 You must keep your desk clean.
→ You ________ ________ keep your desk clean.

2 He doesn't have to meet her directly.
→ He ________ ________ ________ meet her directly.

3 You should cross the road carefully.
→ You ________ ________ cross the road carefully.

4 You shouldn't smoke at the bus stop.
→ You ________ ________ ________ smoke at the bus stop.

VOCA project 기획, 프로젝트 | due date 마감일 | customer 고객 | cross 건너다 | light 신호등 | own 자신의 | meal 식사 | allow 허용하다 | directly 바로, 직접 | carefully 주의해서 | smoke 흡연하다

Ready for Exams

››› 정답 8쪽

My score is

Let's Check It Out ______	/ 19점	0~20점 → Level 1 Test
Ready for Exams ______	/ 11점	21~25점 → Level 2 Test
Total ______	/ 30점	26~30점 → Level 3 Test

1 다음 대화의 빈칸에 알맞은 것은? 2점

A: Do I have to take him this document?
B: ________________. I saved it on the computer. So you can send it by email.

① Yes, you must
② Yes, you have to
③ No, you won't
④ No, you don't have to
⑤ No, you aren't able to

2 Among ①~⑤, which one is grammatically incorrect? 2점

A: ① Should we ② see your parents ③ before we go to the movies?
B: No, I don't ④ think we ⑤ shouldn't.

3 두 문장이 같은 뜻이 되도록 빈칸에 알맞은 말을 쓰시오. 4점

Must you hand in your assignment now?

→ __________ you __________ __________ hand in your assignment now?

4 Rearrange the following words and add one more word in the appropriate place to make a complete sentence. 3점

too, you, not, late, ought, stay up

→ ______________________________

VOCA document 서류, 문서 | save 저장하다 | hand in 제출하다 | assignment 과제 | stay up (자지 않고) 깨어 있다

UNIT 12

would like to, had better, used to

CONCEPT 1 would like to

긍정	부정
would like to+동사원형: ~하고 싶다 'want to+동사원형'과 비슷한 의미이다. 'd like to로 줄여 쓸 수 있다. I would like to apply for a library card.	would not[wouldn't] like to+동사원형: ~하고 싶지 않다 (= don't want to) I wouldn't like to join the contest. (= I don't want to join the contest.)

CONCEPT 2 had better

긍정	부정
had better+동사원형: ~하는 것이 좋겠다 충고와 제안을 나타내며, 'd better로 줄여 쓸 수 있다. You had better do your homework.	had better not+동사원형: ~하지 않는 것이 좋겠다 You had better not cry.

CONCEPT 3 used to

과거의 규칙적인 습관이나 상태를 나타내며, 현재는 그렇지 않다는 의미를 담고 있다.

	긍정	부정	의문
형태	used to+동사원형	didn't use to+동사원형 = used not to+동사원형	Did+주어+use to +동사원형 ~?
과거의 습관 (~하곤 했다)	On weekends, we used to climb the mountain.	We didn't use to go camping. = We used not to go camping.	Did you use to drink river water?
상태 (예전에 ~이었다)	There used to be a pond in the yard, but now there isn't.	There did not use to be a pond, but now there is.	Did there use to be owls here?

GRAMMAR POINT

현재의 의미

- would like to와 had better는 형태는 과거형이지만 현재나 미래의 의미를 갖는다.

had better와 would rather

- had better는 주로 2인칭 주어와 쓰이는 충고에 사용되며, would rather는 주로 1인칭 주어와 쓰이는 선택의 의미를 나타낸다.

  You had better cancel your trip.
  (너는 여행을 취소하는 것이 낫겠다.)

  I would rather stay at home.
  (나는 집에 있는 게 낫겠다.)

would와 used to

- would는 지금도 계속되는지 알 수 없는 과거의 습관을 나타내며, used to는 지금은 지속되지 않는 과거의 습관, 상태를 나타낸다.

  I would sometimes go to the movies alone.
  (나는 가끔 혼자 영화 보러 가곤 했다. - 지금도 가는지는 모름)

  We used to bake potatoes in a hot stove.
  (우리는 화덕에 감자를 구워 먹곤 했다. - 지금은 구워 먹지 않음)

used to의 부정

- used to의 부정 표현은 didn't use to와 used not to 두 가지가 있으나 used not to는 격식적인 표현으로, 자주 쓰이지 않는다.

used to의 세 가지 쓰임

- used to+동사원형: ~하곤 했다

  I used to get up late.
  (나는 늦게 일어나곤 했다.)

- be used to+-ing: ~하는 것에 익숙하다

  I am used to sleeping on the bus.
  (나는 버스에서 자는 것에 익숙하다.)

- be used to+동사원형: ~하기 위해 사용되다

  The cart is used to carry luggage.
  (그 카트는 짐을 옮기기 위해 사용된다.)

VOCA apply for ~을 신청하다 | library card 도서 대출증 | join 참가하다 | cancel 취소하다 | trip 여행 | pond 연못 | owl 올빼미 | alone 홀로, 혼자서 | bake 굽다 | luggage 짐

Let's Check It Out

››› 정답 8쪽

My score is / 18점

A 우리말과 같은 뜻이 되도록 괄호 안의 말을 배열하시오. 각 1점

1 너는 집안에 있는 대신에 산책하는 것이 낫겠다. (better, had, go)

→ You ______________________ for a walk instead of staying indoors.

2 우리 마을에는 작은 개울이 있었어. (be, to, used)

→ There ______________________ a small stream in my village.

3 나는 내 목표를 달성하고 싶다. (would, to, like)

→ I ______________________ achieve my goal.

4 나는 이 영화를 다시 보고 싶지 않아요. (not, like, would, to)

→ I ______________________ watch this film again.

5 너는 단것을 너무 많이 먹지 않는 게 낫겠다. (had, not, better)

→ You ______________________ eat too many sweets.

B 다음 문장을 부정문으로 바꿔 쓰시오. 각 1점

1 I would like to hear your thoughts.

→ ____

2 You'd better wear a vest under your coat.

→ ____

3 Ryan used to lock himself in his bedroom.

→ ____

C 밑줄 친 부분을 어법에 맞게 고치시오. 각 2점

1 <u>Used to you take</u> a vitamin pill every day?

→ ________________________________

2 I <u>would like lie</u> down for a while.

→ ________________________________

3 I think you <u>had better to start</u> now.

→ ________________________________

4 You <u>had not better read</u> the book in the dark.

→ ________________________________

5 We <u>used to playing</u> basketball during lunchtime.

→ ________________________________

VOCA instead of ~ 대신에 | indoors 실내에 | stream 개울, 시내 | achieve 이루다, 달성하다 | goal 목표 | film 영화 | sweet 단것 | vest 조끼 | lock oneself in ~에 틀어박히다 | pill 알약 | lunchtime 점심 시간

Ready for Exams

››› 정답 9쪽

My score is

Let's Check It Out ________	/ 18점	0~20점 → Level 1 Test
Ready for Exams ________	/ 12점	21~25점 → Level 2 Test
Total ________	/ 30점	26~30점 → Level 3 Test

1 다음 문장을 올바르게 고친 학생은? 3점

He didn't use snore before he got married.

① 민희: didn't use를 used not으로 바꾸어야 한다.
② 철수: didn't use를 didn't used로 바꾸어야 한다.
③ 지우: snore를 to snore로 바꾸어야 한다.
④ 영희: snore를 snoring로 바꾸어야 한다.
⑤ 수지: got married를 married로 바꾸어야 한다.

2 Which is the common word for the blanks? 2점

• I ____________ to finish my report yesterday.
• You ____________ better rest right now.

① have ② could ③ had
④ used ⑤ would

3 Write the proper words so that the sentences have the same meaning. 3점

I want to go to a buffet restaurant.

→ I ________ ________ ________ go to a buffet restaurant.

4 다음 두 그림에 대한 설명을 하나의 문장으로 표현하려 한다. 빈칸에 들어갈 알맞은 말을 쓰시오. 4점

· Before I liked the country.
· After I like the city. I don't like the country anymore.

→ I ________ ________ ________ the country, but now I don't.

VOCA snore 코를 골다 | finish 끝내다 | country 시골 | not ~ anymore 더 이상 ~ 않다

CHAPTER 05

Review Test

My score is / 80점
60점 이상 PASS!!

››› 정답 9쪽

U10_3

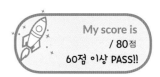

01 밑줄 친 부분의 쓰임이 [보기]와 다른 것은? 2점

보기 You may come here anytime.

① Anyone may use these free of charge.
② You may visit my house tomorrow.
③ The news may be false.
④ Kelly, you may go now.
⑤ May I use your bathroom?

U10_2+3

02 빈칸에 들어갈 말이 순서대로 바르게 짝지어진 것은? 2점

- Tony is tall, so he ________ play basketball well.
- The webcam is cool, but I ________ afford it.

① can – can't ② may – will
③ may not – won't ④ may not – may
⑤ can – can

U10_2+4

03 Which sentence has the same meaning as the one in the box? 2점

한눈에 쏙

Can I borrow your notebook?

① Can you borrow your notebook?
② May I lend your notebook to you?
③ Will you lend your notebook to me?
④ Are you able to borrow the notebook from me?
⑤ Would you lend your notebook from me?

U10_4

04 다음 빈칸에 알맞은 것은? 2점

I cheated during the English test. I know it's a terrible thing to do. I regret it. From now on, I ________ do it again.

① will ② can't
③ may not ④ won't
⑤ am going to

U10_3

05 다음 대화의 빈칸에 알맞지 않은 것은? 2점

A: Why don't you buy Philip this blue cap?
B: No, he may ________.

① want something else
② really love this blue cap
③ have lots of caps
④ not want this cap
⑤ not like it

U12_2

06 다음 두 문장 중 틀린 것을 찾아 바르게 고친 학생은? 2점

함정

ⓐ You'd better to apologize to me.
ⓑ People ought not to drive like that.

① 재석: ⓐ to apologize → apologize
② 태희: ⓑ ought not to → ought to not
③ 동건: ⓐ to apologize → apologizing
④ 소라: ⓑ to drive → drive
⑤ 미소: ⓑ ought → have

U11_1

07 다음 빈칸에 들어갈 말로 알맞은 것은? 2점

함정

You ________ run. We have enough time.

① cannot ② don't have to
③ have to ④ won't
⑤ should

U12_1

08 Which is appropriate for the blank? 2점

I ________ like to learn how to use the oven.

① want ② had
③ used ④ would
⑤ ought

U12_2+U10_4

09 Who chose the correct words for the blanks? 2점

> A: I feel dizzy now.
> B: You ________ drink some water, and then you ________ feel better.

① 보미: had better – will
② 수혜: can – have to
③ 수정: will – used to
④ 보화: would – should
⑤ 진주: should – need to

U11_1

10 다음 중 어법상 어색한 문장은? 2점

① We should help the disabled.
② I used to be lazy a few years ago.
③ Why did you have to invite Clara?
④ He ought to agree to the plan.
⑤ You don't must make any noise here.

U11_1

11 함정 다음 대화에서 문맥상 빈칸 (A)와 (B)에 들어갈 말을 순서대로 나열한 것은? 3점

> Mom: Peter, you __(A)__ drive the car. You are only 15 years old. After you become an adult, you can drive the car.
> Peter: Okay. I won't drive the car. Don't worry, Mom.
> Mom: Joseph, you __(B)__ drive the car because your dad will drive instead of you.
> Joseph: Thanks. I don't want to drive. I am a little bit tired now.

	(A)	(B)
①	must not	must not
②	must not	don't have to
③	don't have to	have to
④	don't have to	don't have to
⑤	have to	don't have to

U11_1+U12_2

12 ★고난도 다음 중 어법상 어색한 것은? (정답 최대 3개) 3점

① Jake has return the book today.
② Katherine has to do her best to pass the exam.
③ Does Sue have to do her homework?
④ Are you going to borrow an umbrella?
⑤ You had better not to stay up late at night.

U11_2+U12_3

13 한눈에 쏙 Choose the correct translations. 3점

> ⓐ 너는 도서 대출증을 신청하고 싶니?
> = Would you like to apply for a library card?
> ⓑ 너는 일찍 자는 것이 낫겠다.
> = You had better sleep early.
> ⓒ 우리는 주말에 교회에 가곤 했다.
> = We used to going to church on weekends.
> ⓓ 예전에는 정원에 소나무가 없었다.
> = There used not to a pine tree in the garden before.
> ⓔ 너는 자기 전에 많은 물을 마시면 안 된다.
> = You ought not to be drink lots of water before sleeping.

① ⓐ, ⓑ
② ⓐ, ⓓ, ⓔ
③ ⓐ, ⓑ, ⓓ, ⓔ
④ ⓑ, ⓒ
⑤ ⓒ, ⓓ, ⓔ

U11_1

14 한눈에 쏙 다음 중 밑줄 친 'must'의 의미가 같은 것끼리 묶인 것은? 3점

> ⓐ You <u>must</u> be good to your friends. Don't be mean or rude to them.
> ⓑ You <u>must</u> improve your English skills if you want to make foreign friends.
> ⓒ You <u>must</u> keep your promise. You should not break it.
> ⓓ The school festival <u>must</u> be fun. There are lots of cool bands coming.
> ⓔ You <u>must</u> be really worried about him. You look deeply concerned.

① ⓐ, ⓑ, ⓓ
② ⓒ, ⓓ
③ ⓓ
④ ⓓ, ⓔ
⑤ ⓑ, ⓓ, ⓔ

U11_1
15 다음 주어진 문장의 부정문을 쓰시오. 3점
함정

He must be a spy. (그는 스파이가 틀림없어.)

→ ____________________

U10_2
16 다음 문장과 의미가 같도록 빈칸을 채우시오. 4점

He couldn't lift the rock.

→ He __________ __________ __________ __________ the rock.

U10_3
17 Rearrange the words correctly. 4점

not, true, the rumor, may, be

→ ____________________

U11_2
18 다음 중 어법상 어색한 것을 찾아 바르게 고치시오. 4점

ⓐ I had to look after my sister yesterday.
ⓑ You ought to not put hot water on a burn.

( ) __________ → __________

U11_1
19 조건에 맞도록 다음 문장을 영작하시오. 5점
★ 고난도

그는 점심을 쌀 필요가 없다.

· 조건 1 어휘 – pack one's lunch
· 조건 2 7단어로 쓸 것

→ ____________________

U11_2
20 주어진 문장과 같은 의미가 되도록 빈칸에 알맞은 말을 1단어로 쓰시오. 3점

Students ought to do their homework by themselves.

→ Students __________ do their homework by themselves.

U10_GP
21 Write the common word for the blanks. 3점

• __________ you come to my house?
• She __________ play the piano when she was young.

→ __________

U12_2
22 주어진 단어 중 1단어를 제외하고 바르게 배열하여 완전한 문장을 쓰시오. 5점

had, time, not, your, waste, to, better, you

→ ____________________

U12_3
23 조동사를 사용해서 다음 두 문장을 한 문장으로 표현하시오. 4점
한눈에 쏙

There was a lemon tree in my yard. There isn't a lemon tree now.

→ There __________ __________ __________ a lemon tree in my yard.

U11_1
24 다음 그림을 보고 'must not'과 'don't have to' 중 알맞은 것을 골라 빈칸에 쓰시오. 3점

→ You __________ enter a house with your shoes on.

시험 직전에 챙겨 보는 비법 노트

››› 정답 9쪽

한눈에 쏙! 아래 노트를 보면서 빈칸을 채워 보세요.

1 추측과 의무의 강도

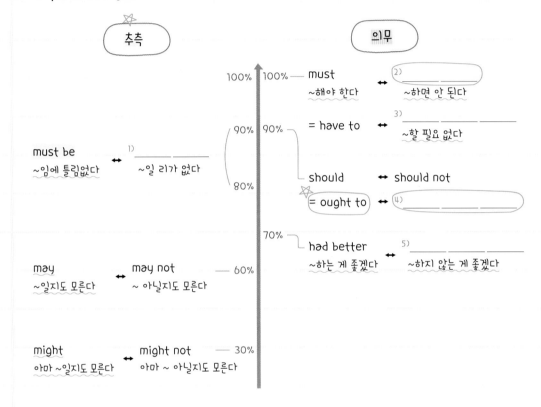

추측

- 100%
- 90% ~ 80%: must be (~임에 틀림없다) ↔ 1) ______ ______ (~일 리가 없다)
- 60%: may (~일지도 모른다) ↔ may not (~ 아닐지도 모른다)
- 30%: might (아마 ~일지도 모른다) ↔ might not (아마 ~ 아닐지도 모른다)

의무

- 100%: must (~해야 한다) ↔ 2) ______ ______ (~하면 안 된다)
- 90%: = have to ↔ 3) ______ ______ ______ (~할 필요 없다)
- should ↔ should not
- = ought to ↔ 4) ______ ______ ______
- 70%: had better (~하는 게 좋겠다) ↔ 5) ______ ______ ______ (~하지 않는 게 좋겠다)

헷갈리지 말자! 초록색으로 표시된 부분을 바르게 고쳐 쓰세요.

1 Are you going participate in the elections?
→

2 He must not be a liar. (그는 거짓말쟁이일 리가 없다.)
→

3 There used to being a pond in the yard.
→

CHAPTER 06

명사, 부정대명사

UNIT 13

명사의 종류, 수량 표현, 소유격

CONCEPT 1 명사의 종류

셀 수 있는 명사	보통명사	사람·사물의 일반적인 명칭	computer, son, nurse
	집합명사	개체가 모인 하나의 집합체	class, family, team
셀 수 없는 명사	고유명사	유일한 사람·사물의 이름	Brian, Tokyo, Christmas
	물질명사	특정한 형태가 없는 명사	paper, air, water, meat
	추상명사	오감으로 감지할 수 없는 명사	beauty, health, hope

Your team is full of excellent players.

Bill doesn't have any hope for the future.

Is it true that hippos have pink milk?

CONCEPT 2 명사의 수량 표현

많은		약간의	거의 없는	종류
a lot of, lots of, plenty of	many	a few	few	셀 수 있는 명사
	much	a little	little	셀 수 없는 명사

I washed a few big trucks, but the boss gave me little money.

There was plenty of food to eat, but few people came to the party.

CONCEPT 3 물질명사의 수량 표현

수사/지시사+단위 명사+of+물질명사		
a cup of coffee	two glasses of water	three pieces of cheese
that bottle of juice	two slices[pieces] of pizza	three pounds of meat
this sheet of paper	two spoonfuls of sugar	three bowls of soup
those lumps of ice	two loaves of bread	three bars of chocolate

I'm so thirsty. Please give me a glass of water.

She eats two pieces of bread every morning.

CONCEPT 4 명사의 소유격

생물	명사+'s	the cat's tail
	복수형-s'	the kids' clothes
무생물	of+명사	the title of the movie

GRAMMAR POINT

명사의 복수형 만들기

- 명사의 복수형 만드는 방법은 〈내공 중학영문법 1 개념이해책〉 p. 28 참조.

집합명사

- 집합명사는 단수 취급하고, 복수형도 가능하다.

My family lives in a small village. Only five families live there. (우리 가족은 작은 마을에 산다. 다섯 가족만이 그곳에 산다.)

수사+하이픈(-)+단위 명사

- 「수사+하이픈(-)+단위 명사」는 명사 앞에서 형용사 역할을 한다.

He is a ~~ten-years-old~~ (→ ten-year-old) boy.

cf. He is ten years old.

수사+piece(s)+of+추상명사

- a piece of advice
- a piece of information
- a piece of furniture
- a piece of news

수사+pair(s)+of+복수 명사

- a pair of pants
- a pair of shoes
- a pair of scissors
- a pair of glasses

명사의 소유격

- -s로 끝나도 복수형이 아니면 -s's로 쓴다.

the boss's computer

Charles's friends

- 시간, 거리, 가격, 무게의 경우 무생물일지라도 's를 붙일 수 있다.

today's topic (오늘의 주제)

five years' experience (5년의 경험)

VOCA village 마을 | hippo 하마 | boss 상사, 사장 | thirsty 목마른 | advice 충고 | scissors 가위 | experience 경험

Let's Check It Out

››› 정답 10쪽

My score is
/ 20점

A 괄호 안의 단어를 빈칸에 알맞은 형태로 쓰시오. 각 1점

1 Ray bought two ________ of apples. (box)
2 About ten ________ were running around in the basement. (mouse)
3 I like ________ the best. (September)
4 I'm afraid you have the wrong ________ about me. (information)
5 I am looking for a 7-________-long nail. (centimeter)

B 빈칸에 알맞은 것을 [보기]에서 골라 쓰되, 한 번씩만 쓰시오. 각 1점

보기	much	a lot of	few	little	a few

1 He has ________ friends, but he doesn't feel lonely.
2 How ________ money do you need?
3 Don't give us ________ homework, please.
4 We raise ________ pigs and goats on the farm.
5 Hurry up! We have ________ time.

C 괄호 안의 단어를 이용하여 알맞은 표현을 쓰시오. 각 1점

1 I had a ________________ this morning. (bowl, rice)
2 There are two ________________ on the table. (glass, juice)
3 He gives me a ________________. (piece, advice)
4 She bought three ________________. (bottle, beer)
5 Amy ate four ________________ just now. (slice, pizza)

D 밑줄 친 표현을 바르게 고치시오. 각 1점

1 I'm wearing Mr. Wilson' gloves. → ________________
2 My sisters's room is so messy. → ________________
3 What are the test of the results? → ________________
4 Did you hear yesterday' news? → ________________
5 What is the best online women' clothing store? → ________________

VOCA run around 이리저리 뛰어다니다 | basement 지하실 | information 정보 | goat 염소 | messy 지저분한 | result 결과 | clothing store 옷 가게

Ready for Exams

››› 정답 10쪽

My score is		
Let's Check It Out ______ / 20점		0~24점 → Level 1 Test
Ready for Exams ______ / 15점	➡	25~29점 → Level 2 Test
Total ______ / 35점		30~35점 → Level 3 Test

1 다음 빈칸에 알맞은 것으로 짝지어진 것은? 3점

• I've already been to Spain ________________ times.
• Could we have ________________ wine, please?

① a few – many ② many – a few ③ a lot of – few
④ a little – little ⑤ a few – a little

2 다음 두 문장 중 어법상 어색한 것을 찾아 바르게 고친 것은? 3점

ⓐ I don't see any meats in my soup.
ⓑ The farmer lost hundreds of sheep last night.

① ⓐ any → some
② ⓐ meats → meat
③ ⓑ lost → has lost
④ ⓑ hundreds → hundred
⑤ ⓑ sheep → sheeps

3 Fill in the blanks to complete the sentence. 4점

하루 지난(어제의) 우유가 Thomas의 가방에 있다.

→ __________ __________ is in __________ __________.

4 다음 그림을 보고 조건에 맞도록 대화를 완성하시오. 5점

· 조건 1 과거형으로 쓸 것
· 조건 2 지시형용사를 사용할 것
· 조건 3 어휘 – throw away, pieces
· 조건 4 빈칸에 6단어로 쓸 것

→ Who ____?

VOCA hundreds of 수백의 | throw away ~을 버리다

UNIT 14

부정대명사

CONCEPT 1 부정대명사

종류	의미와 쓰임	주의할 점	
one	'~한 것'이라는 의미로 막연한 단수 명사를 나타냄	복수는 ones cf. it: 특정한 명사	
each	'각자, 각기'라는 의미로 단수 취급	each of+복수 명사+단수 동사	
every-	'모든 것' 또는 '모든 사람'이라는 의미로 항상 단수 취급	everything/everyone/everybody+단수 동사	
all	'모두, 모든 것'이라는 뜻으로 단수 또는 복수 취급	all (of)+복수 명사+복수 동사 all (of)+단수 명사+단수 동사	
both	'둘 다'의 뜻으로 항상 복수 취급	both (of)+복수 명사+복수 동사	
some(-)	'조금의, 어떤'이라는 의미로 주로 긍정문에 쓰임	의문문: 권유	-one, -body, -thing은 형용사가 뒤에서 수식
any(-)	주로 부정문과 의문문에 쓰임	긍정문: ~라도	

Is there a bank near here? –Yes, there's one over there.

Each of the boys was from a different area.

Everything in this city is very modern.

Both of us want to buy this hair band.

CONCEPT 2 부정대명사의 관용 표현

둘일 때	one ~, the other...
셋일 때	one ~, another..., the other ~
넷 이상일 때	one ~, another..., the[a] third, ~ and the other...
일부는 ~, 다른 일부는 ···	some ~, others...
일부는 ~, 나머지 일부는 ···	some ~, the others...

I have two foreign friends. One can speak Korean, but the other can't.

There are three marbles; one is red, another is green, and the other is blue.

Here are four cards; one is a 5, another is a 0, the third is a 2, and the other is a 6.

Some people are walking, and other people[others] are biking in the park.

There are nine dancers; some (dancers) are practicing the cha-cha, and the others are practicing jive.

GRAMMAR POINT

one과 it

- one은 막연한 명사를, it은 특정한 명사를 나타낸다.

Where is my key?
– I saw it on the table.

every

- every는 형용사로 '모든'이라는 의미이지만 뒤에는 단수 명사가 온다.

Every student at my school knows him.

all의 수 일치

- all (of) 뒤에 복수 명사가 오면 동사도 복수형으로 쓰고, 단수 명사가 오면 동사도 단수형으로 쓴다.

All of these apples taste sweet.

All of the furniture was not in place.

some(-)과 any(-)의 사용

- 의문문에서는 any(-)를 쓰지만 권유의 의미일 때는 some(-)을 쓴다.

Would you like something cold to drink?

- 긍정문에서 any(-)를 쓰면 '어떤 ~라도'라는 뜻이다.

You can take any book from here.
(너는 여기에서 어떤 책이라도 가져갈 수 있다.)

each other와 one another

- each other는 '둘이 서로'이고, one another는 '둘 또는 셋 이상에서 서로'이다.

VOCA area 지역 | modern 현대적인 | in place 제자리에 | marble 구슬 | cha-cha 차차차(라틴 아메리카의 빠른 춤) | jive 자이브(강한 비트의 춤)

Let's Check It Out

››› 정답 10쪽

My score is
/ 14점

A [ ]에서 알맞은 것을 고르시오. 각 1점

1 [All / Every] cook needs a good knife.

2 [Each / Both] of them are very pretty.

3 [Each / All] student has to follow the class rules.

4 Would you like [anything / something] to drink?

5 A: Do you have a favorite number?
B: Yes, I have [one / it].

B 빈칸에 알맞은 말을 [보기]에서 골라 쓰시오. (중복 가능) 각 1점

보기			
	one	another	the other
	some	others	the others

1 I've been to two foreign countries. ____________ is Switzerland, and ____________ is Brazil.

2 She has three sisters; ____________ is 10 years old, ____________ is 12, and ____________ is 27.

3 ____________ people are happy, but ____________ are not.

4 There are 12 people in the garden. Seven of them are kids, and ____________ are adults.

C 밑줄 친 부분을 바르게 고치시오. 각 1점

1 She likes the white shoes, but I like the red one. → ______________

2 Where have everybody gone? → ______________

3 Every persons needs a true friend. → ______________

4 Tim and Maria know each another. → ______________

5 Not everybody love to eat chocolate. → ______________

VOCA rule 규칙 | Switzerland 스위스(Swiss는 형용사형) | adult 성인

Ready for Exams

››› 정답 10쪽

My score is

Let's Check It Out ________ / 14점
Ready for Exams ________ / 11점
Total ________ / 25점

0~17점 → Level 1 Test
18~21점 → Level 2 Test
22~25점 → Level 3 Test

1 다음 빈칸에 알맞은 것은? 2점

> Not all of you can sleep in the room. Only one can, and ________________ should sleep outside.

① another ② the other ③ other
④ the others ⑤ others

2 밑줄 친 우리말을 영어로 바르게 옮길 때 필요하지 않은 것을 모두 고르면? 2점

> Brandon saw three movies last weekend; 하나는 무서웠고, 또 다른 하나는 지루했고, 나머지 하나는 재미있었다.

① one ② another ③ some
④ the other ⑤ the others

3 How many sentences are grammatically incorrect? 3점

> ⓐ All of them helped one another.
> ⓑ Each children has the right to an education.
> ⓒ I want some tomatoes. Give me these big one.
> ⓓ I leave the house every mornings at 7:30.
> ⓔ Both of the women are from Uzbekistan.
> ⓕ Don't just stand there. Do something!

① 1개 ② 2개 ③ 3개
④ 4개 ⑤ 5개

4 그림을 보고 빈칸에 알맞은 말을 쓰시오. 4점

→ Two boys are sitting on the bench. ______________ is reading a book, and ______________ ______________ is talking on the phone.

VOCA right 권리 | education 교육 | Uzbekistan 우즈베키스탄

CHAPTER 06

Review Test

My score is / 60점
51점 이상 PASS!!

>>> 정답 10쪽

U13_1

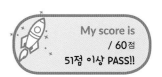

01 다음 중 어법상 올바른 문장은? 3점

★ 고난도

① I went to buy butter, sugar, and two eggs.
② I'd like to have some grape juices.
③ All animals need to drink waters every day.
④ How much sugars do you put in your coffee?
⑤ The foreigner drink *makgeolli* every night.

U13_3

02 다음 중 표현이 어법상 어색한 것의 개수는? 3점

★ 고난도

ⓐ a piece of advice
ⓑ two sheets of paper
ⓒ two pairs of glove
ⓓ a big glass of milk
ⓔ that large slices of pizza
ⓕ three loaves of bread
ⓖ two lumps of sugars

① 2개　② 3개
③ 4개　④ 5개
⑤ 6개

U13_GP

03 Which underlined part is wrong? (2 answers) 2점

① I always carry two two-dollar bills.
② They enjoyed a ten-day-long holiday in Paris.
③ I need four twenty-meter hoses right now.
④ I'd like five ten-thousands-won pens, please.
⑤ Janice has a seven-months-old kitty.

U13_4+U14_1

04 다음 대화의 빈칸에 알맞은 것은? 2점

A: What do you like about this house?
B: Well, I love ________.

① the house green door
② the house's the big windows
③ the house of the large rooms
④ the blue roof of the house
⑤ the house high ceiling

U14_1

05 다음 중 어색한 부분을 모두 찾아 바르게 고친 것은? 3점

한눈에 쏙

Both of my brothers is professional athlete.
One plays soccer, and another plays golf.

① is → are
② is → are, athlete → athletes
③ athlete → athletes, One → The one
④ is → are, athlete → athletes, another → other
⑤ is → are, athlete → athletes, another → the other

U14_1

06 다음 중 밑줄 친 부분이 어법상 어색한 것은? 2점

① All of your friends are so funny.
② Each of them doesn't have a job.
③ Both of them are very kind.
④ Some people are really good at singing.
⑤ Every student have to be present this Sunday.

U14_2

07 빈칸에 들어갈 말이 순서대로 짝지어진 것은? 2점

한눈에 쏙

________ prefer to live in a big city while ________ prefer to live in a small town. Which do you prefer?

① One – some　② One – another
③ Some – others　④ Some – the other
⑤ One – the other

U13_GP+U14_1

08 다음 문장 중 어법상 어색한 부분이 가장 많은 것은? 2점

함정

① Look at that four-leaf clovers.
② Do you like both of the picture?
③ My sisters plays the game every nights.
④ Every girl want to feel like a princess.
⑤ I can't find my shoes. I need new one.

U14_2

09 각 빈칸에 알맞은 말을 쓰시오. (각각 1단어 또는 2단어임) 4점

He hates three subjects. __________ is Korean, __________ is English, and __________ is math.

U13_1

10 두 문장 중 어법상 어색한 것을 찾아 바르게 고치시오. 4점

ⓐ Some children go to school by bicycle.
ⓑ You have to brush your teeth after meal.

(　　) __________ → __________

U13_2

11 (A), (B), (C)의 각 네모에서 알맞은 것을 고르시오. 4점

Sandy is fluent in Japanese, Chinese, French, and Spanish. It's quite (A) [common / rare]. (B) [Few / Many] people can speak (C) [few / several] foreign languages.

U13_GP

12 다음 우리말을 조건에 맞게 영작하시오. 6점

우리는 10시간짜리 연습을 막 끝마쳤다.

- 조건 1 현재완료 시제로 쓸 것
- 조건 2 하이픈(-)을 사용할 것
- 조건 3 어휘 – just, finish, practice
- 조건 4 주어진 어휘를 포함하여 7단어로 쓸 것 (하이픈으로 연결된 단어는 한 단어로 침)

→ __________

U13_4

13 단어 조각을 바르게 배열하여 문장을 완성하시오. 4점

this　attractive　the　cover
of　book　looks

→ __________

U14_1

14 Fill in each blank to make two sentences that have the same meaning. 4점

Cosmos flowers are in full bloom on both __________ of the street.
= Cosmos flowers are in full bloom on __________ side of the street.

U14_2

15 그림을 보고 빈칸 (A)에 이어질 문장을 주어진 단어를 활용하여 4단어로 쓰시오. 5점

W: I invited five friends to my birthday party, but only Laura and Nara came. ___(A)___. (not, come)

(A) __________.

U14_1

16 빈칸에 알맞은 단어를 골라 넣어 문장을 완성하시오. 4점

함정

somebody, anybody, something, anything

→ Does __________ want __________ to drink?

U13_2

17 다음 문장을 조건에 맞게 영작하시오. 6점

이 식물들은 관리가 거의 필요 없고 거의 어디에서나 자랄 수 있다.

- 조건 1 단·복수에 유의할 것
- 조건 2 두 번째 단어는 아래 영영풀이를 참조할 것
  n__________ : to have to have something or to want something very much

→ These __________ n__________ __________ care and can __________ almost __________.

시험 직전에 챙겨 보는 비법 노트

>>> 정답 11쪽

한눈에 쏙! 아래 노트를 보면서 빈칸을 채워 보세요.

1 물질명사의 수량 표현

• a 1)p_ _ _ _ of cheese, two 2)g_ _ _ _ _ _ _ of water, three 3)b_ _ _ _ of soup

2 소유격

생물 → 명사+1)________ / 복수+2)________

무생물 → 3)________+명사

3 부정대명사의 종류

• 1)o_ _ (막연한 것*), 2)e_ _ _ / 3)e_ _ _ _ _-/ 4)a_ _, 5)b_ _ _, some-, any-

*cf. it(특정한 것) → 단수 취급

4 부정대명사 관용 표현

• 둘 → 1)________, 2)________ ________

• 셋 → 3)________, 4)________, the other

• 일부, 다른 일부 → some, 5)________

• 일부, 나머지 일부 → some, 6)________ ________

헷갈리지 말자! 초록색으로 표시된 부분을 바르게 고쳐 쓰세요.

1 He has two pieces of breads every morning.
→

2 Each of the men were from Paju.
→

3 There are two kinds of balls in the box. Some are red. Others are blue.
→

CHAPTER 07

수동태

UNIT 15

수동태의 개념과 시제

CONCEPT 1 수동태의 의미와 형태

태	의미	기본 해석	기본 형태
능동태	주어가 동작을 하는 주체	~을 하다	동사
수동태	주어가 동작을 받는 대상	~되다[-지다]	be+p.p. (by+목적격)

Columbus broke the egg. (깼다: 능동태)

The egg was broken by Columbus. (깨졌다: 수동태)

CONCEPT 2 수동태 전환법

능동태 문장을 수동태 문장으로 전환하는 방법은 다음과 같다.

능동: She teaches math. 수동: Math is taught by her.	① 능동태의 목적어 → 수동태의 주어 ② 능동태의 동사 → be+p.p. ③ 능동태의 주어 → by+행위자(목적격)

A famous singer owns the buildings.

→ The buildings are owned by a famous singer.

The farmers grow sugarcane in Hawaii.

→ Sugarcane is grown by the farmers in Hawaii.

CONCEPT 3 수동태의 시제

수동태의 시제는 be동사로 표현된다.

종류	형태	예문
현재	am/is/are+p.p.	The cake is baked by Mr. Bakery.
과거	was/were+p.p.	The cake was baked by Mr. Bakery.
미래	will be+p.p.	The cake will be baked by Mr. Bakery.

CONCEPT 4 'by+행위자'의 생략

다음과 같은 경우에는 수동태에서 'by+행위자'가 생략될 수 있다.

일반인 행위자	Korean is spoken in Korea (by people).
불분명한 행위자	The grass was cut yesterday (by somebody).
불필요한 행위자	I was invited to Cindy's birthday party (by Cindy).

GRAMMAR POINT

불규칙 동사의 과거분사

- 과거분사 만드는 법은 p. 157 동사 변화표 참조.

be동사의 인칭, 수, 시제

- 수동태(be+p.p.)에서 be동사의 인칭과 수는 수동태의 주어에 따르며, 시제는 능동태의 동사에 따라 결정된다.

Ben made the cookies.

→ The cookies were made by Ben. (3인칭 복수, 과거)

be going to be+p.p.

- be going to be+p.p.도 미래를 나타내는 수동태이다.

Your shoes are going to be washed tomorrow.
(네 신발은 내일 세탁될 거야.)

수동태 부정문

- 수동태의 부정문은 be동사나 조동사 뒤에 not을 쓴다.

We don't carry hammers.

→ Hammers are not carried by us.

VOCA grow 기르다 | sugarcane 사탕수수 | carry 가지고 다니다 | hammer 망치

Let's Check It Out

››› 정답 11쪽

My score is / 20점

A 다음 문장이 능동태이면 A, 수동태이면 P를 쓰시오. 각 1점

1 His wallet was found by the taxi driver. → ________

2 You have the right to remain silent. → ________

3 She's not often invited to parties. → ________

4 He isn't going to give me a discount. → ________

B 괄호 안의 동사를 빈칸에 알맞은 형태로 쓰시오. 각 1점

1 Finally, the problem ________ yesterday. (solve)

2 Those computers ________ these days. (not, use)

3 Dinner is going to ________ soon. (serve)

4 Your hair will ________ by Cindy. (wash)

C 밑줄 친 부분이 어법상 어색하면 알맞게 고치시오. 각 1점

1 The flat tire was changing by Catherine. → ________

2 The flowers were planted by my father. → ________

3 Halloween celebrated in Korea, too. → ________

4 This painting not was drawn by Danwon. → ________

D 다음을 수동태로 전환할 때 빈칸에 알맞은 말을 쓰시오. 각 2점

1 He broke the windows.

→ The windows ______ ______ ______ ______.

2 Genghis Khan attacked Japan.

→ Japan ______ ______ ______ ______ ______.

3 Most teenagers use this cell phone.

→ This cell phone ______ ______ ______ ______ ______.

4 People will invent a time machine soon.

→ A time machine ______ ______ ______ (______ ______) soon.

VOCA remain ~인 채로 있다 | discount 할인 | celebrate 기념하다 | flat tire 펑크 난 타이어 | plant 심다 | attack 공격하다 | invent 발명하다

Ready for Exams

››› 정답 11쪽

My score is		
Let's Check It Out ________ / 20점		0~24점 → Level 1 Test
Ready for Exams ________ / 15점	➜	25~29점 → Level 2 Test
Total ________ / 35점		30~35점 → Level 3 Test

1 다음 문장을 바르게 이해하고 있는 학생은? 3점

History always wrote by the victors.

① 효은: 현재완료가 되도록 wrote를 has written으로 고쳐야 해.
② 정은: be동사가 없으니 주어 뒤에 is를 써야 해.
③ 슬기: wrote가 아니라 written으로 써야 해.
④ 희영: 'by+주격'을 써야 하니까 the victors는 맞아.
⑤ 지원: 주어 다음에 is를 넣고 wrote를 written으로 써야 해.

2 다음 중 어법상 어색한 것끼리 짝지어진 것은? 3점

ⓐ Prizes were given by the principal.
ⓑ This tower built with stone.
ⓒ The film was directed by he.
ⓓ My teacher was sent a long email to me.
ⓔ Math is taught by Mr. Lee.

① ⓐ, ⓒ ② ⓒ, ⓔ ③ ⓑ, ⓒ
④ ⓑ, ⓒ, ⓓ ⑤ ⓒ, ⓓ, ⓔ

3 Look at the picture and complete the sentences. 4점

The dog ______________ the postman just now.
= The postman ______________ ______________ ______________ the dog just now.

4 다음 문장이 능동태면 수동태로, 수동태면 능동태로 고치시오. 5점

Hemingway wrote *The Old Man and the Sea.*

→ ____

VOCA victor 승자 | principal 교장 | film 영화 | direct 감독[연출]하다 | postman 우편집배원

UNIT 16

여러 가지 수동태(1)

CONCEPT 1 조동사의 수동태

기본 형태: 조동사+be+p.p.

Anybody can use Wi-Fi.

→ Wi-Fi can be used by anybody.

We should not destroy nature.

→ Nature should not be destroyed.

GRAMMAR POINT

have to와 ought to

- have to와 ought to는 한 단어처럼 전환한다.

We have to decide the date now.

→ The date has to be decided now.

CONCEPT 2 의문문 수동태

의문사가 없는 경우	be동사+주어+p.p. (by+행위자) ~?	
의문사가 있는 경우	주어가 있을 때	의문사+be동사+주어+p.p. (by+행위자) ~?
	의문사가 주어일 때	By+의문사+be동사+주어+p.p. ~?

Do they grow grapes in California?

→ Are grapes grown in California (by them)?

When did they announce the results?

→ When were the results announced (by them)?

Who interviewed you?

→ By whom were you interviewed?

쉬운 의문문 전환법

- 의문문 → 평서문 → 수동태 → 의문문

Did he buy the hanger?

→ He bought the hanger.

→ The hanger was bought by him.

→ Was the hanger bought by him?

CONCEPT 3 4형식 문장의 수동태 전환

4형식 문장의 수동태 전환에서, 직접 목적어가 주어로 나올 때 간접 목적어 앞에 전치사를 써야 하는 것에 유의한다.

They gave him a special prize.
(him: 간접 목적어, a special prize: 직접 목적어)

→ He was given a special prize (by them).

→ A special prize was given to him (by them).

직접 목적어를 주어로 4형식 문장을 수동태로 바꿀 때 전치사는 동사에 따라 다르다.

to를 쓰는 동사	give, teach, send, sell, write, show, pass, bring
for를 쓰는 동사	sing, find, make, buy, cook, get
of를 쓰는 동사	ask

직접 목적어만 주어로 수동태를 만들 수 있는 동사

- make, read, get, sell, write, buy, send, cook

My mom bought me a soccer ball.

→ I was bought a soccer ball by my mom. (×)

→ A soccer ball was bought for me by my mom. (○)

VOCA destroy 파괴하다 | nature 자연 | announce 발표하다 | result 결과 | interview 면접을 보다, 인터뷰하다 | decide 결정하다 | date 날짜 | hanger 옷걸이

Let's Check It Out

››› 정답 11쪽

My score is
/ 19점

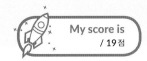

A [ ]에서 알맞은 것을 고르시오. 각 1점

1 The bridge should [is / be] completed soon.
2 This fact must [be remembered / remember].
3 [Does / Is] English spoken in your country?
4 When was the car [repairing / repaired]?
5 Poetry is taught [for / to] us by Mrs. Robinson.

B 밑줄 친 부분이 어색하면 바르게 고치시오. 각 1점

1 The rules may be forgotten quickly. → ________
2 Was the picture painting by Monet? → ________
3 When did the castle destroyed? → ________
4 A copy will be sent for you soon. → ________
5 A special vegetarian breakfast was cooked for us. → ________

C 우리말과 일치하도록 주어진 단어를 빈칸에 알맞은 형태로 쓰시오. 각 1점

1 이 프로젝트는 반드시 제시간에 끝마쳐져야 합니다. (finish)
→ This project must ________ ________ on time.

2 이 칼은 무엇을 위해서 사용되나요? (use)
→ What ________ this knife ________ for?

3 그 학생들에 의해 교통 법규가 지켜졌나요? (observe)
→ ________ the traffic rules ________ by the students?

D 주어진 단어를 어법에 맞게 바르게 배열하시오. 각 2점

1 A watch ________________ as a gift. (to, was, Leo, given)
2 ________________ read? (was, whom, by, the letter)
3 The moon ________________ because it was cloudy. (seen, not, be, could)

VOCA complete 완료하다, 완공하다 | repair 수리하다 | poetry 시 | copy 사본 | destroy 파괴하다 | traffic rule 교통 법규 | observe 준수하다 | cloudy 흐린, 구름 낀

Ready for Exams

>>> 정답 12쪽

My score is

Let's Check It Out _______ / 19점		0~20점 → Level 1 Test
Ready for Exams _______ / 11점	→	21~25점 → Level 2 Test
Total _______ / 30점		26~30점 → Level 3 Test

1 다음을 수동태로 바르게 전환한 것은? 2점

We must not forget today's lesson.

① Today's lesson isn't must forgotten.
② Today's lesson must isn't forgotten.
③ Today's lesson doesn't must forgotten.
④ Today's lesson must not be forgotten.
⑤ Today's lesson doesn't must be forgotten.

2 Which is appropriate for the blank? 2점

When did he design the stadium?
→ When ______________ by him?

① designed the stadium
② the stadium was designed
③ did the stadium designed
④ was the stadium designed
⑤ was the stadium designing

3 주어진 문장과 의미가 같도록 단어 카드에서 필요한 것만 골라 쓰시오. (중복 가능) 각 2점

Ms. Page teaches us English.

is are to taught for English us teach

(1) We ________ ________ ________ by Ms. Page.

(2) English ________ ________ ________ ________ by Ms. Page.

4 Change the sentence into the passive voice with 5 words. 3점

Do they speak French in Quebec?

→ ______________________________

VOCA lesson 교훈 | stadium 경기장 | Quebec 퀘벡(캐나다 동부의 도시)

UNIT 17

여러 가지 수동태(2)

CONCEPT 1 by 이외의 전치사를 쓰는 수동태

be interested in	~에 관심이 있다	be located in[at]	~에 위치하다
be caught in	(비)를 만나다 ~에 갇히다	be disappointed at[in, with, by]	~에 실망하다
be surprised at[by]	~에 놀라다	be shocked at[by]	~에 충격받다
be excited about[at, by]	~에 흥분해 있다	be worried about	~에 대해 걱정하다
be amazed at[by]	~에 놀라다	be covered with	~로 덮여 있다
be satisfied with	~에 만족하다	be scared of	~에 겁먹다
be filled with	~로 가득 차다	be pleased with	~에 기뻐하다
be married to	~와 결혼하다	be crowded with	~로 붐비다
be dressed in	~을 입고 있다	be tired of	~에 질리다
be made of	~로 만들어져 있다 (물리적 변화)	be known for	~로 유명하다
		be known to	~에게 알려져 있다
be made from	~로 만들어져 있다 (화학적 변화)	be known as	~로 알려져 있다
		be known by	~로 알 수 있다

I am very pleased with your performance.

Are you interested in pop art?

My heart is filled with happiness.

I am tired of your old story.

The book is known to every student.

CONCEPT 2 동사구의 수동태

동사구는 한 묶음으로 인식해서 수동태로 전환하며, 마지막의 'by+행위자'에 유의해야 한다.

> Jean takes care of the children.
>
> → The children are taken care of by Jean.

The audience laughed at him.

→ He was laughed at by the audience.

The boss put off the meeting until next week.

→ The meeting was put off by the boss until next week.

The children looked at the butterfly.

→ The butterfly was looked at by the children.

GRAMMAR POINT

원료+be made into+제품

- Milk is made into butter.
  = Butter is made from milk.

자주 쓰이는 동사구 표현

- laugh at: ~을 비웃다
- make fun of: ~을 조롱하다
- put off: ~을 연기하다
- put on: ~을 입다
- take off: ~을 벗다
- bring up: ~을 기르다, (화제를) 언급하다
- run over: ~을 (차로) 치다
- run out of: ~을 다 써버리다
- look for: ~을 찾다
- ask[call] for: ~을 요청하다
- look at: ~을 보다
- pay attention to: ~에 주의를 기울이다
- look up to: ~을 존경하다
- look down on: ~을 경시하다
- make use of: ~을 이용하다
- give up: ~을 포기하다
- call off: ~을 취소하다
- put together: ~을 조립하다
- take apart: ~을 분해하다
- pick up: ~을 줍다, (차로) 태우다
- send for: ~을 부르러 보내다
- carry out: ~을 수행하다
- take out: ~을 가지고 나가다
- turn on/off: ~을 켜다/끄다
- look after(= take care of): ~을 돌보다

VOCA performance 공연; 성과 | pop art 팝아트 | happiness 행복 | take care of ~을 돌보다 | audience 관중 | laugh at ~을 비웃다 | put off ~을 연기하다 | butterfly 나비

Let's Check It Out

››› 정답 12쪽

My score is / 19점

A [ ]에서 알맞은 것을 고르시오. 각 1점

1 Is she interested [by / in] heavy metal?
2 The road was covered [from / with] fog.
3 Jacky was excited [about / in] the smart TV.
4 We weren't surprised [by / about] the news.
5 The picnic table is made [from / of] plastic.

B 다음 문장을 수동태로 전환할 때 빈칸에 알맞은 말을 쓰시오. 각 1점

1 The building staff will take out the garbage.
→ The garbage will ______________ the building staff.
2 Many Koreans look up to Admiral Yi Sun-sin.
→ Admiral Yi Sun-sin ______________ many Koreans.
3 Mr. Kenney didn't put off the project.
→ The project ______________ Mr. Kenney.
4 Did your son turn off the computer?
→ ________ the computer ______________ your son?
5 We will put this chair together.
→ This chair ______________ us.

C 괄호 안의 단어를 주어진 시제에 맞게 빈칸에 쓰시오. 각 1점

1 We ________ ________ ________ the results. (satisfy: 현재)
2 Bread ________ ________ ________ wheat. (make: 현재)
3 The glass ________ ________ ________ water. (not, fill: 과거)
4 The baby pigs ________ ________ ________ ________ by her. (not, look after: 미래)

D 밑줄 친 부분을 바르게 고쳐 쓰시오. 각 1점

1 Your mom is really worried <u>at</u> you. → ______________
2 The roof was covered <u>of</u> snow. → ______________
3 The model plane was made <u>from</u> used paper. → ______________
4 A person can be known <u>as</u> his or her friends. → ______________
5 All of us were surprised <u>with</u> his attitude. → ______________

VOCA heavy metal 헤비메탈 | fog 안개 | staff 직원 | garbage 쓰레기 | admiral 해군 장교 | wheat 밀 | attitude 태도

Ready for Exams

››› 정답 12쪽

My score is

Let's Check It Out ______ / 19점		0~20점 → Level 1 Test
Ready for Exams ______ / 11점	→	21~25점 → Level 2 Test
Total ______ / 30점		26~30점 → Level 3 Test

1 [보기] 중에서 빈칸에 적절하지 않은 것의 개수는? 2점

Was Nicole ______________ at the ranking?

보기 ⓐ shocked ⓑ surprised ⓒ worried ⓓ amazed ⓔ disappointed ⓕ looked

① 1개 ② 2개 ③ 3개 ④ 4개 ⑤ 5개

2 주어진 문장을 수동태로 바르게 바꾼 것은? 2점

The boys made fun of her.

① She was made fun by the boys.
② She did make fun by the boys.
③ She was made fun of by the boys.
④ She was make fun of by the boys.
⑤ She was made fun of the boys.

3 그림을 보고 조건에 맞게 문장을 완성하시오. 4점

- 조건1 빈칸에 4단어로 쓸 것
- 조건2 현재 시제로 쓸 것
- 조건3 어휘 – fill, tears

→ Her eyes ____.

4 우리말과 일치하도록 주어진 단어를 활용하여 영작하시오. 3점

넌 어디서 자랐니?
you, up, where, bring

→ ____

VOCA ranking 순위 | tear 눈물

CHAPTER 07

Review Test

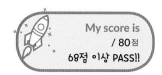

My score is
/ 80점
68점 이상 PASS!!

››› 정답 12쪽

15_1+3

01 다음 빈칸에 알맞은 것은? 2점

This gallery ________ by a famous architect.

① are designed ② is designing
③ was designing ④ was designed
⑤ were designed

U15_2

02 다음 중 주어진 문장과 의미가 같은 문장은? 2점

The subject is not taught by Alan.

① Alan teach the subject.
② Alan didn't teach the subject.
③ Alan doesn't teach the subject.
④ Alan teaches the subject.
⑤ Alan is not taught the subject.

U15_4

03 Which underlined phrase CANNOT be omitted? 2점

한눈에 쏙

① My child was bitten by your dog.
② The man was killed in the war by someone.
③ Beauty can be seen anywhere by people.
④ Many buildings are built by some people.
⑤ The window was broken by someone.

U17_1

04 다음 중 빈칸에 들어갈 말이 [보기]와 같은 것은? 2점

보기 The hall is filled ________ lots of artwork.

① What is silk made ______?
② Are you interested ______ K-pop?
③ He is married ______ my sister.
④ She was surprised ______ his failure.
⑤ The table is covered ______ flour.

U16_2

05 다음을 영어로 바르게 옮긴 학생은? 2점

그 유리잔은 어떻게 깨졌니?

① 유민: How was broken the glass?
② 영록: How was the glass broken?
③ 채리: How did the glass broken?
④ 윤필: How the glass was broken?
⑤ 기준: How was the glass broke?

U15_1

06 다음 중 어법상 올바른 것을 모두 고르시오. 3점

★ 고난도

① The poem was written by Alex.
② She is played the game every night.
③ How much gasoline is storing here?
④ The flowerpot was brought to me by mistake.
⑤ The dishwasher was repaired by he.

U15_2

07 다음 중 문장 전환이 올바르지 않은 것은? (답 2개) 3점

한눈에 쏙

① Sally took the photos.
→ The photos was taken by Sally.
② The firefighter couldn't rescue the cats.
→ The cats couldn't rescued by the firefighter.
③ He destroyed her image.
→ Her image was destroyed by him.
④ Tony polished the window.
→ The window was polished by Tony.
⑤ She draws many pictures.
→ Many pictures are drawn by her.

U17_1

08 Which sentence has a grammatical error? 2점

① The bottle is made of ice.
② The tank was filled with gasoline.
③ *The Little Prince* is known for everybody.
④ Good wine is made from good grapes.
⑤ Those pictures were painted by Hwang Gin-i.

U16_3+GP

09 문장 전환이 올바른 것으로 짝지어진 것은? 3점

함정

ⓐ He bought me a new tablet computer.
→ I was bought a new tablet computer by him.
ⓑ They will send each actor an email.
→ An email will be sent to each actor.
ⓒ George didn't tell your story to Susan.
→ Susan not told your story by George.
ⓓ What did they cook for you?
→ What was cooked for them?

① ⓐ, ⓑ
② ⓑ
③ ⓑ, ⓓ
④ ⓐ, ⓒ, ⓓ
⑤ ⓑ, ⓒ, ⓓ

U16_2

10 괄호 안의 단어들을 활용하여 우리말 뜻과 같도록 문장을 만들 때 빈칸 (A)에 들어갈 말은? 2점

계란은 실온에 보관 가능한가요? (can, keep)
= _______ _______ _______ ___(A)___ at room temperature?

① are
② be
③ eggs
④ kept
⑤ keep

U15_1

11 각 빈칸에 들어갈 말을 바르게 연결한 학생은? 3점

함정

_______ uniform recycling project _______ teenagers.

① 의강: A – was created
② 수인: A – created by
③ 낙연: A – was created by
④ 난정: An – created by
⑤ 유정: An – was created by

U16_3+GP

12 다음 문장을 수동태로 바꿀 때 5번째로 올 단어는? 2점

Jihoo bought me this mug.

① this
② me
③ for
④ to
⑤ by

U17_1

13 각 빈칸에 알맞은 것으로 짝지어진 것은? 2점

• I was interested _______ music.
• The chair is made _______ wood.

① in – of
② of – in
③ in – from
④ of – from
⑤ for – of

U16_3

14 단어들을 조합하여 완전한 문장을 만들 수 없는 것은? 4점

★ 고난도

① me / of / are / ? / tired / you
② born / ? / where / were / you
③ stolen / night / was / last / kickboard / . / my
④ the / zoo / the / be / . / sent / chimps / will
⑤ were / . / one / actor / played / multiple / by / characters

U15_1+U17_1

15 다음 각 빈칸에 들어갈 말이 바르게 연결된 것은? 2점

함정

• The robber wasn't caught _______ the police.
• The whole village was covered _______ snow.
• Nobody was pleased _______ her performance.

① at – with – to
② at – by – by
③ with – with – with
④ by – with – with
⑤ by – with – for

U17_1

16 밑줄 친 부분이 어법상 어색한 것은? (정답 최대 3개) 3점

① What are you scared by?
② Are you interested with UFOs?
③ Cuba is famous for salsa dancing.
④ The office is located in the city center.
⑤ We were shocked of the size of the snake.

U16_2

17 주어진 단어를 활용하여 다음 문장을 영작하시오. 4점

그 자전거는 언제 고쳐졌니? (bike, repair)

→ ____________________

U15_1

18 주어진 단어를 바르게 배열하여 문장을 완성하시오. 4점

respected, everybody, is, no one, by

→ ____________________

U16_3

19 다음 문장을 수동태로 전환하시오. 5점

Agatha wrote him this card.

→ ____________________

U15_2

20 다음은 수동태의 전환법에 대한 혜림의 노트 필기이다. 내용이 잘못된 2곳을 찾아 바르게 고치시오. 5점

한눈에 쏙

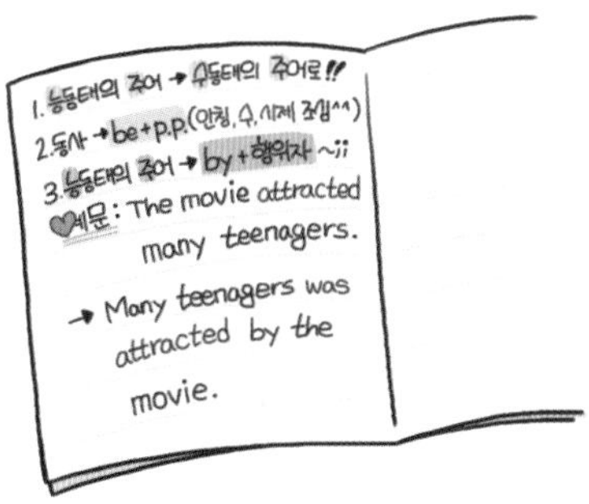

__________ → __________

__________ → __________

U15_1

21 빈칸에 들어갈 말을 [보기]에서 골라 알맞은 형태로 쓰시오. 5점

보기 injure doubt hear survive

→ Last night, I __________ there was a tsunami, but fortunately nobody __________ __________.

U15_4

22 다음 문장에서 생략할 수 있는 단어를 모두 고르고 난 후, 그 단어들을 사용해서 주어진 문장을 완성하시오. 4점

We weren't invited to Karl's goodbye party by Karl.

→ We didn't know __________ lived __________ himself.

U16_2

23 우리말과 같은 뜻이 되도록 주어진 단어를 바르게 배열하시오. 4점

함정

그 시트콤은 누구에 의해 만들어졌니?
the, was, by, whom, sitcom, made

→ ____________________

U17_1

24 빈칸에 공통으로 들어갈 단어의 철자를 이용하여 단어 퍼즐을 완성하시오. 4점

- We were pleased __________ the results of the test.
- The concert hall was crowded __________ many people.

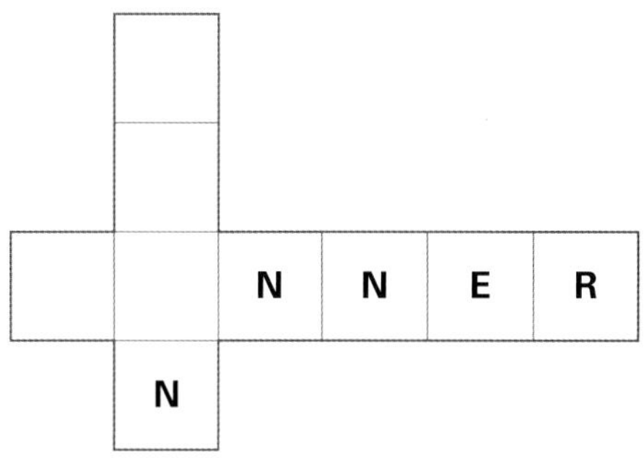

U17_2+GP

25 그림을 보고, 조건에 맞게 문장을 완성하시오. 6점

★ 고난도

- 조건 1 수동태로 쓸 것
- 조건 2 과거형으로 쓸 것
- 조건 3 빈칸에 6단어로 쓸 것

→ ____________________ the boy.

››› 정답 13쪽

한눈에 쏙! 아래 노트를 보면서 빈칸을 채워 보세요.

1 수동태 전환

Edison invented the light bulb.

The light bulb 1) ________ ________ by Edison.

2 수동태의 형태

① 평서문	am/1) __/2) ___+p.p. 3)w__/4)w___+p.p. 조동사+5) ______+p.p. (by+행위자) → 일반인, 불분명, 불확실한 행위자
② 의문문	의문사 무(無): 6) ________+주어+7) ________ 의문사 유(有): – 주어 有 → 8) ________+be동사+주어+p.p. ~? – 의문사=주어 → 9) ________+10) ________+be동사+주어+p.p. ~?

3 4형식 수동태 전환

① to	1)g___, 2)t____, 3)s__d, 4)s__l, 5)w____, 6)sh__
② for	7)s___, 8)f___, 9)m___, 10)b__, 11)c___, 12)g__
③ of	13) ___

헷갈리지 말자! 초록색으로 표시된 부분을 바르게 고쳐 쓰세요.

1 The drone was buying by Sean yesterday.

→

2 By whom were you beating?

→

3 The used car was sold at him by a dealer.

→

CHAPTER 08

관계사

UNIT 18

관계대명사 who, which

CONCEPT 1 관계대명사란?

두 문장을 연결하는 역할을 하며, 앞에 있는 명사나 대명사인 선행사를 수식하는 형용사절을 이끈다.

I have a friend. + My friend can speak French.
→ I have a friend who can speak French.
(a friend: 선행사 / who: 관계대명사 / who can speak French: 형용사절)

CONCEPT 2 관계대명사 who: 선행사가 사람일 때

주격	who	= that	I met a boy. + The boy liked my sister. → I met a boy who[that] liked my sister.
목적격 (생략 가능)	who(m)	= that	I met the boy. + My sister loves him. → I met the boy who(m)[that] my sister loves.
소유격	whose		I know the man. + The man's wallet was stolen. → I know the man whose wallet was stolen.

CONCEPT 3 관계대명사 which: 선행사가 사물 또는 동물일 때

주격	which	= that	She likes the dog. + The dog has fluffy hair. → She likes the dog which[that] has fluffy hair.
목적격 (생략 가능)	which	= that	She likes the dog. + I have the dog. → She likes the dog which[that] I have.
소유격	whose = of which		She likes the dog. The legs of the dog are short. → She likes the dog whose legs are short. (= She likes the dog(,) the legs of which are short.)

CONCEPT 4 관계대명사의 용법

A 제한적 용법

관계대명사절이 선행사를 직접 수식한다.

He has a son who is a singer. (가수가 아닌 아들이 또 있는지 알 수 없는 상황)

B 계속적 용법

관계대명사절이 선행사에 대한 보충 설명을 하며, 앞에 comma(,)가 있다. 계속적 용법의 관계대명사는 '접속사+대명사'로 바꾸어 쓸 수 있다.

He has a son, who (= and he) is a singer. (아들이 하나이고 그 아들이 가수인 경우)

GRAMMAR POINT

주격 관계대명사 수 일치

- 주격 관계대명사 뒤의 동사는 선행사의 수에 일치시킨다.

I like guys who are smart.

의문사 who와 비교

- I don't know who you are.
(의문사: 선행사 없음. '누구'의 뜻)
- I don't know the man who is talking to Suji.
(관계사: 선행사 있음. '~한'의 뜻)

소유격 관계대명사 of which

- 요즘은 사물의 소유격 관계대명사로 대부분 whose를 쓰고 of which는 잘 쓰이지 않는다.

계속적 용법의 관계대명사

- 계속적 용법의 관계대명사 역시 앞에 있는 선행사에 따라 who나 which를 사용하면 된다. 단, that은 계속적 용법으로 사용할 수 없다.

He has a son, that is a singer. (×)

VOCA French 프랑스어 | wallet 지갑 | fluffy 털이 복슬복슬한

Let's Check It Out

>>> 정답 13쪽

My score is
/ 22점

A 다음 문장에서 선행사에 밑줄을 치시오. 각 1점

1 I have a friend who has a cute kitten.

2 I bought a used car which had no air conditioning.

3 A student who studies hard will pass the test.

4 I have a cousin whose hobby is playing the drum.

B [ ]에서 알맞은 것을 고르시오. (둘 다 가능한 경우도 있음) 각 1점

1 I know the boy [who / which] ate your cake.

2 I yelled at the puppy [who / which] was biting my shoe.

3 She is reading a book which [has / have] many interesting drawings.

4 I sold the ring [that / which] he had given me.

5 My father pointed at a driver [whose / who] car was blocking the street.

C 관계대명사를 이용해서 다음을 하나의 문장으로 쓰시오. 각 2점

1 She met the boy. We helped him.

→ ______________________________

2 We found a doll. It looked lonely.

→ ______________________________

3 He has a smartphone. Its case is unique.

→ ______________________________

4 She brought the flowers. They smelled good.

→ ______________________________

5 My mom knew the lady. The lady loved my brother.

→ My mom ______________________________.

D 다음 문장에서 관계대명사가 '제한적 용법'과 '계속적 용법' 중 어느 것으로 사용되었는지 구분하시오. 각 1점

1 I have a lizard which has a sharp tail. → __________

2 I want to visit Canada, which is beautiful in fall. → __________

3 The detective wanted to talk to the man who called the taxi. → __________

VOCA kitten 새끼 고양이 | used car 중고차 | air conditioning 냉방 (기능) | yell 소리 지르다 | puppy 강아지 | bite 물다 | point at ~에게 손가락질하다 | block 막다 | unique 독특한 | lizard 도마뱀 | detective 탐정

Ready for Exams

››› 정답 13쪽

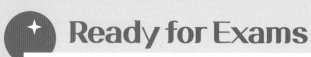

My score is		
Let's Check It Out ______ / 22점		0~24점 → Level 1 Test
Ready for Exams ______ / 13점	→	25~29점 → Level 2 Test
Total ______ / 35점		30~35점 → Level 3 Test

1 빈칸에 알맞은 것은? 2점

> We have a robot ______________ cleans the house.

① when ② that ③ it
④ so ⑤ whose

2 Choose the incorrect sentences. 3점

> ⓐ This is my friend whom lives in Pohang.
> ⓑ I saw the church that Gaudí built.
> ⓒ I know the girl who name is Crystal.
> ⓓ The man we saw yesterday isn't Mike.
> ⓔ Everything that Mr. Kim told us is true.

① ⓐ, ⓑ ② ⓐ, ⓒ ③ ⓑ, ⓒ
④ ⓑ, ⓒ, ⓓ ⑤ ⓒ, ⓔ

3 다음 빈칸에 공통으로 들어갈 단어는? 2점

> • The car ______________ he drives is an electric vehicle.
> • He has a house the roof of ______________ was made of glass.

① who ② which ③ whom
④ what ⑤ whose

4 조건에 맞게 빈칸을 채우시오. 3점

> Once there was a farmer. He was very poor.
>
> ·조건 1 두 문장을 한 문장으로 나타낼 것
> ·조건 2 빈칸에 4단어로 쓸 것

→ Once there was a farmer ______________________________.

5 Write the proper word to make the two sentences have the same meaning. 3점

> Koreans admire King Sejong. He invented Hangeul.

→ Koreans admire King Sejong, ______________ invented Hangeul.

VOCA Gaudí 가우디(스페인의 건축가) | electric vehicle 전기 자동차 | admire 존경하다 | invent 발명하다

UNIT 19

관계대명사 that, what

CONCEPT 1 that을 쓸 수 없는 경우

A that은 소유격이 없다.

I have a squirrel that eyes are yellow. (×) → whose

B 계속적 용법에는 쓰이지 않는다.

Everyone likes Mr. Kim, that is very diligent. (×) → who

C 전치사와 나란히 함께 쓰일 수 없다.

That is the castle in that the princess lives. (×) → in which

That is the castle that the princess lives in. (○)

CONCEPT 2 that을 주로 쓰는 경우

A 선행사에 형용사의 최상급, 서수, the very, the only, the same 등이 있을 때

This is the fastest phone that I have ever used.

B 선행사에 all, every, any, no, -thing 등이 있는 경우

I'll give my children everything that I have.

CONCEPT 3 관계대명사 what = the thing(s) which[that]

관계대명사 what은 '~하는 것'이라는 뜻으로, 선행사를 포함하고 있으며 명사절을 이끈다.

주어	What I have now is only water.
보어	This vegetable pizza is what my mom wants to eat.
목적어	Tell me what you know.

CONCEPT 4 관계대명사의 생략

목적격	타동사의 목적격	He is the man (whom) I met yesterday.
	전치사의 목적격	This is the dog (which) I am fond of.
주격 관계대명사+be동사		The book (which is) on the desk is mine. (on the desk: 형용사구 → The book)

GRAMMAR POINT

전치사+관계대명사

- 관계대명사 who(m)와 which는 전치사와 나란히 쓰일 수 있다.

She is the girl with whom I danced yesterday.

I visited the town in which my father lived.

선행사가 '사람+동물'인 경우

- 선행사가 사람과 동물이 합쳐진 경우에는 that만 쓴다.

I saw a boy and his dog that were running on the ground.

의문사 what과의 비교

- I believe what he told me. (관계사: ~하는 것)
- She told me what he looked like. (의문사: 무엇)

전치사와 관계대명사의 생략

- 관계대명사가 전치사의 목적어로 쓰인 경우, 전치사를 뒤로 보내야만 생략 가능하다.

It is a pen (which) I drew this picture with. (생략 가능)

It is a pen with which I drew this picture. (생략 불가능)

VOCA squirrel 다람쥐 | diligent 부지런한 | castle 성 | princess 공주 | ground 땅, 운동장 | vegetable 야채 | be fond of ~을 좋아하다

Let's Check It Out

››› 정답 14쪽

My score is
/ 21점

A [ ]에서 알맞은 것을 고르시오. 각 1점

1 Mike is the very person [who / that] I trust.
2 Judy is the only student [that / what] passed the test.
3 She went to Paris, [which / that] she always wanted to visit.
4 What is the thing [whose / that] only you can do?
5 I'll give you [that / what] I bought yesterday.
6 She took the bag [which / what] I left on the table.
7 This is not [that / what] she wants to have.
8 [Which / What] surprised me was his attitude toward life.

B 두 문장의 뜻이 같도록 빈칸을 채우시오. 각 1점

1 Show me the thing which you want.
→ Show me __________ you want.
2 She told me the thing that she knew about the accident.
→ She told me __________ she knew about the accident.

C 빈칸에 알맞은 관계사를 넣으시오. (that 또는 what) 각 1점

1 She gave me the watch __________ she had.
2 __________ he said is unbelievable.
3 I sold her the bike __________ I often rode.
4 This is __________ he did at the library.
5 That's the idea __________ she suggested.

D 밑줄 친 부분에 유의하여 문장 전체를 해석하시오. 각 2점

1 She was the very person <u>that achieved the goal</u>.
→ ____
2 <u>All I have</u> is money.
→ ____
3 This is <u>what she sent me yesterday</u>.
→ ____

VOCA trust 믿다 | attitude 태도 | toward ~을 향하여, ~ 쪽으로 | accident 사고 | unbelievable 믿을 수 없는 | suggest 제안하다 | achieve 이루다, 성취하다 | goal 목표

Ready for Exams

››› 정답 14쪽

My score is

Let's Check It Out ______	/ 21점	0~24점 → Level 1 Test
Ready for Exams ______	/ 14점	25~29점 → Level 2 Test
Total ______	/ 35점	30~35점 → Level 3 Test

1 다음 중 밑줄 친 부분을 생략할 수 없는 것은? 2점

① All that I want is your love.

② The boy whom we met was very kind.

③ She is wearing the blouse that I gave her.

④ This is the car that I bought recently.

⑤ I don't like stories which have unhappy endings.

2 다음 중 밑줄 친 'that'의 용법이 같은 것끼리 묶인 것은? 2점

ⓐ K is the letter that comes after J.
ⓑ This is the dog that likes orange juice.
ⓒ I know that the man is honest.
ⓓ I think that the old man is very generous.
ⓔ This is a book, and that is an album.

① ⓐ, ⓑ ② ⓐ, ⓒ ③ ⓑ, ⓒ

④ ⓐ, ⓑ, ⓔ ⑤ ⓐ, ⓒ, ⓓ

3 Which is the different usage of "What[what]"? 2점

① What he said is not true.

② Do you know what this is?

③ That is what we bought for our father.

④ That's just what I'm looking for.

⑤ I don't agree with what you just said.

4 다음 문장에서 생략할 수 있는 말에 괄호로 표시하시오. 3점

We checked everything that we needed.

5 Translate the sentence according to the conditions. 5점

이것은 그녀가 원하는 것이 아니다.

· Condition 1 어휘 – want, not
· Condition 2 6단어로 쓸 것

→ ______________________________

VOCA blouse 블라우스 | recently 최근에 | unhappy 불행한 | ending 결말 | generous 관대한, 너그러운 | check 확인하다

UNIT 20

관계부사

CONCEPT 1 관계부사 = 전시사 + 관계대명사

관계부사는 시간, 장소, 이유, 방법의 선행사를 수식하며, 문장 내에서 '접속사+부사'의 역할을 한다.

용도	선행사	관계부사	전치사+관계대명사
장소	the place, the house 등	where	in[on, at] which
시간	the time, the year 등	when	in[on, at] which
이유	the reason	why	for which
방법	(the way)	how	in which

CONCEPT 2 장소를 나타내는 선행사 + where

선행사가 뒤의 문장에서 장소를 나타내는 부사 역할을 한다.

I know the exact place. He was born in it.

→ I know the exact place which[that] he was born in.

→ I know the exact place in which he was born.

→ I know the exact place where he was born.

CONCEPT 3 시간을 나타내는 선행사 + when

선행사가 뒤의 문장에서 시간을 나타내는 부사 역할을 한다.

The time wasn't known to me. She left for America at that time.

→The time at which she left for America wasn't known to me.

→The time when she left for America wasn't known to me.

CONCEPT 4 이유를 나타내는 선행사 + why

Do you know the reason? He feels so good for the reason.

→ Do you know the reason for which he feels so good?

→ Do you know the reason why he feels so good?

CONCEPT 5 방법을 나타내는 선행사 + how

I don't know the way. She has succeeded in that way.

→ I don't know the way in which she has succeeded. (○)

→ I don't know the way how she has succeeded. (×)

→ I don't know how she has succeeded. (○)

→ I don't know the way she has succeeded. (○)

GRAMMAR POINT

관계대명사와의 비교

- 관계대명사는 선행사가 뒤의 문장에서 명사 역할을 한다.

  I know the house. You built the house. (명사 역할)

  → I know the house which you built.

- 관계부사는 선행사가 뒤의 문장에서 장소, 시간, 이유, 방법을 나타내는 부사 역할을 한다.

  I know the house. You were born in the house. (전치사+명사 = 부사 역할)

  → I know the house where you were born.

관계대명사 that

- 관계대명사 that은 전치사와 나란히 함께 쓰일 수 없다.

  I know the exact place in that he was born. (×)

the way와 how

- the way 와 how는 함께 쓸 수 없고 둘 중 하나만 써야 한다.

VOCA place 장소 | reason 이유 | exact 정확한 | be born 태어나다 | left 떠나다(leave)의 과거형 | succeed 성공하다

Let's Check It Out

››› 정답 14쪽

My score is / 20점

A 빈칸에 알맞은 말을 [보기]에서 골라 쓰시오. 각 1점

보기	where	when	how	why

1 Saturday is the day ___________ she goes shopping.

2 She wants to buy a house ___________ a famous movie star now lives.

3 Sam loves you. That's ___________ he wants to be with you.

4 This is ___________ she solved the problem.

B 두 문장을 한 문장으로 만들 때 빈칸에 알맞은 말을 쓰시오. 각 3점

1 This is the park. + I exercise at the park.

(1) This is the park ___________ I exercise at.

(2) This is the park ___________ ___________ I exercise.

(3) This is the park ___________ I exercise.

2 The way is a secret. + They make Coke.

(1) ___________ ___________ they make Coke is a secret.

(2) ___________ they make Coke is a secret.

3 I remember the day. + I brought my puppy home on the day.

(1) I remember the day ___________ I brought my puppy home ___________.

(2) I remember the day ___________ ___________ I brought my puppy home.

(3) I remember the day ___________ I brought my puppy home.

4 I can explain the reason. + You should eat more vegetables for the reason.

(1) I can explain the reason ___________ ___________ you should eat more vegetables.

(2) I can explain ___________ you should eat more vegetables.

C 빈칸에 알맞은 것을 써 넣으시오. 각 1점

1 Winter is the season ___________ ___________ it rains a lot in California.

2 Tell me ___________ I can contact you.

3 1443 is the year ___________ Hangeul was invented.

4 Don't you know the reason ___________ she went to India?

VOCA secret 비밀 | contact 접촉하다, 연락하다 | invent 발명하다

Ready for Exams

››› 정답 14쪽

My score is

Let's Check It Out ________	/ 20점	0~20점 → Level 1 Test
Ready for Exams ________	/ 10점	21~25점 → Level 2 Test
Total ________	/ 30점	26~30점 → Level 3 Test

1 다음 두 문장을 하나로 연결한 것으로 옳은 것은? (답 2개) 2점

She went to the city. Her friends live in the city.

① She went to the city which her friends live in.
② She went to the city where her friends live in.
③ She went to the city which her friends live.
④ She went to the city in that her friends live.
⑤ She went to the city where her friends live.

2 Who corrects the error properly? 2점

ⓐ Will you show me the room in which you sleep?
ⓑ Today is Saturday, the day on which I go out with my friends.
ⓒ Can you tell me the reason how you are late for class every day?
ⓓ This is the place where my mom works.

① 미나: ⓐ in which → which
② 지호: ⓑ on which → where
③ 현철: ⓒ how → why
④ 희석: ⓓ where → which
⑤ 민서: 틀린 것이 없다.

3 Write the proper words for the blanks to combine the two sentences into one. 3점

Greece is the country. The first Olympic Games were held there.

→ Greece is the country ________ the first Olympic Games ________ ________.

4 우리말과 일치하도록 빈칸에 적절한 한 단어를 쓰시오. 3점

네가 시험에 통과한 방법을 말해 줄래?

→ Can you tell me ________ you passed the test?

VOCA be held 개최되다 | pass a test 시험에 통과하다

Review Test

My score is / 80점
68점 이상 PASS!!

››› 정답 14쪽

U18_2+3

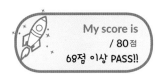

01 빈칸에 알맞은 말이 순서대로 짝지어진 것은? 2점

> • I need someone ________ can help me.
> • The church ________ stands on the hill is closed.

① that – who
② which – that
③ who – which
④ that – whom
⑤ which – which

U18_2+3

02 다음 중 빈칸에 'who'가 들어갈 수 없는 것은? 2점

① I know the girl ______ is playing the piano.
② This is the boy ______ sings very well.
③ The man ______ answered the phone was kind.
④ Soccer is a sport ______ is popular in Korea.
⑤ Look at the man ______ is running without any shoes.

U18_3+U19_3

03 빈칸에 적절한 관계대명사가 순서대로 짝지어진 것은? 2점

함정

> • She read a book ________ story made her cry.
> • He never eats ________ I make for him.

① which – which
② of which – which
③ whose – what
④ whose – that
⑤ of which – of which

U19_4+GP

04 밑줄 친 말을 생략할 수 없는 것을 모두 고르시오. 3점

한눈에 쏙

① The girl with whom I share this room will soon leave for Brazil.
② This is a movie about a boy who fights for freedom.
③ He is a movie star that a lot of people like.
④ The dolls which are on the sofa are my sister's.
⑤ She needs someone that can give her advice.

U18_1+2+GP

05 다음에 대해 바르게 설명한 학생을 모두 고르시오. 3점

한눈에 쏙

> ⓐ The camera which I bought a week ago don't work.
> ⓑ There are many poor people whom we must help them.
> ⓒ These are the blue jeans which James Dean advertised.

① 재우: ⓐ에서 주어가 The camera니까 동사가 doesn't work여야 해.
② 상호: ⓑ에서 them이 앞의 people이라 지워야 해.
③ 민희: ⓒ에서 which는 생략할 수 없어.
④ 태희: ⓐ에서 don't work를 camera 뒤에 써야 해.
⑤ 현빈: ⓑ에서 whom을 that으로 써야 해.

U20_1+2+GP

06 다음 빈칸에 들어갈 알맞은 말은? 2점

> Mina finally found a place ________ she could camp at.

① where ② when
③ which ④ how
⑤ why

U18_GP

07 How many sentences are incorrect? 3점

★ 고난도

ⓐ I like people who knows their worth.
ⓑ He is the boy who come here often.
ⓒ You can read the books that is on the table.
ⓓ He will meet some girls who like him.
ⓔ Do you know anyone who speak English well?

① one ② two
③ three ④ four
⑤ five

U20_5+GP

08 우리말을 영어로 옮긴 것이 어법상 어색한 것을 2개 고르면? 3점

함정

나는 그가 숙제를 빨리 끝마치는 방법을 알고 있다.

① I know the way in which he finishes his homework fast.
② I know the way how he finishes his homework fast.
③ I know the way he finishes his homework fast.
④ I know the way in that he finishes his homework fast.
⑤ I know how he finishes his homework fast.

U20_4

09 우리말과 뜻이 같도록 문장을 만들 때 빈칸 (A)에 들어갈 말은? 2점

너는 그녀가 왜 그렇게 화가 났는지 알고 있니?
= Do you know ________ ________ ___(A)___ ________ ________ so upset?

① reason ② the
③ which ④ she
⑤ why

U20_5+GP

10 다음 중 어법상 어색한 것은? 2점

★ 고난도

① I will show you the way how she did it.
② The school where she studies is nice.
③ He bought the house where his ancestor had lived.
④ She told me why she respected him.
⑤ This is the time of day when she takes a nap.

U18_3+U19_3

11 Which sentences are correct? (There are 1-3 correct answers.) 3점

한눈에 쏙

① I know the man whose eyes are blue.
② Does she like the book which covers are soft?
③ Were there many students whom you knew?
④ That I want to see is a rainbow.
⑤ I remember the exact time when we met yesterday.

U19_3

12 다음 우리말을 영작할 때 필요 없는 단어는? 2점

모차렐라 치즈 피자가 내가 지금 바로 먹고 싶은 것이다.
= Mozzarella cheese pizza ________ ________ ________ ________ ________ ________ right now.

① that ② is
③ want ④ what
⑤ to

U19_3

13 다음의 단어들을 조합하여 완전한 문장을 만들 수 없는 것은? 4점

★ 고난도

① is / this / the / tallest / building / I / . / have / ever / seen
② the / watch / my / bought / . / best / friend / that / is / for / me
③ of / fond / this / . / movie / is / the / she / is
④ me / tell / . / that / get / you / want / to
⑤ is / a / pen / . / it / the / I / drew / with / picture

Challenge! 주관식 서술형

U18_2

14 Rewrite the incorrect sentence correctly. 4점

> ⓐ Do you know the man which is talking to John?
> ⓑ He is a person that keeps his promises.

(   ) ______________ → ______________

U18_2

15 조건에 맞게 다음 문장을 영작하시오. 6점

★ 고난도

> 이분은 내가 함께 일하는 사람이에요.
>
> · 조건 1　어휘 – the person, work, with
> · 조건 2　마지막 단어는 전치사로 쓸 것
> · 조건 3　빈칸에 6단어로 쓸 것

→ This is ______________________________.

U18_3

16 그림을 보고 빈칸에 알맞은 관계대명사를 쓰시오. 3점

→ I cleaned the mirror ____________ was dirty.

U19_3+GP

17 밑줄 친 부분에 유의하여 각 문장을 해석하시오. 각 3점

(1) What I saw there surprised me.

→ ______________________________

(2) Dongjin may know what her job is.

→ ______________________________

U18_3

18 관계사를 사용해서 두 문장을 한 문장으로 쓰시오. 5점

> I bought a new computer. Its monitor is big.

→ ______________________________

____

U19_4

19 다음 문장에서 생략된 관계대명사를 넣어 문장을 다시 쓰시오. 5점

> She ate the curry and rice her son made.

→ ______________________________

____

U19_1

20 어법상 어색한 부분을 찾아 바르게 고치시오. 4점

> On Halloween, that is October 31, children dress up as ghosts and monsters.

______________ → ______________

U18_3+U20_1+2

21 다음 두 문장을 한 문장으로 연결할 때 빈칸에 알맞은 말을 쓰시오. 각 3점

한눈에 쏙

> She often visits the hospital. Her husband works at the hospital.

(1) She often visits the hospital ____________ her husband works ____________.

(2) She often visits the hospital ____________ ____________ her husband works.

(3) She often visits the hospital ____________ her husband works.

U20_3

22 Find the error and correct it. 5점

함정

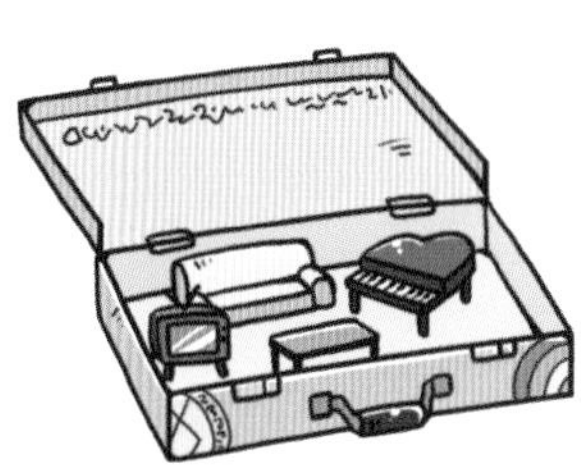

> In the future, we will have a small magic bag. It is a bag in which we can put anything we want. I want a future which everything comes true to come fast.

______________ → ______________

››› 정답 15쪽

한눈에 쏙! 아래 노트를 보면서 빈칸을 채워 보세요.

1 관계대명사의 개념

I have a friend. → 선행사

The ~~friend~~ can speak French. → 주어 자리 / 반복되는 명사 없애기!

사람인가?
- 주어 – 1) ______
- 소유격 – whose
- 목적격 – 2) ______

사물인가?
- 주어 – 3) ______
- 소유격 – whose
- 목적격 – 4) ______

(that)으로 바꾸어 쓸 수 있음!

2 that

쓸 수 없는 경우	쓰는 경우
① 1)______ 자리 → whose로 써야 함	① 선행사가 사람+사물[동물] → 반드시
② 계속적 용법 콤마(,) 다음	② the 3)v___, the 4)o___, 최상급, 서수) 주로
③ 2)______ 다음	③ all, 5)e____, no, -thing이 온 경우) 주로

헷갈리지 말자! 초록색으로 표시된 부분을 바르게 고쳐 쓰세요.

1 I have a friend whom can speak French.
→

2 I'll give my children everything what I have.
→

3 I don't know the way how she has succeeded.
→

CHAPTER 09

비교 구문

UNIT 21

비교 변화, 원급 이용 비교 구문

CONCEPT 1 비교 변화

A 규칙 변화

	원급	비교급	최상급
대부분의 형용사, 부사	small	smaller	smallest
-e로 끝나는 경우	large	larger	largest
'자음+y'로 끝나는 경우	easy	easier	easiest
'단모음+단자음'으로 끝나는 경우	big hot	bigger hotter	biggest hottest
3음절 이상의 형용사, 부사	interesting	more interesting	most interesting
2음절이어도 -ful, -ous, -less, -ish로 끝나는 경우	careful famous useless foolish	more careful more famous more useless more foolish	most careful most famous most useless most foolish
-ing, -ed로 끝나는 경우 (분사 형태의 형용사)	boring tired	more boring more tired	most boring most tired

B 불규칙 변화

good/well(좋은/잘) – better – best

many/much(많은) – more – most

late(시간이 늦은) – later – latest(최근의)

far(거리가 먼) – farther – farthest

bad/ill(나쁜/아픈/나쁘게) – worse – worst

little(작은, 적은) – less – least

late(순서가 늦은) – latter – last(마지막의)

far(정도가 깊은) – further – furthest

CONCEPT 2 원급을 이용한 비교 구문

A ~ as+원급+as B	A는 B만큼 ~하다
A ~ not as[so]+원급+as B (= B ~ 비교급 than A)	A는 B만큼 ~하지 않다 (= B 가 A보다 더 ~하다)
as+원급+as possible (= as+원급+as+주어+can[could])	가능한 한 ~한/하게

These sneakers are as comfortable as those slippers. 

These sneakers are not as comfortable as those slippers. 

=These sneakers are less comfortable than those slippers. 

=Those slippers are more comfortable than these sneakers. 

Please answer the question as soon as possible[you can].

GRAMMAR POINT

원급, 비교급, 최상급

- 원급: 형용사나 부사의 본래 형태를 원급이라고 한다.
- 비교급: '원급+er' 또는 'more+원급'의 형태
- 최상급: '원급+est' 또는 'most+원급'의 형태

more와 -er, most와 -est

- more와 -er 또는 most와 -est를 같이 사용할 수 없다.
- more taller (×) → taller (○)
- most greatest (×) → greatest (○)

열등 비교

- '~보다 덜 …하다'는 「less+원급+than」으로 표현한다.
- 동등 비교의 부정문은 열등 비교로 표현할 수 있다.

Jenny is taller than me.

= I am less tall than Jenny.

비교 대상 일치

- 비교 구문에서는 비교하는 대상이 일치해야 한다.

Your phone is as old as ~~me~~. (×)

→ Your phone is as old as mine. (○)

(네 전화기는 내 것만큼 오래됐다.)

VOCA careful 조심스러운 | useless 쓸모없는 | foolish 바보 같은 | sneakers 운동화 | slippers 슬리퍼 | comfortable 편안한 | possible 가능한

Let's Check It Out

>>> 정답 15쪽

My score is / 19점

A 빈칸에 알맞은 비교급과 최상급을 쓰시오. 각 1점

	원급	비교급	최상급
1	early		
2	great		
3	large		
4	hot		
5	expensive		

B [ ]에서 알맞은 것을 고르시오. 각 1점

1 Dad is [carefuler / more careful] than Mom.
2 My brother is the [smaller / smallest] person in my family.
3 I was the [worse / worst] singer of the three.
4 Bears are [stronger / more strong] than wolves.
5 Sean knows how to make friends [better / well] than I.

C 우리말과 같은 뜻이 되도록 주어진 단어를 활용하여 빈칸을 채우시오. 각 1점

1 폭력이 거짓말보다 더 나쁘다. (bad)
→ Violence is ________ ________ a lie.

2 나는 그의 방식보다 너의 방식을 더 좋아한다. (good)
→ I like your way ________ ________ his.

3 그는 마지막 기회를 놓쳤다. (late)
→ He missed ________ ________ chance.

D 주어진 문장과 같은 뜻이 되도록 빈칸을 채우시오. 각 3점

1 This lake is shallower than that river.
(1) That river is not ________ ________ ________ this lake.
(2) That river is ________ ________ this lake.

2 English is more interesting than math.
(1) Math is ________ interesting than English.
(2) Math ________ ________ as interesting ________ English.

VOCA worst 가장 못한 | bear 곰 | wolves 늑대(wolf의 복수형) | violence 폭력 | chance 기회 | shallow 얕은

Ready for Exams

››› 정답 15쪽

My score is

Let's Check It Out ______ / 19점		0~20점 → Level 1 Test
Ready for Exams ______ / 11점	➡	21~25점 → Level 2 Test
Total ______ / 30점		26~30점 → Level 3 Test

1 밑줄 친 단어들을 올바르게 고친 것은? 2점

ⓐ Bin is as <u>taller</u> as Hyeon.
ⓑ This room is <u>large</u> than that one.

① ⓐ taller – ⓑ largest
② ⓐ tall – ⓑ large
③ ⓐ tall – ⓑ larger
④ ⓐ taller – ⓑ large
⑤ ⓐ taller – ⓑ larger

2 Which sentences are incorrect? (Find ALL.) 2점

① He runs faster than you.
② This building isn't as larger as that one.
③ The yellow car is bigger than the black one.
④ Mike dances better than David.
⑤ She makes more worse noise than you.

3 다음 문장을 바르게 설명한 학생을 모두 고르시오. 3점

My sister saved as much money as possible.

① 미나: much를 many로 바꾸어야 한다.
② 선희: possible은 맞게 쓰였다.
③ 정민: possible은 she could로 바꿀 수 있다.
④ 종윤: possible은 she can으로 바꿀 수 있다.
⑤ 재설: as much ~ as를 more ~ than으로 바꿔야 한다.

4 다음 그림과 설명을 보고, 가장 왼쪽 사람부터 차례대로 이름을 쓰시오. 4점

Jin is not as tall as Sam. Kevin and Daniel are taller than Sam, but Kevin is not as tall as Daniel.

➡ ______________, ______________, ______________, ______________

VOCA save 저축하다

UNIT 22

여러 가지 비교 구문

CONCEPT 1 원급과 비교급을 이용한 최상급 표현

A ~ the+최상급+단수 명사+of[in] …	A는 …(중)에서 가장 ~하다
A ~ 비교급+than any other+단수 명사+of[in] …	…(중)에서 A는 어떤 다른 것보다 더 ~하다
No (other)+단수 명사 ~ 비교급+than A of[in] …	…(중)에서 A보다 더 ~한 것은 없다
No (other)+단수 명사 ~ as[so]+원급+as A of [in] …	…(중)에서 A만큼 ~한 것은 없다

The diamond is the most expensive jewel in the world.

=The diamond is more expensive than any other jewel in the world.

= No other jewel in the world is more expensive than the diamond.

= No other jewel in the world is as expensive as the diamond.

CONCEPT 2 배수사를 이용한 비교 표현

A ~ 배수사+as+원급+as B	…배만큼 ~한
A ~ 배수사+비교급+than B	…배 더 ~한

My bag is twice as big as yours.

= My bag is two times bigger than yours.

CONCEPT 3 기타 비교 구문

The+비교급+주어+동사 ~, the+비교급+주어+동사 …	~하면 할수록, 점점 더 …하다
get/become/grow+비교급+and+비교급	점점 더 ~한/하게 되다
Which[Who] ~ 비교급, A or B?	A와 B 중 어느 것이[누가] 더 ~한가?
A ~ one of the+최상급+복수 명사	A는 가장 ~한 것들 중의 하나이다
A ~ the+최상급+단수 명사+(that)+주어+have ever+p.p.	A는 주어가 …한 중에서 가장 ~하다

The higher you climb, the colder it is.

The weather is getting hotter and hotter.

Which is faster, sound or light?

Harry Potter is one of the most famous characters in the world.

Little Women is the most interesting novel that I have ever read.

GRAMMAR POINT

부정 주어

- 부정 주어로는 Nothing, No one, Nobody 등이 있다.

최상급에서 the의 사용

- 형용사의 최상급 앞에는 the를 쓰고, 부사의 최상급 앞에서는 the를 생략할 수 있다.

  He runs (the) fastest in my class.

of + 복수 명사 / in + 집합, 장소

- of 뒤에는 복수 명사가 오고, in 뒤에는 집합이나 장소가 나온다.

  of my friends (내 친구들 중에서)

  in my class (우리 반에서)

'두 배'일 때 비교 표현

- 두 배를 나타낼 때 twice는 원급과, two times는 비교급과 함께 사용된다.

  My bag is ~~twice~~ bigger than yours. (→ two times)

  My bag is ~~two times~~ as big as yours. (→ twice)

비교 대상 일치

- 배수사를 이용한 비교 표현에서도 비교하는 대상이 일치해야 한다.

  My sword is three times as long as ~~you~~. (→ yours)

비교 구문의 전환

- 「The+비교급+주어+동사 ~, the+ 비교급+주어+동사 …」 구문은 접속사 as(~할수록)를 써서 전환할 수 있다.

  The more you think, the more you understand.

  → As you think more, you understand more.

원급과 비교급의 강조

- 원급은 주로 very로 강조하고, 비교급은 much, even, still, far, a lot 등으로 강조해 준다.

  Mark is <u>very</u> smart.

  Tony is <u>much</u> smarter than Mark.

VOCA diamond 다이아몬드 | expensive 값비싼 | jewel 보석 | climb 오르다 | weather 날씨 | character 등장인물 | novel 소설 | sword 검, 칼

Let's Check It Out

››› 정답 16쪽

My score is / 18점

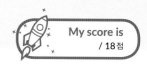

A 우리말과 같은 뜻이 되도록 [ ]에서 알맞은 것을 고르시오. 각 1점

1 바티칸 시국이 세계에서 제일 작은 나라이다.

→ Vatican City is [a / the] smallest country in the world.

2 그녀는 사무실에서 어떤 다른 사람보다 더 부지런하다.

→ She is more diligent than any other person [in / of] the office.

3 건강보다 중요한 것은 없다.

→ [Nothing / Something] is more important than health.

4 민수는 가장 힘이 센 학생 중 하나이다.

→ Minsu is one of the strongest [student / students].

B 주어진 문장과 뜻이 같도록 빈칸을 채우시오. 각 3점

1 To me, basketball is the most exciting sport.

(1) To me, basketball is __________ __________ __________ any other sport.

(2) To me, __________ __________ sport is more exciting __________ __________.

(3) To me, __________ __________ sport is __________ exciting as __________.

2 Seoul is the largest city in Korea.

(1) __________ __________ city in Korea is as large as Seoul.

(2) Seoul is __________ __________ __________ other city in Korea.

3 Japan is four times as large as Korea.

(1) Japan is four times __________ __________ Korea.

(2) Korea is __________ __________ __________ __________ Japan.

C [ ]에서 알맞은 것을 고르시오. 각 1점

1 The more people have, [the most / the more] they want.

2 [Which / What] is better, this or that?

3 Who is [taller / tallest], Daniel or Mike?

4 This is [stranger / the strangest] accident that I've ever seen.

5 Pinocchio's nose grew [longer and longer / more and more long] as he kept lying.

VOCA Vatican City 바티칸 시국(로마 시내에 있는 독립 국가) | country 나라, 국가 | diligent 부지런한 | health 건강 | strange 이상한

Ready for Exams

››› 정답 16쪽

My score is

Let's Check It Out ______ / 18점		0~20점 → Level 1 Test
Ready for Exams ______ / 12점	➡	21~25점 → Level 2 Test
Total ______ / 30점		26~30점 → Level 3 Test

1 주어진 문장과 의미가 다른 것을 고르시오. 2점

No fruit is as delicious as the pear.

① The pear is the most delicious fruit.
② The pear is more delicious than any other fruit.
③ No fruit is more delicious than the pear.
④ No other fruit is as delicious as the pear.
⑤ The pear is as delicious as the other fruits.

2 How many sentences are incorrect? 3점

ⓐ Charlie Chaplin is one of the most famous actor in history.
ⓑ The day is getting short and short.
ⓒ As higher we climb, the thinner the air is.
ⓓ He is one of the most outstanding players that I've ever met.

① zero ② one ③ two
④ three ⑤ four

3 다음 그래프와 일치하도록 빈칸에 알맞은 말을 쓰시오. 각 2점

(1) A lobster lives ________ ________ ________ as a shark.
(2) A human lives ________ ________ ________ than a shark.

4 다음 중 어법상 어색한 문장을 골라 바르게 고치시오. 3점

ⓐ The Taj Mahal is one of the most beautiful building in the world.
ⓑ The weather is getting warmer and warmer.

(　　) ________________ ➡ ________________

VOCA pear 배 | outstanding 뛰어난, 탁월한 | life span 수명 | lobster 바닷가재 | Taj Mahal 타지마할(인도의 건축물)

Review Test

My score is / 70점
60점 이상 PASS!!

››› 정답 16쪽

U21_1+2

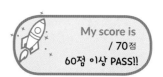

01 빈칸에 들어갈 단어가 순서대로 짝지어진 것은? 2점

- The situation is ________ than I thought.
- He hit the ball as far as ________.

① worse – he can
② worse – possible
③ badder – he could
④ more bad – he can
⑤ the worst – possible

U21_1+U22_3

02 Which sentences are incorrect? 3점

한눈에 쏙

ⓐ Male birds are colorful than female birds.
ⓑ Mr. Lee is much older than my mom.
ⓒ An elephant is one of the biggest animal.
ⓓ A bird flies highlier than a fly.

① ⓐ, ⓑ
② ⓐ, ⓑ, ⓒ
③ ⓐ, ⓒ, ⓓ
④ ⓑ, ⓓ
⑤ ⓑ, ⓒ, ⓓ

U21_2

03 According to the following graph, choose the incorrect sentence. 3점

함정

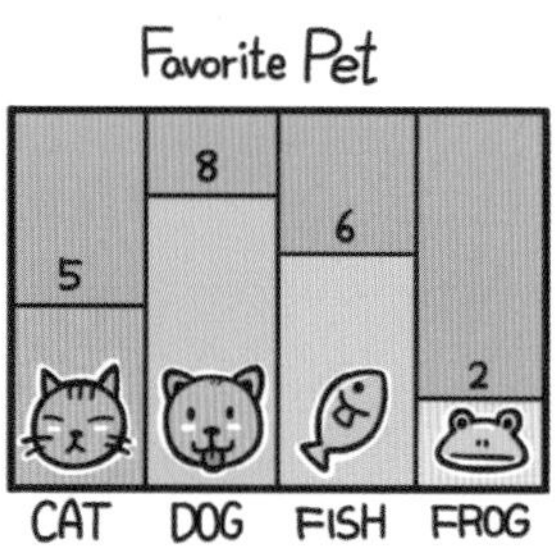

① People like dogs the most.
② People like cats more than frogs.
③ People don't like fish as much as frogs.
④ People like frogs the least.
⑤ No other pet is liked more than dogs.

U22_GP

04 어법상 어색한 부분을 바르게 고친 학생은? 2점

The Pacific is the widest in all ocean.

① 선영: in → of
② 현호: the widest → widest
③ 승훈: in all ocean → of all oceans
④ 예린: ocean → oceans
⑤ 서연: 틀린 부분이 없다.

U22_1

05 다음 중 나머지 네 문장과 의미가 다른 것은? 3점

한눈에 쏙

① Jupiter is the largest planet in the solar system.
② Jupiter is larger than any other planet in the solar system.
③ No planet in the solar system is as large as Jupiter.
④ No planet in the solar system is larger than Jupiter.
⑤ Jupiter is as large as the other planets in the solar system.

U22_GP

06 Which word is NOT proper for the blank? 2점

- You seem ________ more curious than I.
- His hair is ________ longer than mine.

① still
② far
③ much
④ very
⑤ a lot

U21_2+U22_GP

07 다음 중 어법상 어색한 문장을 모두 고르시오. 3점

★ 고난도

① Jane answered as quickly as she can.
② The more you eat, the more you want.
③ The tree is twice as tall as my house.
④ He is getting fatter and fatter.
⑤ He looked quite younger than I expected.

U21_1

08 어법상 어색한 부분을 고쳐 문장을 다시 쓰시오. 5점

함정

I can play chess as good as my dad.

→ ____________________

U21_2

09 빈칸에 알맞은 말을 넣어 다음 영작을 완성하시오. 5점

나는 가능한 한 오랫동안 철봉에 매달려 있었다.

→ I hung on the iron bar ________ ________ ________ ________.

U22_GP

10 주어진 단어를 이용해서 우리말을 영어로 쓰시오. 6점

그녀는 우리 반에서 가장 똑똑한 학생이다.
smart, my class

→ ____________________

U22_1

11 다음 문장을 조건에 맞게 바꾸어 쓰시오. 각 5점

한눈에 쏙

Mt. Everest is the highest mountain.

· 조건 1 Write two sentences that have the same meaning as the given sentence.
· 조건 2 Use the phrase "no mountain."

(1) ____________________
(2) ____________________

U22_3

12 우리말과 같은 뜻이 되도록 빈칸에 알맞은 말을 쓰시오. 5점

네가 책을 많이 읽으면 읽을수록 더욱 똑똑해진다.

→ ________ ________ books you read, ________ ________ you become.

U22_3

13 Rewrite the incorrect part correctly. 4점

The computer is one of the most widely used scientific tool.

________ → ________

[14~15] 다음 그래프를 보고, 질문에 답하시오.

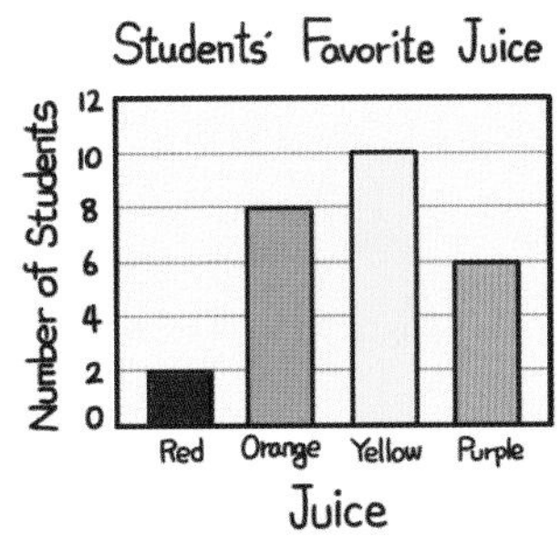

U22_GP

14 위의 그래프와 일치하도록 빈칸을 채우시오. 4점

Students like yellow juice ________.
= Yellow juice is the students' ________ juice.

U21_1+2

15 Compare orange juice and purple juice. 각 3점

(1) Students like purple juice ________ ________ orange juice.

(2) Students like orange juice ________ ________ purple juice.

U22_3

16 그래프와 일치하도록 빈칸에 알맞은 말을 쓰시오. 6점

★ 고난도

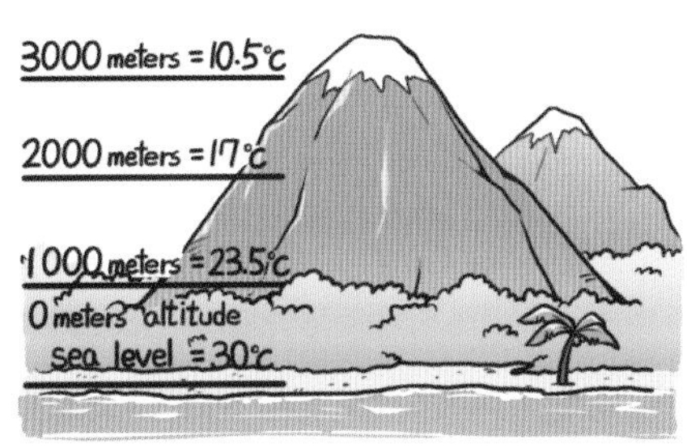

→ ________ ________ we climb the mountain, ________ ________ the temperature gets. (high, low)

시험 직전에 챙겨 보는 비법 노트

››› 정답 16쪽

한눈에 쏙! 아래 노트를 보면서 빈칸을 채워 보세요.

1 원급, 비교급, 최상급

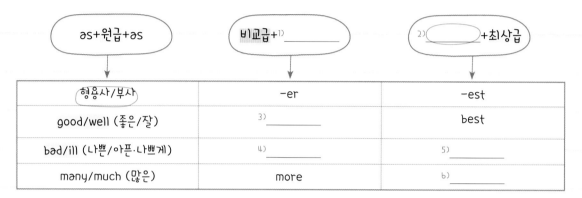

as+원급+as / 비교급+1) ________ / 2) ________+최상급

형용사/부사	-er	-est
good/well (좋은/잘)	3) ________	best
bad/ill (나쁜/아픈·나쁘게)	4) ________	5) ________
many/much (많은)	more	6) ________

2 최상급

= 주어+비교급+1) ________ ________ ________+단수 명사

= 부정 주어+2) ________+3) ________

= 부정 주어+as+4) ________+as

3 중요 비교급 · 최상급 구문

- 1) ________+비교급 ~, 2) ________+비교급: ~하면 할수록 점점 더 …하다
- one 3) ________ the+최상급+복수 명사

헷갈리지 말자! 초록색으로 표시된 부분을 바르게 고쳐 쓰세요.

1 These sneakers are less comfortable as those slippers.

→

2 The diamond is more expensive than any other jewels in the world.

→

3 The higher you climb, colder it is.

→

CHAPTER 10

형용사, 부사, 분사

UNIT 23

형용사와 부사

CONCEPT 1 형용사

A 소수 읽기

정수. 소수 → 기수+point+한 자리씩

3.14: three point one four

0.234: (zero) point two three four

B 분수 읽기

분자 → 기수 / 분모 → 서수(-s)

1/2: one[a] second = (a) half

1/4: one-fourth = a quarter

2/3: two-thirds

4 5/7: four and five-sevenths (대분수)

C 명사를 뒤에서 수식하는 경우

-one, -body, -thing+형용사

I'd like to meet someone tall.

Do you have anything special?

D the+형용사: ~한 사람들

The seat is for the old. (= old people)

CONCEPT 2 부사

A 접속부사와 연결사

however	하지만	therefore	그러므로	in other words	다시 말해
in fact	사실은	as a result	그 결과	on the other hand	반면에
finally (= at last)	마침내	in addition (= besides)	게다가	for example (= for instance)	예를 들면

I was short of money. However, I bought the expensive chair.

My son helps with housework. For example, he takes out the garbage.

B 타동사+부사

타동사+명사+부사	타동사+대명사+부사
타동사+부사+명사	타동사+부사+대명사 (×)

Put on the jacket. (○) Put that on. (○) Put the jacket on. (○) Put on it. (×)

GRAMMAR POINT

분모에 -s 붙이기

- 분수에서 분자가 복수일 경우 분모에 -s를 붙인다.

1/5: one-fifth

2/5: two-fifths

분수에서 over의 사용

- 큰 분수나 구어체에서 over를 사용해 읽는 경우가 있다. (기수+over+기수)

11/13: eleven over thirteen

27/43: twenty-seven over forty-three

서수 읽는 법

- 서수 읽는 법은 〈내공 중학영문법 1 개념이해책〉 p. 86 참조.

분수의 수 일치

- 분수가 명사를 수식할 때 동사는 수식받는 명사에 일치시킨다.

Three-fifths of the apples are good to eat.

Two-thirds of the milk was spilled on the floor.

the+형용사

- 'the+형용사'는 복수로 취급하므로 주어로 사용되었을 때 뒤에 복수 동사가 나온다.

The homeless often become victims of crime.

자동사+전치사

- '자동사+전치사'는 전치사를 뒤로 보낼 수 없다.

I'm looking a cartoon for. (×)

→ I'm looking for a cartoon.

VOCA seat 자리, 좌석 | spill 엎지르다 | be short of ~이 부족하다 | housework 집안일 | garbage 쓰레기 | homeless 집 없는, 노숙하는 | victim 희생자 | crime 범죄 | cartoon 만화

Let's Check It Out

››› 정답 17쪽

My score is / 18점

A 다음 숫자를 읽으시오. 각 1점

1 2,048 → ________________

2 3.58 → ________________

3 7/10 → ________________

4 4 3/4 → ________________

B [ ]에서 알맞은 것을 고르시오. 각 1점

1 Give me [something hot / hot something].

2 Please wait [me for / for me] outside.

3 Can you [turn off it / turn it off]?

C 밑줄 친 부분이 어색하면 바르게 고치시오. 각 1점

1 You have to <u>hand in your homework</u> now.

→ ________________

2 Don't <u>look me at</u> like that.

→ ________________

3 Excuse me. Can I <u>try on this</u>?

→ ________________

D 우리말과 일치하도록 빈칸에 알맞은 말을 쓰시오. (숫자는 영어로 쓸 것) 각 2점

1 난 뭔가 찬 마실 것이 필요해.

→ I need ________ ________ to drink.

2 7/8은 9/10보다 작아, 그렇지?

→ ________-________ is smaller than ________-________, isn't it?

3 마라톤은 왜 42.195km이지?

→ Why is a marathon ________-________ ________ ________ ________ ________ kilometers?

4 그는 외투를 입지 않았다. 그 결과 그는 감기에 걸렸다.

→ He didn't wear a coat. ________ ________ ________, he caught a cold.

VOCA try on 착용해 보다 | marathon 마라톤 | catch a cold 감기에 걸리다

Ready for Exams

››› 정답 17쪽

My score is

Let's Check It Out ________ / 18점
Ready for Exams ________ / 12점
Total ________ / 30점

0~20점 → Level 1 Test
21~25점 → Level 2 Test
26~30점 → Level 3 Test

1 다음 빈칸에 적절한 것을 모두 고르면? 2점

My girlfriend is kind and cute. ________________, she is very smart.

① At last ② In addition ③ Therefore
④ However ⑤ Besides

2 Which is grammatically incorrect? 2점

① Look at the picture on the wall.
② Did you find out the answer?
③ I would like to take this out.
④ She does not care about money.
⑤ Will you take off it inside the room?

3 다음 숫자를 영어로 읽으시오. 각 2점

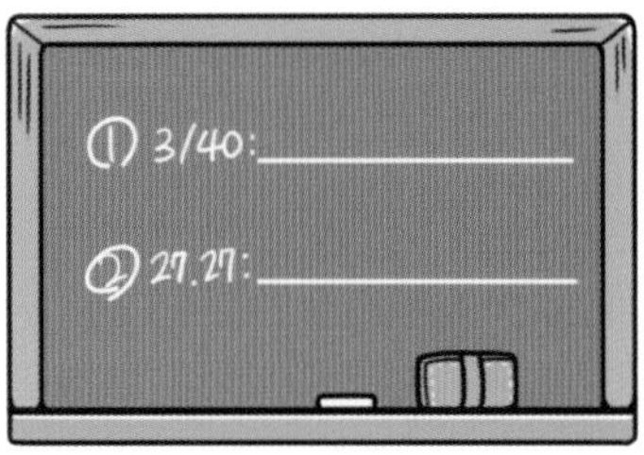

① ________________________________

② ________________________________

4 Translate the following sentence according to the conditions. 4점

그녀는 시각 장애인들을 위한 학교를 설립했다.
·Condition 1 people을 사용하지 말 것 ·Condition 2 아래 어휘를 포함하여 8단어로 쓸 것 ·Condition 3 어휘 – set up, blind

→ ________________________________

VOCA take out 가지고 가다 | find out 알아내다 | set up 설립하다 | blind 눈이 먼

UNIT 24

분사

CONCEPT 1 분사의 의미와 종류

분사란 동사의 성질을 가지면서 형용사 역할을 하는 것을 말한다.

현재분사	-ing	능동: ~하는	I saw a barking dog outside.
		진행: ~하고 있는	We are having fun, aren't we?
과거분사	-ed	완료: ~한	The lady has just repaired the chair.
		수동: ~되는, ~지는	They were raised in the countryside.

CONCEPT 2 분사의 수식

단독 수식	분사+명사	The dancing cowboy is my father. The broken smartphone is mine.
어구 수식	명사+분사	The dog wagging its tail is friendly. The song sung by EM Duo was fantastic.

CONCEPT 3 동명사와 현재분사의 비교

현재분사 (~하는)	형용사 역할 (동작, 상태)	The boy is playing baseball alone. Did you see the swimming seal over there?
동명사 (~하기)	명사 역할 (용도, 목적)	I bought a new pair of running shoes. His only hobby is collecting old coins.

CONCEPT 4 감정을 나타내는 분사

annoying 짜증 나게 하는 annoyed 짜증 난	embarrassing 당황시키는 embarrassed 당황한	boring 지루하게 하는 bored 지루한
confusing 혼란시키는 confused 혼란을 느낀	disappointing 실망시키는 disappointed 실망한	frightening 겁을 주는 frightened 겁먹은
amazing 놀라운 amazed 놀란	depressing 우울하게 하는 depressed 우울한	frustrating 좌절시키는 frustrated 좌절한
pleasing 기쁘게 하는 pleased 기쁜	satisfying 만족시키는 satisfied 만족한	touching 감동적인 touched 감동받은
shocking 충격을 주는 shocked 충격받은	surprising 놀라게 하는 surprised 놀란	tiring 피곤하게 하는 tired 피곤해진

GRAMMAR POINT

어구 수식에서의 수 일치

- 분사(구)가 수식하는 명사에 동사의 수를 일치시킨다.

The men sitting on the bench is (→ are) looking at you.

분사와 본동사

- '~하는/되는'과 '~하다/되다'를 구별한다.

The wallet ~~find~~ (→ found) under the desk ~~belong~~ (→ belongs) to Kate.
(찾는다? → 찾아진, 속한다! → 속한다)

The player ~~shoot~~ (→ shooting) an arrow ~~eat~~ (→ eats) a kimchi burger every day.
(쏜다? → 쏘는, 먹는다! → 먹는다)

현재분사와 동명사의 구별법

- 현재분사: a dancing girl에서 girl = dancing
- 동명사: a dancing room에서 room ≠ dancing

사람이 주어일 때 -ing

- -ing는 주로 사물에, -ed는 주로 사람에 사용하지만 사람을 주어로 -ing도 가능하다.

Your boyfriend is so boring.
(남을 지루하게 하는 사람)

VOCA bark 짖다 | repair 수리하다 | countryside 시골 | wag (개가 꼬리를) 흔들다 | seal 물개 | belong to ~의 것이다 | arrow 화살

Let's Check It Out

››› 정답 17쪽

My score is
/ 24점

A [ ]에서 알맞은 것을 고르시오. 각 1점

1 Have you ever seen a [dancing / danced] monkey?
2 I couldn't find my [stealing / stolen] wallet.
3 He was sweeping up the [breaking / broken] plates.
4 The girl [lives / living] in the house is from Uzbekistan.
5 This is the bridge [building / built] two years ago.
6 She stopped beside a man [worn / wearing] a blue tie.

B 밑줄 친 부분이 '현재분사'인지 '동명사'인지 구분하시오. 각 1점

1 The sun was shining all around me. → ____________
2 The sleeping car was too small to sleep in. → ____________
3 He was just sitting on the floor. → ____________
4 Do not try to catch a running bus. → ____________
5 Is walking up stairs good exercise? → ____________
6 The old man is leaning on a walking stick. → ____________

C 밑줄 친 부분이 어색하면 바르게 고치시오. 각 1점

1 The little girl wants to find her lost doll. → ____________
2 Do you know the girl sung over there? → ____________
3 The man talked to James is my neighbor. → ____________
4 These are new knives importing from Germany. → ____________
5 The pictures taken by him are very impressive. → ____________
6 He showed off his watch made in Switzerland. → ____________

D 괄호 안의 단어를 빈칸에 알맞은 형태로 쓰시오. 각 1점

1 The movie we saw yesterday was __________. (excite)
2 What's up? You look __________. (depress)
3 The news was very __________ to me. (shock)
4 What an __________ scene this is! (amaze)
5 Today's weather is very __________. (please)
6 Your speech was very __________. (touch)

VOCA sweep up 쓸어내다 | plate 접시 | stair 계단 | lean 기대다 | neighbor 이웃 | import 수입하다 | impressive 인상적인 | show off 자랑하다 | scene 장면

Ready for Exams

››› 정답 17쪽

My score is		
Let's Check It Out ______ / 24점		0~24점 → Level 1 Test
Ready for Exams ______ / 11점		25~29점 → Level 2 Test
Total ______ / 35점		30~35점 → Level 3 Test

1 다음 빈칸에 들어갈 말이 순서대로 짝지어진 것은? 2점

- The girl ______________ the brown hat is Janet.
- The man ______________ to the hospital seemed okay.

① wearing – taking
② wearing – taken
③ wears – takes
④ worn – taking
⑤ worn – taken

2 Which of the underlined words is incorrect? 2점

① She was disappointed by the decision.
② Have you heard the shocking news yet?
③ Something surprising happened last night.
④ I think that he has the most bored job.
⑤ The singer was surrounded by excited fans.

3 밑줄 친 부분의 쓰임이 [보기]와 같은 것을 모두 고르시오. 3점

보기 Who is the man talking to Dr. Connors?

① Why were they chasing you?
② Do you know the girl winking at me?
③ The man's hobby is baking bread.
④ A cute baby was in the sleeping car.
⑤ Where did you see the running man?

4 Look at the picture and describe the situation by using the given words. 4점

→The horse __________ to the tree looks very __________. (tie, tire)

VOCA decision 결정 | be surrounded by ~로 둘러싸이다 | chase 쫓다 | wink 윙크하다 | tie 묶다

Review Test

My score is / 70점
60점 이상 PASS!!

››› 정답 17쪽

U23_1B

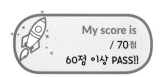

01 다음 중 분수를 잘못 읽은 것을 모두 고르면? 2점

① 1/3: a third
② 2/3: two-thirds
③ 4/5: four-fifth
④ 1/4: a quarter
⑤ 3/7: three-sevens

U23_1D

02 Who corrects the error properly? 2점

> The young are usually kind to the old. However, he sometimes aren't.

① 원동: are usually → usually are
② 윤동: the old → old person
③ 채연: However → Therefore
④ 제영: he → they
⑤ 서연: aren't → doesn't

U23_2A

03 다음 빈칸에 적절한 것은? 2점

> You can save electricity at home easily. ________, you can turn on the printer only when you need to print copies.

① In fact ② At last
③ For example ④ In the end
⑤ On the other hand

U23_1C+GP

04 다음 우리말을 올바르게 영작한 것은? 2점

> 그는 특별한 누군가를 찾고 있었다.

① He was looking someone special for.
② He was looking for special someone.
③ He was looking into someone special.
④ He was looking at special someone.
⑤ He was looking for someone special.

U24_1

05 빈칸에 들어갈 말이 순서대로 짝지어진 것은? 3점

함정

> A cute boy ________ on a ________ bus.

① was stood – crowded
② standing – crowded
③ standing – crowding
④ was standing – crowded
⑤ was standing – crowding

U24_4

06 다음 우리말을 영어로 바르게 바꾼 것은? 2점

> 그녀는 놀라고 실망한 것처럼 보였다.

① She looked surprise and disappointed.
② She looked surprised and disappointed.
③ She looked surprising and disappointing.
④ She looked surprised and disappointing.
⑤ She looked surprising and disappointed.

U24_3

07 밑줄 친 부분의 쓰임이 다른 하나는? 3점

한눈에 쏙

① He told everyone his shocking story.
② Please wait for me in the waiting room.
③ When do I put it in the boiling water?
④ It is the smallest living animal in this area.
⑤ We had to just watch the burning house.

U24_1+4

08 다음 중 어법상 어색한 것끼리 짝지어진 것은? 3점

★ 고난도

> ⓐ I often buy using things on the Internet.
> ⓑ I'll have the fried chicken with mashed potatoes.
> ⓒ The man weeping in the rain looks very frustrating.

① ⓐ ② ⓐ, ⓑ
③ ⓑ, ⓒ ④ ⓐ, ⓒ
⑤ ⓐ, ⓑ, ⓒ

U23_1A+1B
09 Write the words for the number. 각 3점

(1) 0.124: ______________________

(2) 3/4: ______________________

U23_1D+U24_1
10 Find ALL of the errors and correct them. 4점

The wounded was taking to a nearby hospital.

__________ → __________

U23_1C
11 Rearrange the words to make a sentence. 4점

한눈에 쏙

happened, something, has, her, to, wonderful

→ ______________________

U23_1B+GP
12 조건에 맞게 다음 우리말을 영작하시오. 7점

★ 고난도

엄마, 반 아이들의 90퍼센트가 이 스마트폰을 갖고 있어요.

· 조건 1 분수를 사용하되 영어로 쓸 것
· 조건 2 수 일치에 유의할 것
· 조건 3 어휘 – my classmates

→ Mom, ______________________
______________________.

U08_3+U24_1C
13 밑줄 친 ⓐ~ⓓ 중 어색한 것을 2개 찾아 고치시오. 4점

Mrs. Sims ⓐis worked at the same bank for 7 years. She does the ⓑsame things again and again. Now, she doesn't enjoy her job ⓒany longer. She would like to do ⓓdifferent something.

( ) → ______________________

( ) → ______________________

U24_1+4
14 괄호 안의 단어를 빈칸에 알맞은 형태로 쓰시오. 4점

The new game __________(release) last week is very __________(excite).

U23_2
15 다음 빈칸에 알맞은 표현을 [보기]에서 골라 쓰시오. 4점

보기		
	In addition	At last
	In fact	However

Let me see. Your computer has a terrific graphics card. __________, it only has 4 gigabytes of RAM. That makes your computer perform slowly.

U23_1C+U24_4
16 조건에 맞게 다음 우리말을 영작하시오. 6점

그가 뭔가 재미있는 것을 말했니?

· 조건 1 interest를 활용할 것
· 조건 2 say, anything

→ ______________________

U23_2
17 다음 중 어법상 어색한 문장을 찾아 바르게 고치시오. 4점

ⓐ Let me pick your friends up in my truck.
ⓑ Who turned on the TV and didn't turn off it?

( ) __________ → __________

U24_1+2
18 Look at the picture and complete the sentence according to the conditions. 7점

· Expressions wait in line, look like
· Condition 1 Change the forms of the verbs if necessary.
· Condition 2 The sentence should be 9 words in total.

→ The people ______________________
______________________ a family.

시험 직전에 챙겨 보는 비법 노트

››› 정답 18쪽

한눈에 쏙! 아래 노트를 보면서 빈칸을 채워 보세요.

1 형용사가 명사를 뒤에서 수식할 때

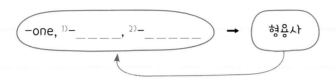

-one, 1)-_____, 2)-______ → 형용사

2 the+1)________ : ~한 사람들 (복수 취급)

3 분사

현재분사	능동, 1)________	현재분사	3)________, 상태 예) a swimming fish
과거분사	수동, 2)________	동명사	4)________, 목적 예) a swimming suit

4 감정 분사

현재분사(-ing)	주로 1)________, 가끔 사람	뜻: 2)~________
과거분사(-ed)	주로 3)________	뜻: 4)~________

헷갈리지 말자! 초록색으로 표시된 부분을 바르게 고쳐 쓰세요.

1 Do you need new something?

→

2 The cat finding under the car looked lonely.

→

3 It was a very touched moment.

→

CHAPTER 11

접속사

UNIT 25

명사절, 때의 부사절, 상관 접속사

CONCEPT 1 명사절을 이끄는 접속사

명사절은 주어와 동사를 갖춘 문장의 형태로, 문장 내에서 명사의 역할을 한다.

that	주어: ~하는 것은	That he is alive is certain. = It is certain that he is alive.
	목적어: ~하는 것을, ~라고	I think (that) he is a great hero.
	보어: ~하는 것이다	His strength is that he is honest.
if	~인지 (아닌지)	I don't know if it is wrong.
whether	~인지 (아닌지)	I wonder whether he is married (or not).

CONCEPT 2 때의 부사절을 이끄는 접속사

when	~할 때	When you go to England, don't forget to have fish and chips.
as	~할 때, ~하면서	She came in as I was cooking dinner.
before	~하기 전에	Before I had dinner, I washed my hands.
after	~한 후에	After she retired from running a shop, she became a nurse.
while	~하는 동안	While I was speaking, he stood still.
until	~할 때까지	He helped many other people until he died.
as soon as	~하자마자	As soon as I finish my homework, I'm going to meet my friend.
since	~한 이래로	I have known her since she was a child.

CONCEPT 3 상관 접속사

both A and B	A와 B 둘 다	Both my sister and I wear glasses.
either A or B	A와 B 둘 중의 하나	Either she or I have to go there.
neither A nor B	A도 B도 아닌	Jane likes neither math nor English.
not only A but (also) B	A뿐만 아니라 B도	Not only you but also he was wrong. (= He as well as you was wrong.)
not A but B	A가 아니라 B	It is not red but yellow.

GRAMMAR POINT

가주어-진주어

- 주어로 쓰인 that절이 긴 경우에는 문장의 맨 앞에 가주어 it을 쓰고 that절은 문장의 맨 뒤로 이동한다.

that의 생략

- 목적어 역할을 하는 명사절에서 접속사 that은 생략할 수 있다.

whether와 if의 차이

- whether 뒤에는 바로 or not을 쓸 수 있지만 if 뒤에는 쓸 수 없다.
- whether는 주절, 목적어절, 보어절로 모두 쓰이지만, if는 목적어절로만 쓰일 수 있다.

현재 시제가 미래를 나타냄

- 시간을 나타내는 부사절에서는 현재 시제가 미래를 나타낸다.

  She will wait there until he ~~will come~~. (×)

  → She will wait there until he comes. (○)

상관 접속사의 수 일치

- 「both A and B」는 항상 복수로 취급한다.
- 「either A or B」, 「neither A nor B」는 B에 수를 일치시킨다.
- 「not only A but (also) B」는 「B as well as A」로 바꾸어 쓸 수 있으며, B에 수를 일치시킨다.
- 「not A but B」는 B에 수를 일치시킨다.

VOCA alive 살아 있는 | hero 영웅 | strength 강점, 장점 | fish and chips 피시 앤 칩스(생선 튀김과 감자 튀김을 함께 먹는 영국 음식) | retire 은퇴하다 | still 가만히

Let's Check It Out

>>> 정답 18쪽

My score is
/ 19점

A 우리말과 같은 뜻이 되도록 [ ]에서 알맞은 것을 고르시오. 각 1점

1 나는 그녀가 친절하다고 생각한다.
→ I think [that / whether] she is kind.

2 나는 그가 집에 있는지 궁금했다.
→ I wondered [that / if] he was at home.

3 나는 그들이 올지 아닐지 알지 못한다.
→ I don't know [if / whether] or not they will come.

B 빈칸에 가장 알맞은 말을 [보기]에서 골라 한 번씩만 쓰시오. 각 1점

보기	until	after	before	while	when	since

1 ________ he was four years old, he got polio.
2 ________ I go to school, I have breakfast at home.
3 I was sleeping ________ my sister was reading.
4 I brush my teeth ________ I have lunch.
5 We will wait for you ________ you come.
6 He has been blind ________ he was two years old.

C 우리말과 같은 뜻이 되도록 빈칸에 알맞은 말을 쓰시오. 각 2점

1 엄마는 커피와 차 둘 다 좋아하신다.
→ My mom likes ________ coffee ________ tea.

2 그 소문은 진실이거나 거짓이거나 둘 중 하나이다.
→ The rumor is ________ true ________ false.

3 그는 술도 마시지 않고 담배도 피우지 않는다.
→ He ________ drinks ________ smokes.

4 나는 춤추는 것뿐만 아니라 노래도 잘한다.
→ I'm good at ________ ________ dancing ________ ________ singing.

5 저 사람은 David가 아니라 Colin이다.
→ That person is ________ David ________ Colin.

VOCA polio 소아마비 | blind 눈이 먼 | rumor 소문 | be good at ~을 잘하다

Ready for Exams

››› 정답 18쪽

My score is

Let's Check It Out ________ / 19점
Ready for Exams ________ / 16점
Total ________ / 35점

0~24점 → Level 1 Test
25~29점 → Level 2 Test
30~35점 → Level 3 Test

1 Which is proper for the blank? 2점

I hope ________ you like your new teacher.

① if ② whether ③ that
④ when ⑤ until

2 다음 중 밑줄 친 부분이 의미상 어색한 것은? 3점

① When we got to his house, his mom was in the garden.
② Whether he is rich is not important.
③ Before you answer the question, think twice.
④ The mouse ran away as soon as the cat appeared.
⑤ After it rains, take in the laundry.

3 다음 중 어법상 어색한 문장으로만 묶인 것은? 3점

ⓐ He lived in both Canada and America.
ⓑ Neither Jane nor I are tired.
ⓒ You can either go there or stay here.
ⓓ She as well as I don't eat kimchi.

① ⓐ, ⓑ ② ⓐ, ⓒ ③ ⓑ, ⓒ
④ ⓑ, ⓓ ⑤ ⓒ, ⓓ

4 Find the error and correct it. 4점

When I will go to Rome, I will eat pizza.

________ → ________

5 조건에 맞게 우리말을 영작하시오. 4점

아이들뿐만 아니라 그들의 엄마들도 방학을 손꼽아 기다린다.

· 조건 1 우리말 순서대로 단어를 쓸 것
· 조건 2 빈칸에 7단어로 쓸 것

→ ________________________ look forward to vacation.

VOCA think twice 두 번 생각하다 | run away 도망치다 | appear 나타나다 | laundry 빨래 | look forward to ~을 손꼽아 기다리다

UNIT

26 조건, 양보, 이유, 결과의 부사절

CONCEPT 1 조건의 부사절을 이끄는 접속사

if	만약 ~한다면	If you take the subway, you will get there on time.
unless (= if ~ not)	만약 ~하지 않는다면	I will not go unless you go with me. = I will not go if you don't go with me.

CONCEPT 2 양보의 부사절을 이끄는 접속사

though	~하지만, ~일지라도	Though they are poor, they seem happy together. = Although they are poor, they seem happy together. = Even though they are poor, they seem happy together.
although		
even though		

CONCEPT 3 이유의 부사절을 이끄는 접속사

because	~하기 때문에, ~해서	I had no time to text you because I was busy.
as		As it's raining, we'll have to stay inside.
since		Since she was tired, she didn't feel like going out.

CONCEPT 4 결과의 부사절을 이끄는 접속사

so ~ that...	너무 ~해서 …하다	The monkeys looked so funny that everybody laughed.

GRAMMAR POINT

조건절과 명사절에서 if절의 시제

- 조건절에서는 현재 시제가 미래를 대신한다.

  If it ~~will rain~~ tomorrow, we will not go on a picnic. (×)

  → If it rains tomorrow, we will not go on a picnic. (○)

- 명사절로 사용된 if절에서는 미래 시제 그대로 쓴다.

  I don't know if he will come to the party. (○)

because와 because of

- because 다음에는 절이 오고, because of 다음에는 구가 온다.

  I was late because there was a car accident.

  I was late because of a car accident.

since의 두 가지 뜻

- ~하기 때문에(이유)

  I was here a bit early since there were no traffic jams.

- ~한 이래로(시간)

  He has known me since I was a child.

so ~ that...과 so that ~

- so ~ that...: 너무 ~해서 …하다(결과)

  The baby was so cute that I kissed him on the forehead. (그 아기가 너무 귀여워서 나는 이마에 키스했다.)

- so that ~: ~하기 위해서(목적)

  Stir constantly so that it does not stick to the pan. (그것이 팬에 달라붙지 않도록 계속 저어 주세요.)

so와 because 비교

- so+결과

  I studied all weekend, so I passed my exam.

- because+이유

  Because I studied all weekend, I passed my exam.

VOCA on time 제시간에 | accident 사고 | text 문자를 보내다 | traffic jam 교통체증 | forehead 이마 | stir 젓다 | constantly 끊임없이, 계속해서 | stick 달라붙다

Let's Check It Out

››› 정답 19쪽

My score is / 18점

A 우리말과 같은 뜻이 되도록 빈칸에 알맞은 말을 쓰시오. 각 1점

1 서두르지 않으면 너는 늦을 것이다.

→ __________ you don't hurry, you'll be late.

2 Tom은 비록 슬펐지만 웃었다.

→ Tom smiled __________ he was sad.

3 배터리가 없기 때문에 내 휴대폰은 작동하지 않는다.

→ __________ the battery is dead, my cell phone doesn't work.

4 날씨가 더워서 그는 외투를 벗었다.

→ The weather was hot, __________ he took off his coat.

B [ ]에서 알맞은 것을 고르시오. 각 1점

1 [If / Unless] I don't feel well tomorrow, I'll cancel all of my plans.

2 [As / Even though] penguins are birds, they can't fly.

3 [If / Because] the restaurant is expensive, I don't eat there.

4 I studied so hard [since / that] I passed the exam.

C 두 문장을 한 문장으로 만들 때 빈칸에 알맞은 접속사를 [보기]에서 찾아 쓰시오. 각 2점

보기	so	though	that	as	unless

1 Jane was tired. She got some rest.

→ Jane was tired, __________ she got some rest.

2 He had a bad cold. He took some medicine.

→ __________ he had a bad cold, he took some medicine.

3 I was sick. I went to school.

→ __________ I was sick, I went to school.

4 If we cannot get tickets, we won't go to the concert.

→ __________ we can get tickets, we won't go to the concert.

5 Because the river is clean, I can swim there.

→ The river is so clean __________ I can swim there.

VOCA work 작동하다 | cancel 취소하다 | plan 계획 | get some rest 휴식을 취하다 | take medicine 약을 복용하다

Ready for Exams

››› 정답 19쪽

My score is

Let's Check It Out ______ / 18점
Ready for Exams ______ / 17점
Total ______ / 35점

0~24점 → Level 1 Test
25~29점 → Level 2 Test
30~35점 → Level 3 Test

1 Which is the common word for the blanks? 2점

• It is raining, ______________ I am closing the window in my room.
• He got up early ______________ that he could finish packing.

① although ② since ③ that
④ because ⑤ so

2 다음 중 밑줄 친 부분이 의미상 어색한 것을 고르시오. 2점

① Because Mary likes animals, she often goes to the zoo.
② Even if I am very thirsty, I want to drink water.
③ Unless you exercise, you won't stay healthy.
④ Since I have a stomachache, I have to go to the hospital.
⑤ My mom has gained some weight, so she is on a diet.

3 다음 문장에서 어법상 어색한 부분을 찾아 바르게 고치시오. 4점

If it will snow tomorrow, I will go skiing.

______________ → ______________

4 두 문장이 같은 뜻이 되도록 빈칸에 알맞은 말을 6단어로 쓰시오. 4점

If I am not busy this summer, I will go to Italy.

→ ______________________________, I will go to Italy.

5 Translate the sentence according to the conditions. 5점

안개가 너무 심해서 나는 아무것도 볼 수 없었다.

· Condition 1 어휘 – foggy, anything
· Condition 2 so ~ that...을 사용할 것
· Condition 3 줄임말을 쓰지 말 것

→ ______________________________

VOCA pack 짐을 싸다 | thirsty 목이 마른 | healthy 건강한 | have a stomachache 배가 아프다 | gain weight 체중이 늘다 | be on a diet 다이어트를 하다 | foggy 안개 낀

Review Test

My score is / 70점
60점 이상 PASS!!

››› 정답 19쪽

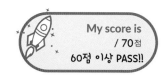

[01~02] 다음 빈칸에 알맞은 것을 고르시오. 각 2점

U25_1

01 I think ________ you made the right choice.

① when ② whether
③ because ④ so
⑤ that

U25_2

02 He sang for me ________ we were walking.

① if ② that
③ while ④ and
⑤ although

U25_1

03 밑줄 친 'that'의 쓰임이 나머지와 다른 하나는? 2점

한눈에 쏙

① I think that he is a good actor.
② It is true that the world is round.
③ I hope that you like it, too.
④ This is the book that I bought yesterday.
⑤ You will find that there's no place like home.

U25_1+U26_1

04 Which is the common word for the blanks? 2점

한눈에 쏙

• Buy me some milk ________ you go to the supermarket.
• I'm not sure ________ I will pass the test.

① when ② if
③ whether ④ although
⑤ as

U25_3+GP

05 Which sentence is incorrect? 3점

★ 고난도

① She can speak both Chinese and Spanish.
② Either you or I are to blame.
③ Not only he but also I like to play games.
④ She is not my niece but my sister.
⑤ I am neither tall nor handsome.

U26_1

06 빈칸에 알맞은 것은? 2점

If it doesn't rain, I will pick you up at 6.
= ________, I will pick you up at 6.

① Unless it rains
② Since it rains
③ Though it doesn't rain
④ As soon as it rains
⑤ That it doesn't rain

U26_2

07 Which is NOT appropriate for the blank? (2 answers) 2점

________ the flower is beautiful, it has many thorns.

① Though ② Although
③ Until ④ Even though
⑤ Unless

U26_GP

08 빈칸에 알맞은 것은? 2점

함정

내가 돈을 많이 번다면, 아름다운 새 집을 지을 것이다.
= If I ________ a lot of money, I will build a beautiful new house.

① will make ② made
③ make ④ makes
⑤ won't make

U25_2+U26_3

09 빈칸에 알맞은 말이 차례대로 연결된 것은? 2점

• ________ the band played my favorite song, I was so happy.
• People quarrel ________ they have opposite points of view.

① If – until ② After – before
③ Until – so ④ When – because
⑤ As – though

U25_GP
10 다음 문장에서 어법상 어색한 곳을 찾아 바르게 고쳐 문장을 다시 쓰시오. 5점

함정

After I will eat dinner, I'm going to do my homework in my room.

→ ______________________________

U25_1
11 우리말과 같은 뜻이 되도록 빈칸을 채우시오. 4점

나는 그가 살아 있는지 알지 못한다.

→ I don't know ________ he is alive.

[12~13] 주어진 문장과 같은 뜻이 되도록 빈칸에 알맞은 말을 쓰시오. 각 4점

U25_3
12

Not only Jane but also Mary plays the cello.

→ Mary ________ ________ ________ Jane plays the cello.

U26_1
13

I can't hear you if you don't turn down the radio.

→ I can't hear you ________ you turn down the radio.

U25_GP+U26_GP
14 Find TWO errors and correct them. 5점

★ 고난도

ⓐ He will get up before the sun will rise.
ⓑ If she will come, I will give a gift to her.

( ) ________ → ________
( ) ________ → ________

U26_2
15 다음 두 문장을 알맞은 접속사로 연결하여 쓰시오. 4점

It rained heavily. He climbed the mountain.

→ ______________________________

U26_4
16 조건에 맞게 우리말을 영작하시오. 6점

★ 고난도

그 차가 너무 뜨거워서 나는 그것을 마실 수가 없다.

- 조건 1 완전한 문장으로 쓸 것
- 조건 2 so, that, hot, drink를 이용할 것
- 조건 3 10단어로 쓸 것

→ ______________________________

U25_1
17 Rewrite the sentence correctly by changing ONE word. 5점

I think if people drink too much coffee.

→ ______________________________

U25_3
18 우리말과 일치하도록 필요한 어휘만 골라 배열하시오. 4점

그도 나도 기상 과학자가 아니다.
I, am, neither, not, nor, climate scientist, a, he, or, and

→ ______________________________

U25_2+U26_3
19 Write the common word for the blanks. 4점

한눈에 쏙

- I saw James ________ I was getting off the bus.
- ________ he was too busy, he couldn't hang out with his friends.

→ ________

U26_3
20 그림을 보고 [보기]에서 알맞은 접속사를 골라 사용해서 빈칸을 채우시오. 6점

보기 Since Though That Whether

· 어휘 – toothache

→ ______________________________, he can't eat candy or chocolate.

시험 직전에 챙겨 보는 비법 노트

》》》 정답 19쪽

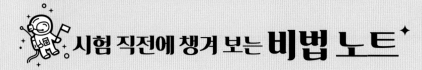

한눈에 쏙! 아래 노트를 보면서 빈칸을 채워 보세요.

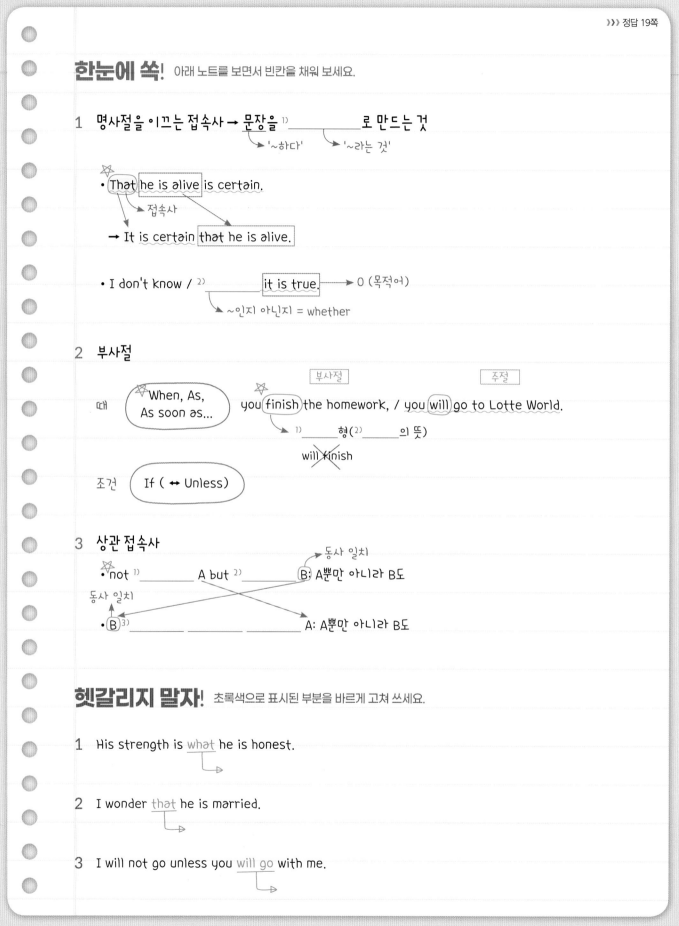

1 명사절을 이끄는 접속사 → 문장을 1) ________로 만드는 것
'~하다' → '~라는 것'

- That he is alive is certain.
  That: 접속사
  → It is certain that he is alive.

- I don't know / 2) ________ it is true. → O (목적어)
  ~인지 아닌지 = whether

2 부사절

부사절 / 주절

때: When, As, As soon as... — you finish the homework, / you will go to Lotte World.
finish → 1) ________형(2) ________의 뜻)
will finish

조건: If (↔ Unless)

3 상관 접속사

- not 1) ________ A but 2) ________ B: A뿐만 아니라 B도 (B: 동사 일치)
- B 3) ________ ________ ________ A: A뿐만 아니라 B도 (B: 동사 일치)

헷갈리지 말자! 초록색으로 표시된 부분을 바르게 고쳐 쓰세요.

1 His strength is what he is honest.
→

2 I wonder that he is married.
→

3 I will not go unless you will go with me.
→

CHAPTER 12

의문문

UNIT 27

선택의문문, 부가의문문

CONCEPT 1 선택의문문

선택의문문은 or를 사용하여 둘 중 하나의 선택을 묻는 의문문이다.

be동사	be동사+주어 ~, A or B?	Is she a dentist or a surgeon? – She's a surgeon.
조동사	조동사+주어+동사원형 ~, A or B?	Does she play the violin or the cello? – She plays the cello.
의문사	의문사+조동사+주어+동사원형 ~, A or B?	Which do you like better, *kimbap* or ramen? – I like *kimbap* better.
	의문사 ~ 비교급, A or B?	Which is more delicious, pizza or hamburgers? – Pizza is more delicious.

CONCEPT 2 부가의문문

「be동사/조동사+대명사 주어」의 형태로 문장 끝에 붙여 상대방에게 동의를 구하거나 사실을 확인할 때 쓰인다. 부가의문문을 만드는 방법은 다음과 같다.

긍정 → 부정(항상 줄임말로) 부정 → 긍정	Jack is energetic, isn't he? You don't have English class today, do you?
be동사/조동사 → 그대로	It's cold, isn't it? Jane can ski and snowboard, can't she?
일반동사 → do/does/did로	You have a bus card, don't you?
완료형(have/has+p.p.) → have/has	Joe has seen a panda, hasn't he?
Let's ~ → shall we?	Let's be optimistic, shall we?
명령문 → will you?	Go to bed right now, will you?

GRAMMAR POINT

선택의문문에 대한 대답

- 선택의문문에 대한 대답은 Yes나 No로 하지 않고 A나 B 중 하나로 답한다.

Are you going to Seoul or Busan?
- I am going to Seoul. (○)
- Yes, I am going to Seoul. (×)
- No, I am not going to Seoul. (×)

this, that, these, those

- 주절에 쓰인 this/that은 it으로, these/those는 they로 받는다.

This is your umbrella, isn't it?

These are your notebooks, aren't they?

there is 구문의 부가의문문

- there가 주어는 아니지만 부가의문문에서는 주어 역할을 한다.

There is something wrong, isn't there?

VOCA dentist 치과 의사 | surgeon 외과 의사 | which 어떤, 어느 (것) | energetic 활동적인 | optimistic 낙관적인

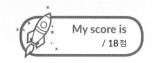

Let's Check It Out

››› 정답 20쪽

My score is / 18점

A 우리말과 같은 뜻이 되도록 [ ]에서 알맞은 것을 고르시오. 각 1점

1 이것은 돌고래인가요 아니면 상어인가요?
→ Is this a dolphin [or / but] a shark?

2 넌 우유와 주스 중 어느 것을 더 좋아하니?
→ Which do you like better, milk [or / and] juice?

3 백두산과 한라산 중 어느 산이 더 높니?
→ [Which / How] is higher, Mt. Baekdu or Mt. Halla?

B 빈칸에 알맞은 부가의문문을 쓰시오. 각 1점

1 You aren't a good soccer player, ____________?
2 He can keep a secret, ____________?
3 Mary painted her house yesterday, ____________?
4 Let's practice the piano together, ____________?
5 Don't play mobile games, ____________?
6 You have drawn cartoons for many years, ____________?

C 대화의 빈칸에 알맞은 말을 쓰시오. 각 1점

1 A: Should we have ice cream __________ pie for dessert?
B: I'd prefer pie.

2 A: __________ season do you like better, spring __________ autumn?
B: I like autumn better.

3 A: How would you like to pay, with cash __________ a credit card?
B: A credit card, please.

D 밑줄 친 부분을 어법에 맞게 고치시오. 각 1점

1 You are very strong, <u>are you</u>? → ______________
2 Jenny will go to the party tomorrow, <u>does she</u>? → ______________
3 He visited his grandparents last week, <u>do he</u>? → ______________
4 David hasn't seen a rainbow, <u>did he</u>? → ______________
5 Let's feed the dog, <u>can we</u>? → ______________
6 Stand in line, <u>shall we</u>? → ______________

VOCA keep a secret 비밀을 지키다 | mobile 핸드폰 | cartoon 만화 | cash 현금 | credit card 신용 카드 | feed 먹이를 주다 | stand in line 줄을 서다

Ready for Exams

››› 정답 20쪽

My score is

Let's Check It Out ________ / 18점 | 0~20점 → Level 1 Test
Ready for Exams ________ / 12점 | 21~25점 → Level 2 Test
Total ________ / 30점 | 26~30점 → Level 3 Test

1 Which is suitable for the blank? 2점

A: ________________ is more important, fame or money?
B: I think fame is more important.

① How ② Which ③ Whose
④ Where ⑤ When

2 다음 중 어법상 어색한 것끼리 짝지어진 것은? 2점

ⓐ Ms. Kim was born in France, isn't she?
ⓑ Jane can't solve the problem, can she?
ⓒ Give me that money, sweetie, will you?
ⓓ Rick hasn't finished his homework yet, did he?
ⓔ Let's hike in the woods, shall we?

① ⓐ ② ⓑ, ⓓ ③ ⓐ, ⓓ
④ ⓑ, ⓔ ⑤ ⓐ, ⓒ, ⓓ

3 다음 대화에서 밑줄 친 부분 중 어법상 어색한 것은? 2점

A: What ① would you like ② to eat, a tuna sandwich ③ or an egg sandwich?
B: ④ Yes, I'd like to eat ⑤ a tuna sandwich.

4 Write the proper tag question(부가의문문). 3점

Yuna went on a diet again, ________________?

5 다음 조건에 맞게 우리말을 영작하시오. 3점

우리 낚시 하러 가자, 그럴래?

· 조건 1 어휘 – go fishing
· 조건 2 부가의문문을 사용할 것

→ ____, ________________?

VOCA fame 명성, 명예 | woods 숲 | tuna 참치 | go on a diet 다이어트를 하다 | go fishing 낚시를 하러 가다

UNIT 28

간접의문문

CONCEPT 1

간접의문문이란?

주절 뒤에 목적어절로 의문문이 포함될 때 이를 간접의문문이라고 한다.

I wonder if he will come. 주절 + 간접의문문 (의문사 없는 경우) I don't know where he lives. 주절 + 간접의문문 (의문사 있는 경우)

CONCEPT 2

의문사가 없는 간접의문문

의문사가 없는 의문문이 다른 문장의 일부가 될 때 의문문 앞에 if나 whether를 쓴다. if와 whether는 '~인지 (아닌지)'의 의미이다.

if[whether]+주어+동사+(or not)

Is Sora at home?

→ Do you know if Sora is at home?

= Do you know whether Sora is at home (or not)?

Do you know Nick?

→ I wonder whether you know Nick (or not).

CONCEPT 3

의문사가 있는 간접의문문

의문사+주어+동사

Where is he?

→ Do you know where he is?

Who are they?

→ Can you tell me who they are?

When are they leaving?

→ I don't know when they are leaving.

How did she come here?

→ We will figure out how she came here.

GRAMMAR POINT

간접의문문의 if와 조건절의 if

- I don't know if she accepted his proposal.
  (간접의문문: ~인지 아닌지)
- You won't be able to buy a new phone if you don't save any money.
  (조건절 if: 만약 ~한다면)

의문사가 주어인 간접의문문

- 의문사가 주어로 쓰인 경우에는 직접의문문의 어순인 「주격 의문사+주어+동사」를 그대로 유지한다.
  Who broke the window?
  → I wonder who broke the window.

생각·추측을 나타내는 동사

- 간접의문문이 포함된 문장에서 주절의 동사가 think, guess, believe와 같이 생각이나 추측을 나타내는 동사일 때 간접의문문의 의문사는 문장의 맨 앞에 위치한다.
  Do you think what he did yesterday? (×)
  → What do you think he did yesterday? (○)

VOCA wonder 궁금해하다 | accept 받아들이다 | proposal 제안 | save 절약하다, 저축하다

Let's Check It Out

››› 정답 20쪽

My score is / 22점

A 다음 직접의문문을 간접의문문으로 바꾸시오. 각 2점

1 Is Emily at her office now?

→ I don't know ________ ________ ________ ________ ________ ________ now.

2 Do they live here?

→ Tell me ________ ________ ________ ________.

3 Does he have a car?

→ I don't remember ________ ________ ________ ________ ________.

4 Is she married?

→ Do you know ________ ________ ________ ________?

B 다음 직접의문문을 간접의문문으로 바꾸시오. 각 2점

1 How old is he?

→ Do you know ________ ________ ________ ________?

2 What time is it now?

→ Can you tell me ________ ________ ________ ________ ________?

3 Why did she go home early?

→ I wonder ________ ________ ________ ________ ________.

4 Who invented the computer?

→ I don't remember ________ ________ ________ ________.

5 Where did Ted go yesterday?

→ I don't know ________ ________ ________ ________.

C 어법상 어색한 부분을 바르게 고쳐 문장을 다시 쓰시오. 각 2점

1 Do you think what we should do?

→ ________________________________

2 Do you guess who can solve the problem?

→ ________________________________

VOCA office 사무실 | be married 결혼한 상태이다, 기혼이다 | invent 발명하다 | solve a problem 문제를 풀다

Ready for Exams

››› 정답 20쪽

My score is

Let's Check It Out ________ / 22점
Ready for Exams ________ / 13점
Total ________ / 35점

0~24점 → Level 1 Test
25~29점 → Level 2 Test
30~35점 → Level 3 Test

1 Which is suitable for the blank? (2 answers) 2점

Can you tell me ____________ they can go there?

① if ② or ③ and
④ what ⑤ whether

2 주어진 문장을 빈칸에 넣을 때 알맞은 것은? 2점

Whose dictionary is this?
→ I wonder ____________.

① if whose dictionary is this
② whether whose dictionary this is
③ whose dictionary this is
④ whose dictionary is this
⑤ this is whose dictionary

3 다음 중 어법상 옳은 문장끼리 묶인 것은? 2점

ⓐ She asked if he knew Matt.
ⓑ I don't remember where she works.
ⓒ Do you think who will go to the party?

① ⓐ ② ⓐ, ⓑ ③ ⓐ, ⓒ
④ ⓑ, ⓒ ⑤ ⓐ, ⓑ, ⓒ

4 Combine the two given sentences into one. 4점

I don't know. + What are they talking about?

→ ________________________________

5 우리말을 영어로 옮긴 문장에서 어법상 어색한 부분을 바르게 고쳐 문장을 다시 쓰시오. 3점

너는 그가 운동하는 것을 좋아하는지 아니?
= Do you know he likes to play sports?

→ ________________________________

VOCA dictionary 사전 | remember 기억하다

Review Test

My score is / 60점
51점 이상 PASS!!

>>> 정답 20쪽

U27_1

01 다음 빈칸에 알맞은 것은? 2점

Which do you prefer, e-books ________ paper books?

① but
② and
③ or
④ if
⑤ whether

U27_2

02 Which has a grammatical error? 2점

한눈에 쏙

① David wasn't angry, was he?
② They will get up at 6 o'clock, won't they?
③ Helen speaks Italian, does she?
④ Let's have lobster, shall we?
⑤ This is your bicycle, isn't it?

U27_2

03 빈칸에 들어갈 말이 순서대로 짝지어진 것은? 2점

• You haven't taken your medicine yet, ________?
• Don't waste your time, ________?

① have you – will you
② haven't you – will you
③ didn't you – shall you
④ did you – shall you
⑤ doesn't you – will you

U28_2+3

04 다음 중 어법상 어색한 문장으로 짝지어진 것은? 3점

★ 고난도

ⓐ I don't remember if I turned off the oven.
ⓑ Do you know whether can he drive?
ⓒ Can you tell me what you saw?
ⓓ Do you think what it means?

① ⓐ, ⓑ
② ⓐ, ⓒ
③ ⓑ, ⓒ
④ ⓐ, ⓑ, ⓓ
⑤ ⓑ, ⓓ

U27_2

05 다음 문장을 잘못 이해한 학생은? 3점

함정

Nick likes traveling by plane, doesn't he?

① 은희: doesn't he?는 부가의문문이다.
② 동수: 주절이 긍정문이므로 부정의 부가의문문이 쓰였다.
③ 소라: 동사 likes는 일반동사이므로 부가의문문에서 does가 쓰였다.
④ 나리: 주절의 주어 Nick은 남자이고 3인칭이므로 부가의문문에서 he로 받았다.
⑤ 진호: 동사 likes는 일반동사이므로 do를 써서 don't he?라고 해야 한다.

U28_2

06 밑줄 친 단어와 바꾸어 쓸 수 있는 것은? 2점

함정

I don't know if Jim will be here tomorrow.

① or
② whether
③ and
④ so
⑤ but

U28_2+3

07 다음 우리말을 영어로 바르게 옮긴 학생은? 2점

나는 세상에 얼마나 많은 식물들이 있는지 알고 싶다.

① 희정: I want to know how many plants there are in the world.
② 준호: I want to know if how many plants there are in the world.
③ 지수: I want to know whether there are how many plants in the world.
④ 슬기: I want to know there are how many plants in the world.
⑤ 하늘: I want to know that there are how many plants in the world.

U28_GP

08 'Where[where]'가 들어가기에 알맞은 곳은? 2점

(①) do you (②) think (③) she (④) is going (⑤)?

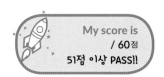

U27_1

09 다음 우리말과 같은 뜻이 되도록 주어진 단어들을 빈칸에 배열하시오. 4점

너는 학교에 버스를 타고 가니, 아니면 걸어서 가니? on, bus, by, or, foot

→ Do you go to school ______________?

U27_1

10 그림을 보고, 조건에 맞게 주어진 문장을 완성하시오. 5점

·조건 1 선택의문문을 만들 것 ·조건 2 어휘 – cookies, chocolate

→ __________ should I eat first, __________ __________ __________?

U27_2

11 주어진 단어를 활용하여 우리말을 바르게 영작하시오. 4점

우리 함께 그 음악회에 가자, 그렇게 할까? let's, concert, together

→ ______________________________, ______________?

U28_3

12 다음 의문문을 빈칸에 알맞게 바꾸어 쓰시오. 5점

How do you swim so well?

→ Can you tell me ______________________?

U27_2

13 ★고난도 다음 문장에서 어법상 어색한 부분을 모두 바르게 고쳐 문장 전체를 다시 쓰시오. 5점

Sarah and her family moved to Toronto, does she?

→ ______________________________
____

U28_2

14 ★고난도 다음 두 문장을 한 문장으로 합칠 때 빈칸에 알맞은 말을 쓰시오. (가능한 문장을 2개 쓰시오.) 각 3점

Do you know? + Is the store open today?

(1) Do you know ______________________?

(2) Do you know ______________________
______________?

U28_GP

15 함정 Find the error and rewrite the sentence correctly. 4점

Do you think what it is?

→ ______________________________

U27_2

16 Choose the <u>necessary</u> words and rearrange them to make a sentence with a tag question(부가의문문). 4점

close, the window, will, shall, we, you

→ ______________________, ______________?

U27_2

17 ★고난도 Rewrite the sentence according to the conditions. 5점

Amy hasn't been to China. ·Condition 1 부가의문문을 덧붙여 쓸 것 ·Condition 2 모두 7단어로 쓸 것

→ ______________________________

시험 직전에 챙겨 보는 비법 노트

››› 정답 21쪽

한눈에 쏙! 아래 노트를 보면서 빈칸을 채워 보세요.

1 직접의문문

(의문사) + 동사 + 주어 ~?

(When) / (Why)

Is she a violinist?
Was she a violinist?
→ be동사

Does she play the violin?
Did she play the violin?
Can't she play the violin?
→ 조동사

→ 부가의문문

She is ~, isn't she?
She was ~, 1) ________ she?
She plays ~, doesn't she?
She played ~, didn't she?
She can't play ~, 2) ________ ________?

2 간접의문문

I wonder + 접속사 + 주어 + 동사 ~?

if she is a violinist.
1) w______ she plays the violin.
의문사 she can't play the violin.
→ where, what, when, why...

헷갈리지 말자! 초록색으로 표시된 부분을 바르게 고쳐 쓰세요.

1 You don't have English class today, aren't you?
→

2 I wonder if do you know Nick.
→

3 Can you tell me who are they?
→

CHAPTER 13

가정법

UNIT 29

조건문과 가정법 과거

CONCEPT 1 가정법 과거

의미	현재 사실과 반대되는 내용을 가정
형태	If+주어+과거 동사 ~, 주어+조동사의 과거형+동사원형 ….
해석	만일 ~라면, …할 텐데.

If it were not cold, I would go out.

Brian would get a promotion if he worked harder.

What would your mom say if she were here now?

CONCEPT 2 가정법 과거의 문장 전환

If+주어+과거 동사 ~, 주어+조동사의 과거형+동사원형 ….
→ As[Because] 주어+현재 동사 ~, 주어+현재 동사 …. [긍정 ↔ 부정]
→ 주어+현재 동사 ~, so 주어+현재 동사 …. [긍정 ↔ 부정]

If he were not lazy, he could get a good job.

→ As[Because] he is lazy, he can't get a good job.

→ He is lazy, so he can't get a good job.

If I had more time, I would study math.

→ As[Because] I don't have more time, I won't study math.

→ I don't have more time, so I won't study math.

CONCEPT 3 직설법 조건문과 가정법 과거

조건문 현재	If+주어+현재 동사 ~, 주어+will+동사원형 ….	불확실한 현재와 미래를 가정
가정법 과거	If+주어+과거 동사 ~, 주어+조동사의 과거형 + 동사원형 ….	확실한 현재 사실의 반대를 가정

If she is at home, I will tell her about it. (집에 있는지 불확실함)

If she were at home, I would tell her about it. (집에 없음이 확실함)

If you love flowers, you will love the festival. (꽃을 좋아하는지 불확실함)

If you loved flowers, you would love the festival. (꽃을 좋아하지 않음이 확실함)

GRAMMAR POINT

가정법 과거에서 be동사

- 가정법 과거에서 be동사는 were가 원칙이나, 구어체에서는 was도 가능하다.

If the weather were[was] fine, I would go to the beach.

would와 could

- would는 '의도, 소망', could는 '능력'을 표현할 때 사용한다.

She would be angry with me if I weren't honest. (내가 솔직하지 않다면 그녀는 나에게 화를 낼 텐데.)

If you helped them, they could finish it soon. (네가 만약 그들을 도와주면 그들은 그것을 곧 끝낼 수 있을 텐데.)

명령문이 조건문의 주절인 경우

- 조건문의 주절에 명령문도 올 수 있다.

If you see him, say hi to him. (그를 보면 안부 전해 줘.)

조건문에서 can의 사용

- 조건문의 주절에는 can도 사용할 수 있다.

If you are good today, you can watch TV tonight. (오늘 말 잘 들으면 밤에 TV 볼 수 있어.)

VOCA promotion 승진 | be angry with ~에게 화가 나다 | lazy 게으른 | say hi to ~에게 안부 전하다 | be good 착하게 굴다

Let's Check It Out

››› 정답 21쪽

My score is / 22점

A [보기]에서 빈칸에 알맞은 것을 골라 쓰시오. 각 1점

보기	gets	regret	would	came	hurried

1 If I __________ home earlier, I would prepare dinner.

2 We could catch the bus if we __________.

3 If he __________ there before me, ask him to wait.

4 If you bought the computer, you would __________ it soon.

5 __________ you help me if you were here?

B [ ]에서 알맞은 것을 고르시오. 각 1점

1 If I [am / were] not sick, I could come to your party.

2 If Jason found some money, he [will / would] not keep it.

3 I [wouldn't / didn't] invite them if I were you.

4 I'd buy a new car if I [would have / had] enough money.

5 What [did / would] you do if you saw a theft?

C 두 문장의 의미가 같도록 빈칸을 채우시오. 각 2점

1 If I weren't so busy, I could take a long holiday.

→ As I __________ so busy, I __________ __________ a long holiday.

2 As he is sick, he can't go to the concert.

→ If he __________ sick, he __________ __________ to the concert.

3 As she doesn't know the truth, she doesn't tell me.

→ If she __________ the truth, she __________ __________ me.

4 He doesn't have any tools, so he can't fix the machine.

→ If he __________ some tools, he __________ __________ the machine.

D 우리말과 일치하도록 빈칸을 채우시오. 각 2점

1 지금 눈이 오면, 내가 너에게 눈사람을 만들어 줄 텐데.

→ If it __________ now, I __________ __________ you a snowman.

2 네가 런던을 방문한다면, London Eye에 가 봐.

→ If you __________ London, __________ to the London Eye.

VOCA prepare 준비하다 | regret 후회하다 | theft 절도 | truth 진실 | tool 도구 | snowman 눈사람 | London Eye 런던아이(영국 런던 템스 강변의 관람차)

Ready for Exams

››› 정답 21쪽

My score is

Let's Check It Out ______	/ 22점	0~24점 → Level 1 Test
Ready for Exams ______	/ 13점	25~29점 → Level 2 Test
Total ______	/ 35점	30~35점 → Level 3 Test

1 다음 문장을 바르게 분석한 학생은? 2점

Peter would get better results if he studies harder for his exams.

① 경민: 뒤쪽에 if가 있으니까 직설법 조건문이야.
② 민정: 가정법이니까 would get을 got으로 바꿔야 해.
③ 서영: Peter는 공부를 아예 안 한다는 뜻이야.
④ 소원: if절의 studies를 studied로 바꿔야 해.
⑤ 현정: 가정법 과거 문장이니까 would study로 써야 해.

2 How many sentences are <u>incorrect</u>? 3점

ⓐ I wouldn't do that if I were you.
ⓑ If I were the president, I'd reduce taxes.
ⓒ If you are in my position, you'd understand.
ⓓ He wouldn't agree if I asked him.
ⓔ If we lived in the country, we needed a second car.

① one ② two ③ three
④ four ⑤ five

3 Look at the picture and fill in the blanks. 4점

→ I wonder why Superman wears his underwear outside his clothes. If I ________ Superman, I ________ ________ it inside.

4 주어진 단어들을 바르게 배열하여 의문문을 만드시오. 4점

you, it, how, had, you, a million dollars, spend, would

→ If ______________________, ______________________?

VOCA result 결과 | reduce 줄이다 | tax 세금 | position 입장 | agree 동의하다 | underwear 속옷

UNIT 30

I wish 가정법 과거, as if 가정법 과거

CONCEPT 1 I wish 가정법과거

의미	현재나 미래의 실현될 수 없는 소망을 표현
형태	I wish (that) 주어+가정법 과거 동사 ~.
해석	~하면 좋을 텐데.

I wish I were a genius.

I wish I could see her again.

I wish I had a friend like me.

CONCEPT 2 I wish 가정법 과거의 문장 전환

I wish (that) 주어+가정법 과거 동사 ~.
→ I am sorry (that) 주어+현재 동사 ~. [긍정 ↔ 부정]

I wish I had a laptop computer.

→ I am sorry I don't have a laptop computer.

I wish every day were Sunday.

→ I am sorry that every day is not Sunday.

CONCEPT 3 as if 가정법 과거

의미	현재 사실과 반대인 상황을 가정
형태	as if+주어+가정법 과거 동사
해석	마치 ~인 것처럼

He looks as if he knew something about it.

My sister talks as if she knew everything.

CONCEPT 4 as if 가정법 과거의 문장 전환

as if+주어+가정법 과거 동사
→ In fact, 주어+현재 동사 ~. [긍정 ↔ 부정]

I feel as if I were dreaming.

→ In fact, I am not dreaming.

She smiles as if she were not sad.

→ In fact, she is sad.

GRAMMAR POINT

wish의 주어

- wish의 주어는 I가 아닐 수도 있다.

  She wishes she weren't busy today.

hope, wish, want

- I hope she comes.
  (실현 가능성이 큼)
- I wish she would come.
  (실현 가능성이 적음)
- I want her to come.
  (that절을 쓰지 못함)

as if와 as though

- as if는 as though로 바꾸어 쓸 수 있다.

  She acts as though she were my girlfriend.

VOCA genius 천재 | laptop computer 노트북 컴퓨터 | act 행동하다

Let's Check It Out

››› 정답 22쪽

My score is / 17점

A [ ]에서 알맞은 것을 고르시오. 각 1점

1 I wish I [am / were] a baby again.

2 I wish I [could / can] do something for him.

3 I [wish / hope] she were here now.

4 She talks as if she [were / is] my mother.

B 두 문장이 같은 뜻이 되도록 빈칸에 알맞은 말을 쓰시오. 각 1점

1 I wish he agreed with me.

→ I'm sorry he ___________ agree with me.

2 I wish Mrs. Kim were a careful driver.

→ I'm sorry Mrs. Kim ___________ ___________ a careful driver.

3 He talks as if he ruled the world.

→ In fact, he ___________ ___________ the world.

4 She talks as if she didn't know anything.

→ In fact, she ___________ something.

C 괄호 안에 주어진 단어를 빈칸에 알맞은 형태로 쓰시오. 각 1점

1 I wish my father ___________ a new car. (have)

2 She wishes she ___________ ___________ ___________ work tonight. (don't have to)

3 You talk as if you ___________ a lot about her. (know)

D 우리말과 같은 뜻이 되도록 빈칸에 알맞은 말을 쓰시오. 각 2점

1 내가 영어를 유창하게 말할 수 있으면 좋을 텐데.

→ I wish I ___________ ___________ English fluently.

2 그는 마치 정답을 아는 것처럼 말해.

→ He talks ___________ ___________ ___________ ___________ the answer.

3 때때로 할머니는 아이처럼 행동하신다.

→ Sometimes Grandma acts ___________ ___________ ___________ ___________ a child.

VOCA agree 동의하다 | careful 신중한, 주의 깊은 | rule 지배하다 | fluently 유창하게

Ready for Exams

››› 정답 22쪽

My score is

Let's Check It Out ______ / 17점		0~20점 → Level 1 Test
Ready for Exams ______ / 13점	→	21~25점 → Level 2 Test
Total ______ / 30점		26~30점 → Level 3 Test

1 Which is suitable for the blank? 2점

I wish I ______________ a motorcycle now.

① can ride ② could ride ③ am riding
④ have ridden ⑤ will ride

2 두 문장이 같은 의미가 되도록 할 때 빈칸에 알맞은 것은? 2점

You look as if you were hungry.
→ In fact, you ______________ hungry.

① are ② were ③ are not
④ were not ⑤ haven't been

3 밑줄 친 부분이 어법상 어색한 것을 모두 고르면? 3점

① I wish I were a famous singer.
② I wish he lives near my house.
③ I wish you can make it, too.
④ I wish I could stay a little longer.
⑤ He wished he won't fail this time.

4 Look at the picture and fill in the blanks. 3점

→ I wish ______________ ______________ Friday today.

5 다음 문장을 직설법으로 바꾸어 쓰시오. 3점

She looks as if she were angry.

→ In fact, ______________________________.

VOCA motorcycle 오토바이 | fail 실패하다, 낙제하다

CHAPTER 13
Review Test

My score is / 70점
60점 이상 PASS!!

››› 정답 22쪽

U29_1

01 Which is proper for the blank? 2점

> If my daughter ________ to be a pro-gamer, I would let her.

① want ② wants
③ wanted ④ will want
⑤ have wanted

U29_1

02 다음 대화의 빈칸에 알맞은 것으로 짝지어진 것은? 2점

> A: I need more money. What should I do?
> B: If I ________ you, I ________ a job.

① were – would get
② was – got
③ am – get
④ would be – get
⑤ would be – would get

U29_2

03 다음 주어진 문장과 의미가 같은 것은? 2점

> As Ellen is not here now, she can't help me.

① If Ellen were here now, she can help me.
② If Ellen were here now, she could help me.
③ If Ellen is not here now, she can't help me.
④ If Ellen were not here now, she can help me.
⑤ If Ellen were here now, she couldn't help me.

U29_1

04 어법상 어색한 부분을 찾아 바르게 고친 것은? 2점

> My mom works until 9 p.m. every weekday. If she didn't work late at night, my family can spend more time together.

① works → worked
② weekday → weekdays
③ late → lately
④ can → could
⑤ more → many

U29_2

05 다음 중 문장 전환이 어색한 것을 모두 고르면? 3점

★ 고난도

① As I am busy, I can't help you.
→ If I weren't busy, I could help you.
② If I were your friend, I wouldn't feel sad.
→ I feel sad because I'm not your friend.
③ She is talented, so she can be a singer.
→ If she weren't talented, she could be a singer.
④ If you tried harder, you could get better.
→ You don't try harder, so you can't get better.
⑤ If the hat were not expensive, I would buy it.
→ The hat was expensive, so I didn't buy it.

U30_1

06 실현 불가능한 다음 소망을 영작할 때 필요 없는 단어는? (답 2개) 2점

함정

> 모두가 나를 매력적이라고 생각하면 좋겠어.

① wish ② am
③ me ④ did
⑤ found

U30_4

07 다음 문장의 의미를 바르게 분석한 학생은? 2점

> He yells at me as if I were deaf.

① 율희: He doesn't like my voice.
② 서린: I'm pretending that I'm deaf.
③ 시영: In fact, I'm not deaf.
④ 아진: I feel sad that he yells at me.
⑤ 예찬: He thinks that his voice is attractive.

U30_1+3

08 Which sentence is incorrect? (Find ALL.) 3점

★ 고난도

① I wish the world has no crime.
② Carl wishes he didn't have a cold today.
③ She treats me as if I'm her younger brother.
④ Fred tries to look as if he were working hard.
⑤ If he played, we would win the game.

U29_2
09 두 문장이 같은 뜻이 되도록 빈칸을 채우시오. 5점

If you told me the truth, I could help you.

→ You ____________ ____________ me the truth, so I ____________ help you.

U29_1
10 다음 빈칸에 들어갈 말을 조건에 맞게 쓰시오. 6점

She is too angry to listen to my excuses.

· 조건 위 문장에 사용된 단어를 활용할 것

→ If ____________ ____________ ____________, she ____________ ____________ ____________ my excuses.

U29_1
11 주어진 단어 중 필요한 것만 골라 문장을 완성하시오. 5점
함정

rides, so, she, carefully, bike, rode, as, her, more, if, many

→ ________________________________, she would have fewer accidents.

U29_1
12 조건에 맞도록 우리말을 영작하시오. 7점

Kate가 뛰고 있다면, 경기는 더 흥미진진할 텐데.

· 조건 1 가정법 과거로 쓸 것
· 조건 2 The game으로 시작할 것
· 조건 3 어휘 – exciting, play

→ ________________________________
____

U30_3
13 다음 우리말을 조건과 힌트에 맞게 영작하시오. 7점
★ 고난도

그는 마치 술에 취한 것처럼 걷는다.

· 조건 1 현재 사실과 반대인 상황을 가정할 것
· 조건 2 3번째와 4번째 단어의 글자 수를 일치시킬 것
· 힌트 drunk는 서술적 용법으로, drunken은 한정적 용법으로만 사용된다.

→ ________________________________

U30_1
14 우리말과 일치하도록 빈칸을 채우시오. 5점

네가 지금 여기 나와 함께 있으면 좋을 텐데.

→ I ____________ you ____________ here with me now.

U29_3
15 빈칸에 들어갈 말이 나머지 넷과 다른 것을 찾아 그 단어를 쓰시오. 4점
한눈에 쏙

ⓐ I wish it ________ not snowing.
ⓑ If she ________ sick, she couldn't be here.
ⓒ What would he say if he ________ here?
ⓓ They treat me as if I ________ a kid.
ⓔ If he ________ free, he will join us.

( ) ________________

U30_1+GP
16 Rewrite the sentence by using "wish." 7점

Sharon doesn't have confidence in herself. She doesn't like it.

→ Sharon ________________________________
________________________________.

U30_3
17 그림을 보고 주어진 어구를 바르게 배열하시오. 5점

is sitting, a chair, it, the lady, were, on a tiger, as if

→ ________________________________
____

시험 직전에 챙겨 보는 비법 노트

››› 정답 22쪽

한눈에 쏙! 아래 노트를 보면서 빈칸을 채워 보세요.

1 가정법 과거 → 1) ________ 사실과 반대

- If+주어+2) ________ 동사 ~, 주어+조동사의 3) ________ 형+동사원형

→ As[Because]+주어+4) ________ 동사, 주어+조동사의 5) ________ 형+동사원형 (긍정 ↔ 부정)

2 직설법과 가정법

- 조건문 현재: 1) ________ 한 현재와 2) ________ 를 가정
- 가정법 과거: 3) ________ 한 4) ________ 사실의 반대를 가정

3 I wish 가정법 과거 → 1) ________ 나 2) ________ 의 실현 불가능한 3) ________ 을 표현

- I wish+주어+가정법 4) ________ 동사

→ I'm sorry+주어+5) ________ 동사 (긍정 ↔ 부정)

4 as if 가정법 과거 → 1) ________ 사실과 반대 상황을 가정

→ In fact, 주어+2) ________ 동사 (긍정 ↔ 부정)

헷갈리지 말자! 초록색으로 표시된 부분을 바르게 고쳐 쓰세요.

1 If the weather is better, we could ride on horses.

└→

2 I wish I have a friend like me.

└→

3 He looks as if he were upset. = In fact, he wasn't upset.

└→

불규칙 동사 변화표

불규칙 동사도 외우는 방법이 있다!

1 A – A – A 형태 동일

*표시는 필수 기본 동사들

원형	뜻	과거	과거분사
broadcast	방송하다	broadcast	broadcast
bet	돈을 걸다	bet	bet
burst	파열하다	burst	burst
cast	던지다	cast	cast
cost	비용이 들다	cost	cost
*cut	자르다	cut	cut
forecast	예고하다	forecast	forecast
*hit	치다	hit	hit
hurt	아프게 하다	hurt	hurt
let	~하게 하다	let	let
*put	놓다	put	put
quit	~을 그만두다	quit	quit
*read	읽다	read [red]	read [red]
rid	~을 제거하다	rid	rid
set	놓다	set	set
shed	흘리다	shed	shed
shut	닫다	shut	shut
spit	침을 뱉다	spit	spit
split	쪼개다	split	split
spread	펴다	spread	spread
thrust	찌르다	thrust	thrust
upset	뒤엎다	upset	upset

2 A – A – A' 과거분사만 살짝 바뀜

원형	뜻	과거	과거분사
beat	때리다, 이기다	beat	beaten

3 A – B – A 과거형에서 모음만 바뀜

원형	뜻	과거	과거분사
*come	오다	came	come
*become	되다	became	become
*run	달리다	ran	run

4 A – B – A' 과거형은 모음 변화, 과거분사형은 원형에 -n 붙임

원형	뜻	과거	과거분사
arise [əráiz]	(일이) 일어나다	arose [əróuz]	arisen [ərizn]
*be (am, is, are)	~이다	was, were	been
blow	불다	blew [bluː]	blown [bloun]
*do, does	하다	did	done
draw	당기다, 그리다	drew [druː]	drawn [drɔːn]
*drive	운전하다	drove [drouv]	driven [drivn]
*eat	먹다	ate	eaten
fall	떨어지다	fell	fallen
forbid	금지하다	forbade	forbidden
forgive	용서하다	forgave	forgiven
forsake	그만두다, 저버리다	forsook	forsaken
*give	주다	gave [geiv]	given [givn]
*go	가다	went [went]	gone [gɔːn]
*grow	자라다	grew [gruː]	grown [groun]
*know	알다	knew [njuː]	known [noun]
ride	(차, 말 등을) 타다	rode [roud]	ridden [ridn]
rise	일어서다	rose [rouz]	risen [rizn]
*see	보다	saw [sɔː]	seen [siːn]
shake	흔들다	shook [ʃuk]	shaken [ʃeikn]
show	보여주다, 보이다	showed	shown, showed
sow [sou]	(씨를) 뿌리다	sowed [soud]	sown [soun]
strive	노력하다	strove [stouv]	striven [strivn]
*take	잡다	took [tuk]	taken [teikn]
thrive	번영하다	throve [θrouv], thrived	thriven [θrivn], thrived
*throw	던지다	threw [θruː]	thrown [θroun]
withdraw	물러나다	withdrew [wiðdruː]	withdrawn [wiðdrɔ́ːn]
*write	쓰다	wrote [rout]	written [ritn]

5 A – B – B 원형에 -t 붙임

원형	뜻	과거	과거분사
bend	구부리다	bent	bent
*build	세우다	built	built
burn	태우다	burnt, burned	burnt, burned
deal	다루다	dealt [delt]	dealt
dwell	거주하다, 살다	dwelt, dwelled	dwelt, dwelled
lend	빌려주다	lent	lent
mean	의미하다	meant [ment]	meant
*send	보내다	sent	sent
smell	냄새 맡다, 냄새가 나다	smelt, smelled	smelt, smelled

spend	소비하다	spent	spent
spoil	망쳐놓다	spoilt, spoiled	spoilt, spoiled

6 A – B – B 원형의 자음 + ought/aught

원형	뜻	과거	과거분사
*bring	가져오다	brought [brɔːt]	brought
*buy	사다	bought [bɔːt]	bought
*catch	잡다	caught [kɔːt]	caught
*fight	싸우다	fought [fɔːt]	fought
seek	찾다	sought [sɔːt]	sought
*teach	가르치다	taught [tɔːt]	taught
*think	생각하다	thought [θɔːt]	thought

7 A – B – B 원형의 자음 + ound

원형	뜻	과거	과거분사
bind	묶다	bound [baund]	bound
*find	발견하다	found [faund]	found

8 A – B – B 원형의 모음이 하나로 줄고 + t

원형	뜻	과거	과거분사
creep	기다, 포복하다	crept [krept]	crept
*feel	느끼다	felt	felt
*keep	유지하다	kept	kept
kneel [niːl]	무릎 꿇다, 굴복하다	knelt [nelt]	knelt
*leave	떠나다	left	left
*lose [luːz]	잃다	lost [lɔːst]	lost
*sleep	자다	slept	slept
sweep	쓸다	swept [swept]	swept

9 A – B – B 원형의 모음이 하나로 줄어듦

원형	뜻	과거	과거분사
feed	먹이다	fed [fed]	fed
*meet	만나다	met [met]	met
shoot [ʃuːt]	쏘다	shot [ʃɑt]	shot

10 A – B – B y를 i로 바꾸고 -d를 붙임

원형	뜻	과거	과거분사
lay	두다	laid [leid]	laid
*pay	지불하다	paid [peid]	paid
*say	말하다	said [sed]	said

11 A – B – B 원형에서 모음만 바뀜

원형	뜻	과거	과거분사
behold	~를 보다	beheld	beheld
bleed	피를 흘리다	bled	bled
breed	기르다	bred	bred
cling	달라붙다	clung	clung
dig	파다	dug [dʌg]	dug
fling	내던지다	flung	flung
hang	걸다	hung	hung
*hold	잡다, 손에 들다	held	held
lead	이끌다	led	led
shine	빛나다	shone [ʃoun]	shone
*sit	앉다	sat [sæt]	sat
spin	(실을) 잣다	spun [spʌn]	spun
*stand	서다	stood [stud]	stood
stick	찌르다	stuck	stuck
sting	쏘다	stung	stung
strike	때리다	struck [strʌk]	struck
*win	이기다	won [wʌn]	won
wind [waind]	감다	wound [waund]	wound
withhold	보류하다	withheld	withheld

12 A – B – B 모음 변화, 끝에 -d 붙임

원형	뜻	과거	과거분사
flee	도망치다	fled [fled]	fled
*have, has	가지다	had	had
*hear [hiər]	듣다	heard [həːrd]	heard
*make	만들다	made	made
*sell	팔다	sold	sold
slide	미끄러지다	slid	slid
*tell	말하다	told	told

13 A – B – B' 모음 변화, 과거형 + n

원형	뜻	과거	과거분사
awake [əwéik]	깨다	awoke [əwóuk]	awoken [əwoukn]
*bear [bɛər]	낳다	bore [bɔər]	born [bɔːrn]
bite	물다	bit [bit]	bitten [bitn]
*break	깨뜨리다	broke [brouk]	broken [broukn]
*choose	고르다	chose [tʃouz]	chosen [tʃouzn]
*forget	잊다	forgot [fərgát]	forgotten [fərgátn]
freeze	얼음이 얼다	froze [frouz]	frozen [frouzn]
*get	얻다	got [gɑt]	gotten [gɑtn]
*hide	감추다	hid [hid]	hidden [hidn]
*speak	말하다	spoke [spouk]	spoken [spoukn]
steal	훔치다	stole [stoul]	stolen [stouln]
swear	맹세하다	swore [swɔər]	sworn [swɔːrn]
tear [tɛər]	찢다	tore [tɔər]	torn [tɔːrn]
tread [tred]	걷다, 짓밟다	trod [trɑd]	trodden [trɑdn]
wake	깨다	woke	woken
*wear	입다	wore [wɔər]	worn[wɔːrn]

14 A – B – C

원형	뜻	과거	과거분사
*begin	시작하다	began [bigǽn]	begun [bigʌ́n]
*drink	마시다	drank [dræŋk]	drunk [drʌŋk]
*fly	날다	flew [fluː]	flown [floun]
lie	가로눕다	lay [lei]	lain [lein]
cf. lie (규칙 변화)	거짓말하다	lied	lied
*ring	울리다	rang [ræŋ]	rung [rʌŋ]
shrink	줄어들다	shrank [ʃræŋk]	shrunk [ʃrʌŋk]
*sing	노래하다	sang [sæŋ]	sung [sʌŋ]
sink	가라앉다	sank [sæŋk]	sunk [sʌŋk]
spring	뛰다	sprang [spræŋ]	sprung [sprʌŋ]
*swim	수영하다	swam [swæm]	swum [swʌm]

15 조동사

원형	뜻	과거
*must	~해야 한다	(had to)
*can	~할 수 있다	could [cud]
*may	~해도 좋다	might [mait]
shall	~할 것이다	should [ʃud]
*will	~할 것이다	would [wud]

16 뜻에 따라 활용이 달라지는 불규칙 동사

원형	뜻	과거	과거분사
bear	참다	bore	borne
	낳다	bore	born
bid	명령하다	bade	bidden
	말하다	bid	bid
hang	걸다	hung	hung
	교수형에 처하다	hanged	hanged

17 혼동하기 쉬운 불규칙 동사와 규칙 동사

원형	뜻	과거	과거분사
bind	묶다	bound [baund]	bound
bound [baund]	되튀다	bounded	bounded
fall	떨어지다, 쓰러지다	fell	fallen
fell	쓰러뜨리다	felled	felled
find	발견하다	found [faund]	found
found [faund]	세우다, 창립하다	founded	founded
fly	날다	flew [flu:]	flown [floun]
flow	흐르다	flowed	flowed
lie	눕다	lay	lain
lay	눕히다, 낳다	laid	laid
see	보다	saw	seen
saw [sɔ:]	톱질하다	sawed [sɔ:d]	sawed, sawn [sɔ:n]
sew [sou]	바느질하다	sewed [soud]	sewed, sewn [soun]
sit	앉다	sat	sat
set	두다	set	set
wind	감다	wound [waund]	wound
wound [wu:nd]	상처를 입히다	wounded	wounded
welcome	환영하다	welcomed	welcomed
overcome	이겨내다, 극복하다	overcame	overcome

MEMO

신영주

2급 외국어 정교사 자격증, UCSD TESOL 취득(국제영어교사 교육자격증, University of California)
(전) EBSi 온라인 강사, 대치 시대인재, 이강학원 강사
(현) 프라우드 세븐 어학원 원장, 리딩타운 원장
저서: 체크체크, 올백(천재교육), 투탑 영어(디딤돌), Grammar 콕, VOCA콕(꿈을담는틀), 중학 영문법 클리어(동아) 등 다수의 교재 공저

이건희

쥬기스(http://jugis.co.kr) 대표
저서: 맨처음 수능 시리즈 – 맨처음 수능 영문법, 맨처음 수능 영어(기본, 실력, 독해, 완성)
내공 시리즈 – 내공 중학영문법, 내공 중학 영어구문, 내공 중학영어듣기 모의고사 20회
체크체크(천재교육), Grammar In(비상교육) 외 다수
instagram@gunee27

최신개정판

내신공략 중학영문법 2 개념이해책

지은이 신영주, 이건희
펴낸이 정규도
펴낸곳 (주)다락원

개정판 1쇄 발행 2021년 3월 15일
개정판 7쇄 발행 2024년 8월 26일

편집 김민주
디자인 구수정
조판 박선영
영문 감수 Michael A. Putlack
삽화 김진용

다락원 경기도 파주시 문발로 211
내용문의: (02)736-2031 내선 532
구입문의: (02)736-2031 내선 250~252
Fax: (02)732-2037
출판등록 1977년 9월 16일 제406-2008-000007호

ISBN 978-89-277-0891-9 54740
978-89-277-0888-9 54740(set)

http://www.darakwon.co.kr

다락원 홈페이지를 방문하시면 상세한 출판 정보와 함께 동영상 강좌, MP3 자료 등 다양한 어학 정보를 얻으실 수 있습니다.

내신공략

중학영문법

신영주 ✦ 이건희 지음

최신개정판

개념이해책 2

정답 및 해설

DARAKWON

내신공략

중학영문법

개념이해책 2

정답 및 해설

CHAPTER 01
문장의 형식

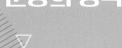

UNIT 01 1형식, 2형식, 3형식

Let's Check It Out p. 13

A 1 There goes a nice car. (goes: V, a nice car: S)
2 The turtle walks slowly. (The turtle: S, walks: V)
3 There were a lot of children at the park. (were: V, a lot of children: S)
4 It is getting dark. (It: S, is getting: V, dark: C)
5 Earth moves around the sun. (Earth: S, moves: V)

B 1 good 2 quickly
3 quietly 4 comes the bus
5 terrible 6 sour
7 easily 8 lovely

C 1 She put the phone on the table.
2 Mina explained the meanings of the words.
3 We enjoyed taking pictures.

D 1 어색한 곳 없음
2 making → to make
3 어색한 곳 없음
4 sad → sadly

Ready for Exams p. 14

1 ⑤ 2 ⑤
3 ③ 4 He laughed very rudely.
5 good → well

해설

1 smell은 감각동사로 뒤의 형용사와 함께 '~한 냄새가 나다'라는 의미가 된다. sweetly는 부사이므로 형용사인 sweet가 와야 한다.
2 틀린 문장은 ⓒ와 ⓔ이다. ⓒ는 There가 문장 앞에 있으므로 '동사+주어'의 순서로 goes my day가 알맞고, ⓔ는 감각동사 다음에 형용사가 와야 하므로 부사 well 대신 good이 알맞다.
3 a funny story가 명사이므로 sounds like가 와야 한다.
4 시제가 과거이므로 laughed를 쓰고, 1형식 문장이므로 부사 rudely를 써야 알맞다.
5 '물건을 잘 판다'는 의미이므로 형용사 good이 아니라 '잘'이라는 의미의 부사 well이 되어야 한다.

UNIT 02 4형식, 5형식

Let's Check It Out p. 16

A 1 You should keep yourself warm. (yourself: O, warm: OC)
2 I will get you something to eat. (you: IO, something to eat: DO)
3 Will you pass me the salt? (me: IO, the salt: DO)
4 We found the movie boring. (the movie: O, boring: OC)

B 1 lent me some money
2 send an invitation to you
3 didn't buy a laptop for me
4 make her sad
5 found the question hard

C 1 his tablet PC to me
2 ask something of you
3 a ring for his fiancée
4 get something for you
5 some pizza for us

Ready for Exams p. 17

1 ④ 2 ③
3 ② 4 prettily → pretty
5 I found him friendly.

해설

1 ask동사는 간접 목적어 앞에 전치사 of가 온다.
2 ⓐ make동사는 간접 목적어 앞에 전치사 for를 취한다. (to the children → for the children) ⓓ 「tell+간접 목적어+직접 목적어」이므로 to me에서 to를 빼야 한다. ⓔ 목적격 보어로 부사가 아닌 형용사 happy가 와야 한다.
3 buy동사는 간접 목적어 앞에 전치사 for가 오고, 나머지는 to가 온다.
4 her hair는 목적어이고 목적격 보어로는 형용사 pretty가 알맞다.
5 5형식 동사 find(~이 …라고 생각하다) 뒤에는 목적격이 오고, 그 뒤에 목적격 보어 자리에는 형용사가 온다.

UNIT 03 5형식

Let's Check It Out p. 19

A 1 I found the rumor false.
2 We named the girl Nancy.
3 She wanted me to become a judge.
4 They let me use their hair dryer.
5 He helped the old lady carry the luggage.

B 1 to come 2 help

3 to say
4 scream
5 to put up

C 1 to empty
2 (to) search
3 sent
4 to do
5 to make

D 1 to bring
2 realize
3 어색한 곳 없음
4 called
5 어색한 곳 없음

Ready for Exams

p. 20

1 ③
2 ④
3 to
4 throw away

해설

1 ⓑ 준사역동사 help의 목적격 보어는 climb이나 to climb이 알맞다. ⓕ 사역동사 let은 목적격 보어로 동사원형 help가 온다.

2 사역동사 make는 목적격 보어로 동사원형 go가 와야 한다.

3 • 5형식 동사(tell)+목적어+목적격 보어(to부정사)
• 3형식 동사(show)+직접 목적어+to+간접 목적어

4 사역동사 made의 목적격 보어로 동사원형 throw away가 오는 것이 알맞다.

Review Test

p. 21

01 ②
02 ②
03 ⑤
04 ③
05 ②
06 ④
07 ②
08 ②
09 ② ③
10 ①
11 ②
12 ③
13 ④
14 ②
15 ⑤
16 ④
17 Here are
18 heavy → heavily / differently → different
19 It looks angry.
20 (1) for (2) of
21 He had the computer fixed.
22 The librarian told me to return the book by Saturday.
23 He will make a unique bag for
24 cool
25 miss
26 He felt something come[coming] close to him.

해설

01 safely는 부사(안전하게)이고 나머지는 명사에 -ly가 붙은 형용사이다.

02 ⓐ ⓒ 감각동사 다음에 형용사 (safely → safe, sharply → sharp) ⓔ 1형식 동사 work(작동하다) 뒤에는 부사 well이 알맞다.

03 ⑤는 2형식 동사 become(~이 되다) 다음에 주격 보어로 a soldier가 쓰였고, 나머지는 목적어 역할을 하고 있다.

04 look은 감각동사로 형용사가 보어로 온다. well은 부사이므로 빈칸에 알맞지 않다.

05 3형식 문장에서 give동사는 간접 목적어 앞에 전치사 to를, cook동사는 전치사 for를 쓴다.

06 1형식 문장인 ④를 제외하고는 모두 3형식 문장이다.

07 teach동사 다음에 간접 목적어 앞에 전치사 to가 오고, expect동사 다음에 목적어로 to부정사가 온다.

08 지각동사 watch의 목적격 보어 자리에 동사원형 run이나 running이 알맞다. (ran → run 또는 running)

09 ② want 다음에는 to부정사가 목적어 역할을 한다. (eating → to eat) ③ finish 다음에 목적어로 동명사 playing이 알맞다. (to play → playing)

10 advise동사는 목적격 보어로 to부정사가 오므로 cry는 to cry가 되어야 알맞다.

11 look은 감각동사로 뒤의 형용사와 함께 '~하게 보이다'라는 의미가 된다. fantasy는 명사이므로 형용사인 fantastic이 와야 한다.

12 5형식 동사 find(~이 …라고 생각하다) 뒤에는 목적격이 오고, 그 뒤에 목적격 보어 자리에는 형용사가 온다.

13 I downloaded a very useful application on my smartphone. (나는 내 스마트폰에 매우 유용한 앱을 깔았다.) 동사를 먼저 찾고 그 앞에 올 수 있는 명사형 주어와 뒤에 오는 명사형 목적어를 찾아 문장을 의미에 맞게 연결한다. 3형식 문장에 부사 on my smartphone이 첨가된 문장의 형태이다.

14 ask동사 다음에 간접 목적어 앞에 전치사 of가 오고, promise는 to부정사를 목적어로 취한다.

15 ⑤ My dad had the box carried by me.로 목적격 보어로 수동의 의미인 carried가 필요하다. ① Did you give him a present? ② The doctor advised me to rest. ③ We will get her to help us. ④ He heard someone call his name.

16 ⓐ, ⓒ는 4형식 문장에서 직접 목적어 역할을, ⓑ, ⓓ, ⓔ는 5형식 문장에서 목적격 보어 역할을 하고 있다.

17 1형식 문장에 쓰인 「Here+be동사+주어」는 '여기에 ~이 있다'는 의미이다. 주어가 other examples로 복수형이므로 be동사는 are가 알맞다.

18 1형식 문장에서 부사 heavily(심하게)가 알맞다. 감각동사 look 다음에 형용사 different가 알맞다.

19 감각동사 look 다음에 형용사 angry가 알맞다.

20 cook동사는 간접 목적어 앞에 전치사 for가 오고, ask는 of가 온다.

21 컴퓨터가 수리되는 것이므로 목적어 computer 뒤에 목적격 보어 자리에는 과거분사 fixed가 오는 것이 알맞다.

22 tell동사의 목적어로 me, 목적격 보어로 to부정사가 와야 알맞다.

23 make동사는 간접 목적어가 문장 뒤로 갔을 때 전치사 for와 함께 쓴다.

24 주격 보어, 명사를 꾸며줄 때, 목적격 보어로 공통적으로 쓰일 수 있는 품사는 형용사이고, 내용상 '시원한, 멋진'의 뜻을 가진 cool이 알맞다.

25 사역동사 make는 목적격 보어로 동사원형이 온다.

26 지각동사 feel은 목적격 보어로 동사원형이나 현재분사 둘 다 올 수 있다.

시험 직전에 챙겨 보는 비법노트

p. 24

한눈에 쏙!

1 1) to+동사원형(to부정사) 2) -ing(동명사) 3) C(보어) 4) look 5) sound 6) smell 7) get 8) become 9) grow 10) turn

2 1) call 2) keep 3) make 4) find 5) want 6) ask 7) make 8) let 9) see 10) hear 11) help

헷갈리지 말자!

1 strange

2 scream 또는 screaming

해설

1 sound는 감각동사로 뒤의 형용사와 함께 '~하게 들린다'라는 의미가 된다. strangely는 부사이므로 형용사인 strange가 와야 한다.

2 지각동사 hear는 목적격 보어로 동사원형 또는 현재분사가 와야 알맞다.

CHAPTER 02 to부정사

UNIT 04 명사적, 형용사적, 부사적 용법

Let's Check It Out

p. 27

A 1 ⓒ 2 ⓕ 3 ⓑ 4 ⓐ 5 ⓓ

B 1 명사 2 명사 3 부사 4 형용사 5 부사

C 1 ⓑ 2 ⓓ 3 ⓒ 4 ⓔ 5 ⓐ

D 1 to live in

2 in order to meet my friend 또는 so as to meet my friend

Ready for Exams

p. 28

1 ④ 2 ④ 3 ③ 4 to write with

해설

1 ④는 보어로 쓰인 명사적 용법이고 나머지는 부사적 용법(목적)이다.

2 ④는 '그것'이란 의미의 대명사이고 나머지는 가주어이다.

3 ⓐ, ⓓ는 명사적 용법, ⓒ, ⓕ는 형용사적 용법, ⓑ, ⓔ는 부사적 용법이다.

4 '뭔가 가지고 쓸 것'이란 의미로 anything to write with로 쓰면 된다. 의문문에서는 something 대신 anything을 쓴다.

UNIT 05 의미상의 주어, 부정, 기타 용법

Let's Check It Out

p. 30

A 1 of 2 for 3 of 4 me

B 1 not to buy 2 never to be 3 not to touch 4 not to eat 5 for me not to like

C 1 too 2 enough 3 없음 4 couldn't

D 1 so nervous / he couldn't sing

2 so large / we can stay / it

Ready for Exams

p. 31

1 ① 2 ③ 3 ④ 4 too strong to drink

해설

1 일반 형용사에는 for, 성품 형용사에는 of를 쓴다.

2 Our captain decided not to change the plan.으로 영작할 수 있다.

3 ① very → too ② so → too ③ escaping → to escape ⑤ enough clean → clean enough

4 남자는 커피가 너무 진해서 마시기를 원하지 않으므로 too strong to drink를 이용해 문장을 완성할 수 있다.

Review Test

p. 32

01 ② 02 ③
03 ⑤ 04 ④
05 ③ 06 ①
07 ③ 08 ① ④ ⑤
09 ③
10 I should solve
11 to eat
12 I'm[I am] pleased to get more than 70.
13 You are too young to download this movie.
14 (1) in (2) to (3) with
15 His wife decided not to buy anything from the Home Shopping Channel.
16 I went to the outlet in order to buy a cheap T-shirt.
17 It is possible to complete the bridge this year.

해설

01 to부정사의 부정은 to 앞에 not을 쓴다.

02 ③은 부사적 용법(감정의 원인)이고 나머지는 형용사적 용법이다.

03 '어디에 ~해야 할지'는 'where+to부정사'로 쓴다.

04 ④는 인칭대명사이고 나머지는 가주어이다.

05 too ~ to... 자체에 부정의 의미가 있으므로 not을 빼야 한다. scary는 '~을 무섭게 하는'의 뜻이다.

06 I ran hard not to be late for the appointment.로 영작할 수 있으며, 부정은 일반동사가 아니라 to부정사에 해야 한다.

07 ③은 성품 형용사(clever)가 있으므로 of, 나머지는 for가 들어간다.

08 ① enough smart → smart enough ④ it 삭제 ⑤ buy → buy it

09 ⓐ ⓔ 명사적 용법 ⓑ ⓕ 형용사적 용법 ⓒ ⓓ 부사적 용법

10 「의문사+to부정사」는 「의문사+주어+should+동사원형」으로 바꾸어 쓸 수 있다.

11 A와 B 모두 배가 고프므로 '먹을 것'이라는 말을 쓰면 된다.

12 to부정사의 부사적 용법(감정의 원인)으로 표현한다.

13 「too+형용사(young)+to+동사원형(download)」으로 쓰면 된다.

14 (1) live in (a house) (2) dance to (music) (3) live with (a roommate)로 답을 찾으면 된다.

15 주어는 His wife, 동사는 decided이고, to부정사를 목적어로 취하며, '사지 않기로'는 not to buy로 쓴다.

16 [보기]처럼 to부정사의 부사적 용법 중 '목적'을 이용하여 나타내면 된다.

17 긴 주어의 to부정사는 뒤로 보내고 It(가주어)–to(진주어) 구문으로 전환할 수 있다.

시험 직전에 챙겨 보는 비법노트

p. 34

한눈에 쏙!

1 1) 보어 2) 목적어 3) 주어 4) should 5) 명사 6) 부사적 7) 목적 8) 원인 9) 결과

2 1) for 2) of

3 1) not 2) never

4 1) so 2) that 3) cannot[can't] 4) so 5) that 6) can

헷갈리지 말자!

1 to talk with[to]

2 use it

해설

1 talk이 자동사이므로 talk with[to]로 써야 한다.

2 that절로 전환할 때 to부정사의 목적어를 대명사로 써야 한다.

CHAPTER 03 동명사

UNIT 06 동명사의 쓰임, 동명사와 to부정사

Let's Check It Out

p. 37

A 1 ⓐ 2 ⓓ 3 ⓒ 4 ⓑ 5 ⓒ

B 1 Making 또는 To make 2 protecting 3 playing

C 1 어색한 곳 없음 2 bothering 3 giving 4 어색한 곳 없음 5 to go

D 1 to keep 2 to turn 3 learning

Ready for Exams

p. 38

1 ④ 2 ④

3 ⓐ to cook → cooking

4 remember seeing

해설

1 [보기]와 ④는 동명사의 주어 역할이다. ①, ②, ③은 동사의 목적어, ⑤는 보어이다.

2 ⓒ to jump → jumping ⓓ to have → having

3 finish는 동명사를 목적어로 취한다.

4 남자를 역에서 보았던 기억이 나는 것이므로 remember+-ing로 쓴다.

UNIT 07 동명사와 현재분사, 관용적 표현

Let's Check It Out

p. 40

A 1 waiting 2 crying 3 running 4 shopping 5 smiling

B 1 동명사 2 현재분사 3 현재분사 4 동명사 5 동명사

C 1 D 2 S 3 S 4 D 5 S

D 1 skating 2 어색한 곳 없음
3 buying 4 following
5 renting

Ready for Exams

p. 41

1 ⑤ 2 ③
3 ②
4 (a)는 동명사이고 → (a)는 현재분사이고

해설

1 ⓐ와 ⓓ는 명사를 수식하는 현재분사이고 나머지는 동명사이다.
2 ③은 현재분사이고 나머지는 동명사이다.
3 feel like 다음에는 -ing를 쓴다.
4 (a)는 진행형으로 쓰인 현재분사이고 (b)는 용도를 나타내는 동명사이다.

Review Test

p. 42

01 ④ ⑤ 02 ①
03 ⑤ 04 ③
05 ④ 06 ②
07 ③ 08 ⑤
09 ① ⑤ 10 taking
11 ⓐ Watch → Watching[To watch]
12 to dance → dancing
13 Eating / is
14 [a] w [e] [s] o [m] e
15 keep[kept] entering / wrong
16 Edward denied eating the chicken.
17 We had a hard time cleaning the house.
18 (가) ⓐ (나) ⓒ

해설

01 주어가 될 수 있는 것은 동명사나 to부정사이다.
02 want는 to부정사를, enjoy는 동명사를 목적어로 취한다.
03 try to ~는 '~하려고 노력하다'이고 try+-ing는 '시험 삼아 ~해보다'이다.
04 전치사 뒤에는 명사나 동명사가 온다.
05 ④는 현재분사, 나머지는 동명사이다.
06 would like는 to부정사를 목적어로 취한다.
07 remember+-ing는 '~했던 것을 기억하다'이다.
08 I did not have difficulty[a hard time] mastering Wing Chun.으로 영작할 수 있다.
09 ① dislike는 동명사만 목적어로 취한다. (to chat → chatting) ⑤ need는 to부정사를 목적어로 취한다. (going → to go)
10 • take care of: ~을 돌보다
• take a picture of: ~ 의 사진을 찍다
둘 다 빈칸이 전치사 뒤에 왔으므로 동명사 형태로 써야 한다.
11 주어 자리이므로 동명사나 to부정사로 써야 한다.
12 '~하는 것을 멈추다'는 stop+-ing이다.
13 '많은 야채를 먹는 것은 당신의 건강에 좋다'라고 한 문장으로 말할 수 있으므로 동명사를 주어로 쓰고 이때 동사는 단수 동사를 쓴다.
14 동명사(watching)를 목적어로 취하는 동사(ⓐ, ⓑ, ⓓ, ⓕ)를 찾아서 알맞은 단어가 되도록 넣으면 된다.
15 할머니가 계속 잘못된 비밀번호를 입력해서 오류가 났으므로 keep+-ing '계속 ~하다'의 표현을 쓰면 된다.
16 deny(부인하다)는 동명사를 목적어로 취한다.
17 주어를 쓰고 have a hard time+-ing '~하는 데 어려움을 겪다'로 완성하면 된다.
18 remember+-ing는 '~한 것을 기억하다'이고 try to ~는 '~하려고 애쓰다'이다.

시험 직전에 챙겨 보는 비법노트

p. 44

한눈에 쏙!

1 1) 보어 2) 목적어 3) 목적어
2 1) enjoy 2) mind 3) dislike 4) quit
5) avoid 6) finish 7) want[wish] 8) plan
9) hope 10) promise 11) expect
12) decide 13) like 14) begin 15) start
16) continue 17) love 18) hate 19) try
20) remember 21) stop 22) forget
3 1) 목적 2) 동작 3) 진행형

헷갈리지 말자!

1 was
2 to close
3 ⓐ의 watching은 현재분사, ⓑ의 watching은 동명사이다.

해설

1 동명사 주어는 단수 취급한다.
2 '~할 것을 잊다'라는 의미로 to부정사가 와야 한다.
3 ⓐ는 진행형으로 쓰인 현재분사이고, ⓑ는 보어로 쓰인 동명사이다.

CHAPTER 04
현재완료

UNIT 08 현재완료의 의미와 용법

Let's Check It Out

p. 47

A 1 caught 2 have
3 hasn't 4 Have
5 for

B 1 has just made a mistake
2 have already eaten lunch

3 has lost for a week
4 has not thrown the ball yet
5 Have you fixed

C 1 have lost 2 have seen
3 have / finished drawing
4 has lived here for

Ready for Exams
p. 48

1 ③ 2 ④
3 ④ 4 has fallen down

해설

1 과거(last Friday)부터 현재까지 영향을 미치므로 현재완료형을 써야 하며, 주어가 3인칭 단수이므로 has+p.p. 형태를 선택해야 한다.
2 Have ~로 물으면 have를 사용하여 답한다. B의 마지막 말로 보아 긍정으로 답해야 한다.
3 ⓐ 결과 또는 완료 ⓑ ⓓ 완료 ⓒ ⓕ 경험 ⓔ 계속
4 주어가 3인칭 단수이므로 has+p.p.로 쓰며, fall동사는 fall-fell-fallen으로 변화한다.

UNIT 09 주의해야 할 현재완료

Let's Check It Out
p. 50

A 1 visited 2 has stayed
3 in 4 How long
5 did he go

B 1 been 2 gone
3 gone 4 been / was

C 1 moved 2 in
3 have been 4 went
5 did you meet

D 1 haven't had[eaten] / since
2 bought / in
3 have had / since

Ready for Exams
p. 51

1 ② 2 ③
3 has gone to
4 When did she return home?

해설

1 • 내용상 과거이므로 과거형이 알맞다.
• Have ~로 시작하면서 경험을 묻고 있으므로 been이 알맞다.
2 ⓐ에서 과거 시점(last night)이 있으므로 과거 시제(lost)로 써야 한다.
3 Sarah가 푸켓에 가고 없으므로 has gone to를 쓴다.
4 특정한 과거 시점을 묻는 when은 현재완료와 어울리지 않는다. 과거 시제로 써야 한다.

Review Test
p. 52

01 ④ 02 ②
03 ③ ⑤ 04 ②
05 ⑤ 06 ⑤
07 ③ 08 ②
09 They have never had a merry Christmas.
10 Have you heard
11 have been
12 just now / yet / already
13 I have never seen such a tiny puppy before.
14 has played golf since (has been playing golf since도 가능)
15 Carmen has been on a diet for two days.
16 ⓐ has visited → visited
17 has worn / for

해설

01 현재완료의 부정은 have와 p.p.사이에 not 또는 never를 쓴다.
02 과거의 상태가 현재까지 이어지므로 현재완료를 쓴다. (lose-lost-lost)
03 ③ have gone to는 일반적으로 I를 주어로 쓰지 않는다. ⑤ become의 과거분사는 become이다.
04 just와 already가 현재완료에 쓰일 때는 have와 p.p. 사이에 쓰이며 yet은 문장 끝에 쓰인다. just now는 과거 시제에 사용된다.
05 just, already, yet이 있으면 완료 용법이다. ⑤는 경험 용법이다.
06 과거의 동작이 현재까지 이어지므로 현재완료를 쓰며, for 다음에는 시간이 온다. (teach-taught-taught)
07 [보기]와 ③은 계속 용법이고 ①, ④는 경험 용법, ②는 결과 또는 완료 용법, ⑤는 완료 용법이다.
08 ⓐ has he gone → did he go ⓑ hasn't come → didn't come
09 현재완료의 부정은 have와 p.p. 사이에 not이나 never를 쓴다.
10 B가 No, I haven't.로 답했으므로 현재완료로 물어야 하고, B의 말에서 heard라는 단어를 이용하여 질문을 완성하면 된다.
11 아직 병원에 있으므로 현재완료로 써야 한다.
12 첫 번째는 과거 시제이므로 just now가 알맞다. 두 번째와 세 번째는 현재완료에서 의문문에는 yet을 쓰고, 긍정문에는 already가 주로 쓰인다.
13 현재완료 중 경험 용법에 해당하므로 have+p.p. 구문을 이용한다.
14 과거의 동작이 현재까지 영향을 미치므로 현재완료로 쓰고, 과거 시점 앞에는 since를 쓴다.
15 과거의 일이 현재까지 이어지므로 현재완료를 쓰며, 'for+기간'으로 쓴다.
16 과거 시점(five years ago)이 있으면 과거 시제를 쓴다.
17 모자를 너무 오랫동안 쓰고 있어서 머리가 아프다는 내용으

로 계속 용법의 현재완료로 써야 하며, 기간 앞에는 for를 쓴다. (wear – wore – worn)

시험 직전에 챙겨 보는 비법노트

p. 54

한눈에 쏙!

1 1) 과거 2) 현재 3) 완료 4) 경험 5) 계속 6) 결과
2 1) not 2) never
3 1) Have 2) Has
4 1) 부사구 2) been 3) gone

헷갈리지 말자!

1 for
2 Did they leave
3 have been to

해설

1 'for+기간', 'since+시점'으로 쓰인다.
2 yesterday라는 과거 부사구가 있으므로 과거형으로 써야 한다.
3 have gone to는 결과 용법으로 1인칭을 주어로 거의 쓰지 않는다.

CHAPTER 05 조동사

UNIT 10 can, may, will

Let's Check It Out

p. 57

A
1 can
2 may
3 May
4 will

B
1 was able to
2 Are you going to
3 won't

C
1 can't be sick
2 will be back
3 He's not going to follow
4 will be able to see

Ready for Exams

p. 58

1 ④
2 ④
3 ①
4 Are / able to
5 What are you going to do

해설

1 과학 노트를 빌려달라는 말에 벌써 민수한테 빌려줬다는 것으로 보아 부정의 답이 알맞다.
2 ⓐ 같은 의미의 조동사 could와 be able to를 나란히 쓸 수 없다. ⓒ said동사와 시제가 일치하는 과거 조동사 would가 알맞다. ⓓ 조동사 might 다음에 동사원형 be가 필요하다.
3 요청과 의지를 나타내는 will이 알맞다.
4 능력을 묻는 Are you able to ~?가 알맞다.
5 대답에서 be going to로 대답했으므로 미래의 계획을 묻는 의문사 what이 포함된 be going to 의문문이 알맞다.

UNIT 11 must, have to, should, ought to

Let's Check It Out

p. 60

A
1 have
2 ought
3 lying
4 have to
5 must not

B
1 don't have[need] to
2 had to
3 Do / have to
4 must be
5 ought not to

C
1 have to
2 doesn't need to
3 ought to
4 ought not to

Ready for Exams

p. 61

1 ④
2 ⑤
3 Do / have to
4 You ought not to stay up too late.

해설

1 문서를 가져가야 하는지 묻는 A의 질문에 B가 이메일로 보낼 수 있다고 했으므로, 빈칸에는 불필요를 나타내는 응답이 들어가는 것이 알맞다.
2 부정의 응답은 I don't think we should.로 나타낸다. I don't think we shouldn't.의 경우 이중 부정이므로 알맞지 않다.
3 의무를 나타내는 must는 have to로 바꾸어 쓸 수 있다. 의문문은 「Do/Does+주어+have to ~?」로 쓴다.
4 ought to의 부정은 ought not to이고, 다음에 동사원형 stay를 쓴다.

UNIT 12 would like to, had better, used to

Let's Check It Out

p. 63

A
1 had better go
2 used to be
3 would like to
4 would not like to
5 had better not

B
1 I would not like to hear your thoughts.

2 You'd better not wear a vest under your coat.
3 Ryan did not use to lock himself in his bedroom. 또는 Ryan used not to lock himself in his bedroom.

C 1 Did you use to take
2 would like to lie
3 had better start
4 had better not read
5 used to play

Ready for Exams p. 64

1 ③	2 ③
3 would like to	4 used to like

해설

1 didn't use 다음에 to가 와야 used to의 부정문(~하지 않곤 했다)이다. used not to를 써도 된다.
2 have to의 과거형 had to(~해야 했다), 충고의 had better(~하는 게 좋겠다)가 알맞다.
3 want to = would like to: ~하고 싶다
4 used to+동사원형: '~하곤 했다' (과거에 했었는데 지금은 더 이상 하지 않는 것을 의미)

Review Test p. 65

01 ③	02 ①
03 ③	04 ④
05 ②	06 ①
07 ②	08 ④
09 ①	10 ⑤
11 ②	12 ① ⑤
13 ①	14 ④

15 He cannot[can't] be a spy.
16 wasn't able to lift
17 The rumor may not be true.
18 ⓑ ought to not → ought not to
19 He doesn't have[need] to pack his lunch.
20 should
21 Would[would]
22 You had better not waste your time.
23 used to be
24 must not

해설

01 [보기]와 나머지는 '~해도 좋다'는 허락을 나타내고, ③은 '~일지도 모른다'는 추측을 나타낸다.
02 첫 번째 문장은 능력을 나타내는 긍정의 can 또는 추측을 나타내는 may가 알맞다. 두 번째 문장은 접속사 but으로 보아 부정적인 의미의 can't가 알맞다.
03 '빌리다'라는 뜻을 가진 동사 borrow를 써서 요청을 의미하는 Can I borrow ~? 는 '빌려주다'라는 뜻을 가진 동사 lend를 써서 Will you lend ~?로 바꿀 수 있다. '나에게' 빌려주는 것이므로 to me를 쓴다.
04 '~하지 않겠다'라는 주어의 의지를 나타내야 하므로 will의 부정형인 won't가 들어가는 것이 알맞다.
05 Philip에게 파란 모자를 사주는 것이 어떠냐는 권유에 부정적인 대답을 했으므로, 이 파란 모자를 무척 좋아할 것이라는 대답은 어울리지 않는다.
06 ⓐ had better 다음에 동사원형이 와야 하므로 to apologize는 apologize가 되어야 알맞다.
07 시간이 충분하니 뛸 필요가 없다는 의미이므로 'don't have to+동사원형(~할 필요 없다)'이 알맞다.
08 would like to+동사원형: '~하고 싶다'
09 어지럽다는 말에 물을 마시는 것이 좋겠고 그러면 나아질 것이라고 하는 것이 자연스럽다. (had better+동사원형: '~하는 게 좋겠다')
10 ⑤ must(~해야 한다)의 부정은 'must not+동사원형'이다.
11 (A) 엄마가 Peter에게 15살 밖에 안 되었으니 운전하면 안 된다는 금지의 표현 must not(~하면 안 된다)을 쓰는 것이 알맞다. (B) Joseph에게는 아빠가 대신 운전해 줄 수 있으니 운전할 필요 없다고 하는 것이 자연스러우므로 don't have to(~할 필요 없다)가 알맞다.
12 ① has to(~해야 한다)이므로 has to return이 알맞다. ⑤ 'had better not+동사원형(~하지 않는 것이 좋겠다)'이므로 to stay는 동사원형 stay로 바뀌어야 알맞다.
13 ⓒ used to+동사원형(~하곤 했다) ⓓ 'used not to+동사원형(예전에 ~ 없었다)'이므로 동사원형 be가 필요하다. ⓔ ought not to+동사원형(~하면 안 된다)이므로 be가 필요 없고 drink가 와야 알맞다.
14 ⓓ, ⓔ는 강한 추측(~임에 틀림없다)을 나타내고, 나머지는 의무(~해야 한다)를 나타낸다.
15 must be(~임에 틀림없다)의 부정은 cannot[can't] be(~일 리가 없다)이다.
16 can't는 be not able to와 바꾸어 쓸 수 있고, 과거형 could는 be동사의 과거형으로 쓴다.
17 「주어(the rumor)+조동사(may)+not+동사원형(be true)」의 순서로 배열한다. (그 소문은 사실이 아닐지도 모른다.)
18 ought to의 부정은 ought not to(~하면 안 된다)이다.
19 '~할 필요 없다'는 don't have[need] to이고, 주어가 3인칭 단수이므로 don't는 doesn't로 써야 알맞다.
20 ought to를 한 단어로 바꾸면 should가 된다.
21 첫 번째는 요청의 would이고, 두 번째는 과거의 습관을 나타내는 would이다.
22 had better not+동사원형: ~하지 않는 게 좋겠다
23 과거에 있었는데 지금은 없는 상태를 나타낼 때는 'used to+동사원형'으로 나타낸다.
24 신발을 신고 집안에 들어가면 안 된다는 내용으로, 금지를 나타내는 must not(~하면 안 된다)이 알맞다.

시험 직전에 챙겨 보는 비법노트 p. 68

한눈에 쏙!

1 1) cannot[can't] be 2) must not
3) don't have to 4) ought not to
5) had better not

헷갈리지 말자!

1 to participate
2 cannot[can't]
3 be

해설

1 will(~할 것이다) = 'be going to+동사원형'으로 to participate 가 알맞다.
2 must not은 '~하면 안 된다'라는 뜻이고 cannot[can't] be 가 '~일리가 없다'의 뜻이다.
3 being은 동사원형 be로 써야 한다. (used to+동사원형: 예전에 ~이었다, ~하곤 했다)

CHAPTER 06
명사, 부정대명사

UNIT 13 명사의 종류, 수량 표현, 소유격

Let's Check It Out p. 71

A 1 boxes 2 mice
3 September 4 information
5 centimeter

B 1 few 2 much
3 a lot of 4 a few
5 little

C 1 bowl of rice 2 glasses of juice
3 piece of advice 4 bottles of beer
5 slices of pizza

D 1 Wilson's
2 sisters' 또는 sister's
3 the results of the test
4 yesterday's news
5 women's

Ready for Exams p. 72

1 ⑤ 2 ②
3 Yesterday's milk / Thomas's bag
4 threw away these pieces of pizza 또는 threw these pieces of pizza away

해설

1 time(-번)은 셀 수 있는 명사이고 wine은 셀 수 없는 명사이다.
2 meat는 셀 수 없는 명사이므로 복수형으로 쓸 수 없다.
3 생물의 소유격은 -'s로 쓰고, 무생물일지라도 시간의 소유격은 -'s로 쓴다.
4 주어는 who이고, 동사는 과거형으로 threw away이며, 목적어는 지시 형용사와 pieces를 이용해야 하므로 these pieces of pizza로 쓰면 된다.

UNIT 14 부정대명사

Let's Check It Out p. 74

A 1 Every 3 Both
3 Each 4 something
5 one

B 1 One / the other
2 one / another / the other
3 Some / others
4 the others

C 1 ones 2 has
3 person 4 other
5 loves

Ready for Exams p. 76

1 ④ 2 ③⑤
3 ③ 4 One / the other

해설

1 여러 명 중 한 명을 제외한 나머지이므로 the others로 써야 한다.
2 셋을 하나씩 나열하므로 one was scary, another was boring, and the other was fun[interesting]이라고 영작할 수 있다.
3 ⓑ children → child ⓒ one → ones ⓓ mornings → morning
4 둘 중 하나는 one, 나머지 하나는 the other로 쓴다.

Review Test p. 77

01 ① 02 ②
03 ④⑤ 04 ④
05 ⑤ 06 ⑤
07 ③ 08 ③
09 One / another / the other
10 ⓑ meal → meals (또는 each[every] meal)
11 (A) rare (B) Few (C) several
12 We have just finished a ten-hour practice.
13 The cover of this book looks attractive.
14 sides / each
15 The others didn't come
16 anybody / something
17 plants need little / grow / anywhere

해설

01 ② juices → juice ③ waters → water ④ sugars

→ sugar ⑤ foreigner → foreigners (또는 drink → drinks)

02 ⓒ glove → gloves ⓔ that → those (또는 slices → slice) ⑨ sugars → sugar

03 ④ thousands → thousand ⑤ months → month

04 무생물 주어는 B of A, 즉 'A의 B'로 표현한다.

05 Both는 복수 취급하고 보어도 복수로 써야 하며, 둘 중 하나는 one, 나머지 하나는 the other로 표현한다.

06 Every는 단수 취급하므로 have를 has로 써야 한다.

07 동사가 복수 동사이고 막연한 일부와 다른 일부를 나타내므로 ③이 적절하다.

08 ① that → those (또는 clovers→ clover) (1개) ② picture → pictures (1개) ③ plays → play, nights → night (2개) ④ want → wants (1개) ⑤ one → ones (1개)

09 셋을 나열할 때는 one, another, the other 순으로 쓴다.

10 breakfast, lunch, dinner[supper]는 셀 수 없지만, meal(식사)은 셀 수 있는 명사로 meals로 쓰거나 each[every] meal로 써야 한다.

11 (A) 4개국어에 유창한 것은 드물며(rare), (B) 이에 따라서 부정을 의미하는 few가 와야 하고, (C) 흐름상 몇몇(several)이 알맞다.

12 현재완료는 have just finished로 나타내고, '10시간짜리 연습'은 a ten-hour practice로 나타낸다.

13 무생물의 소유격은 B of A로 표현하며 'A의 B'로 해석한다.

14 both와 each가 명사를 직접 꾸밀 때는 뒤에 각각 복수와 단수가 온다.

15 5명 중 2명만 오고 나머지가 오지 않았으므로 the others를 사용한다.

16 의문문에서 anybody를 써야 하며, 권유할 때는 something을 쓴다.

17 식물들이므로 plants, 영영풀이는 '무엇인가를 가져야 하거나 매우 많이 원하다'로 need가, 셀 수 없는 명사(care)를 부정으로 수식하므로 little, '자라다'의 의미인 grow, 긍정문에서 '어디에서든지'의 의미인 anywhere를 쓰면 된다.

시험 직전에 챙겨 보는 비법노트 p. 78

한눈에 쏙!

1 1) piece 2) glasses 3) bowls
2 1) -'s 2) -s' 3) of
3 1) one 2) each 3) every 4) all 5) both
4 1) one 2) the other 3) one 4) another 5) others 6) the others

헷갈리지 말자!

1 two pieces of bread
2 was
3 The others

해설

1 물질명사(bread)는 셀 수 없고 단위명사(piece)로 세야 한다.
2 주어가 each이고 단수 취급하므로 was로 써야 한다.
3 나머지 일부를 가리키므로 the others로 써야 한다.

CHAPTER 07 수동태

UNIT 15 수동태의 개념과 시제

Let's Check It Out p. 81

A 1 P 2 A 3 P 4 A

B 1 was solved 2 are not used 3 be served 4 be washed

C 1 changed 2 어색한 곳 없음 3 is celebrated 4 was not drawn

D 1 were broken by him
2 was attacked by Genghis Khan
3 is used by most teenagers
4 will be invented (by people)

Ready for Exams p. 82

1 ⑤ 2 ④
3 bit / was bitten by
4 *The Old Man and the Sea* was written by Hemingway.

해설

1 주어가 동작을 받으므로 수동태(is always written)로 써야 한다.
2 ⓑ built → was built ⓒ he → him ⓓ was sent → sent
3 개가 우편집배원을 물었으므로 bite - bit - bitten을 활용하면 되며, just now는 과거 시제와 함께 쓰인다.
4 주어진 문장은 능동태이므로 수동태로 바꿔야 한다. *The Old Man and the Sea*는 책 제목으로 단수 취급한다.

UNIT 16 여러 가지 수동태(1)

Let's Check It Out p. 84

A 1 be 2 be remembered 3 Is 4 repaired 5 to

B 1 어색한 곳 없음 2 painted 3 was 4 to 5 어색한 곳 없음

C 1 be finished
2 is / used

3 Were / observed

D 1 was given to Leo
2 By whom was the letter
3 could not be seen

Ready for Exams p. 85

1 ④ 2 ④
3 (1) are taught English
(2) is taught to us
4 Is French spoken in Quebec?

해설

1 조동사의 수동태는 「조동사+(not)+be+p.p.」이며 ‘by+목적격’은 필요하지 않으면 생략할 수 있다.

2 (when) he designed the stadium → (when) the stadium was designed를 의문문 어순으로 하면 된다.

3 첫 번째는 간접 목적어를, 두 번째는 직접 목적어를 주어로 하여 수동태로 바꾼 것이며, teach는 전치사 to를 쓴다.

4 평서문 → 수동태 → 의문문으로 바꾸면 조금 쉽다. They speak French in Quebec. → French is spoken in Quebec (by them). → Is French spoken in Quebec (by them)?

UNIT 17 여러 가지 수동태(2)

Let’s Check It Out p. 87

A 1 in 2 with
3 about 4 by
5 of

B 1 be taken out by
2 is looked up to by
3 wasn’t[was not] put off by
4 Was / turned off by
5 will be put together by

C 1 are satisfied with 2 is made from
3 wasn’t filled with
4 won’t be looked after

D 1 about 2 with
3 of 4 by
5 at 또는 by

Ready for Exams p. 88

1 ② 2 ③
3 are filled with tears
4 Where were you brought up?

해설

1 be worried는 about을 쓰고, looked at을 쓰면 수동의 의미가 되어 문장이 어색하다.

2 make fun of는 ‘~을 놀리다’라는 뜻의 동사구로, 한 덩어리로 인식하여 수동태를 만든다.

3 그림에서 눈에 눈물이 가득 고여 있으므로 be filled with tears로 쓴다.

4 bring up(기르다)의 수동형이므로 어순에 맞게 「의문사+be동사+주어+p.p.」로 쓰면 된다.

Review Test p. 89

01 ④ 02 ③
03 ① 04 ⑤
05 ② 06 ① ④
07 ① ② 08 ③
09 ② 10 ④
11 ③ 12 ③
13 ① 14 ④
15 ④ 16 ① ② ⑤
17 When was the bike repaired?
18 No one is respected by everybody.
19 This card was written to him by Agatha.
20 1. 능동태의 주어 → 능동태의 목적어 /
예문: Many teenagers was → Many teenagers were
21 heard / was injured
22 Karl / by
23 By whom was the sitcom made?
24

	T				
	H				
W	I	N	N	E	R
	N				

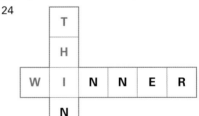

25 The light was turned on by

해설

01 주어가 동작을 받는 것이므로 수동태로 써야 한다. 미술관이 설계된 것은 과거의 일이므로 과거 시제로 쓴다.

02 by Alan이 능동태의 주어가 되고, is not taught는 doesn’t teach로 쓰고, 목적어로 the subject를 쓴다.

03 행위자가 일반인, 불필요, 불확실한 경우에는 생략할 수 있다.

04 [보기]와 ⑤는 with가 들어간다. ① from ② in ③ to ④ at[by]

05 의문사가 있는 수동태는 「의문사+be동사+주어+p.p. ~?」로 쓴다. (break-broke-broken)

06 ② is played → plays ③ storing → stored ⑤ he → him

07 ① was → were ② rescued → be rescued

08 ‘~에게 알려지다’는 be known to이다.

09 ⓐ buy는 직접 목적어를 주어로 하는 수동태로 전환될 수 없다. (→ A new tablet computer was bought for me by him.) ⓒ not → was not ⓓ for them → (by them) for you

10 조동사가 있는 의문문 수동태로 「조동사+주어+be+p.p.」인 Can eggs be kept at room temperature?로 영작하면 된다.

11 uniform[jú:nəfɔ̀:rm]은 첫 발음이 모음이 아니므로 A가 옳고, 기본적으로 수동태는 「be+p.p.+by+행위자」로 표현한다.

12 buy는 간접 목적어만 주어로 수동태로 전환 가능하기 때문에 This mug was bought for me by Jihoo.로 전환할 수 있다.

13 be interested in(~에 관심이 있다)을 쓰고, 나무는 물리적 변화에 의해 의자로 만들어졌으므로 be made of를 쓴다.

14 ④ The chimps will be sent to the zoo.처럼 to가 필요하다. ① Are you tired of me? ② Where were you born? ③ My kickboard was stolen last night. ⑤ Multiple characters were played by one actor.

15 첫 번째는 일반적인 수동태의 행위자라 by가 어울리고, 나머지는 by 이외의 전치사로 with가 어울린다.

16 ① by → of ② with → in ⑤ of → at 또는 by로 써야 한다.

17 의문사가 있는 문장의 수동태는 「의문사+be동사+주어+p.p. ~?」로 쓴다.

18 주어를 No one으로 해야 적절한 문장이 된다. (누구도 모든 사람에게 존경받지는 않는다.)

19 write는 간접 목적어를 주어로 해서 수동태로 전환할 수 없다.

20 1. 능동태의 목적어를 수동태의 주어로 쓴다.
예문: 수동태의 주어가 복수이고 시제가 과거이므로 be동사를 were로 써야 한다.

21 글의 흐름상 빈칸에 필요한 단어는 hear와 injure이다. 첫 번째는 last night이 있으므로 과거형으로 쓰고, 두 번째는 주어가 동작을 받으므로 수동태로 써야 한다.

22 by와 불필요한 행위자는 생략할 수 있다. by oneself는 '혼자'의 뜻이다. (우리는 Karl이 혼자 사는 것을 몰랐다.)

23 의문사가 주어인 의문문의 수동태로 「By+의문사+be동사+주어+p.p. ~?」로 쓰면 된다.

24 be pleased with, be crowded with로 with의 철자를 빈칸에 적절하게 넣으면 된다.

25 '소년이 전등을 켰다(The boy turned on the light[the light on].)'에서 동사구 turn on을 한 묶음으로 해서 수동태로 전환하면 된다.

시험 직전에 챙겨 보는 비법노트 p. 92

한눈에 쏙!

1 1) was invented

2 1) is 2) are 3) was 4) were 5) be
6) be동사 7) p.p. 8) 의문사 9) By 10) 의문사

3 1) give 2) teach 3) send 4) sell 5) write
6) show 7) sing 8) find 9) make 10) buy
11) cook 12) get 13) ask

헷갈리지 말자!

1 was bought

2 beaten

3 to

해설

1 드론이 구입된 것이므로 수동형인 bought으로 고쳐야 한다.

2 의문사가 주어인 Who beat you?의 수동태로 beaten이 되어야 한다.

3 sell은 수동태 전환 시에 전치사 to를 쓴다.

CHAPTER 08 관계사

UNIT 18 관계대명사 who, which

Let's Check It Out p. 95

A
1 I have a friend who has a cute kitten.
2 I bought a used car which had no air conditioner.
3 A student who studies hard will pass the test.
4 I have a cousin whose hobby is playing the drum.

B
1 who 2 which
3 has
4 that, which (둘 다 가능)
5 whose

C
1 She met the boy who[whom, that] we helped.
2 We found a doll which[that] looked lonely.
3 He has a smartphone whose case is unique.
4 She brought the flowers which[that] smelled good.
5 knew the lady who[that] loved my brother

D
1 제한적 용법
2 계속적 용법
3 제한적 용법

Ready for Exams p. 96

1 ② 2 ②
3 ② 4 who[that] was very poor
5 who

해설

1 뒤의 절에서 cleans의 주어 역할을 하고 앞의 a robot을 수식하는 말이 필요하므로 주격 관계대명사 that이 알맞다. (which도 가능)

2 ⓐ 관계대명사 다음에 동사 lives가 왔으므로 주격 who가 알맞다. ⓒ 관계대명사 다음에 명사가 왔으므로 소유격 whose가 알맞다.

3 • 사물 선행사의 목적격 관계사 which 또는 that이 알맞다.
• 사물 선행사의 소유격 관계사 of which가 알맞다.
따라서 공통으로 들어갈 단어는 which이다.

4 공통되는 부분이 a farmer와 He(사람)이므로 주격 관계대명사 who를 사용하여 문장을 연결해야 한다. (that도 가능)

5 관계대명사의 계속적 용법은 콤마 다음에 관계대명사를 쓰며, 이때 선행사가 사람이면 who로 쓴다.

UNIT 19 관계대명사 that, what

Let's Check It Out p. 98

A 1 that 2 that
3 which 4 that
5 what 6 which
7 what 8 What

B 1 what 2 what

C 1 that 2 What
3 that 4 what
5 that

D 1 그녀는 그 목표를 성취한 바로 그 사람이다.
2 내가 가진 모든 것은 돈이다. (내가 가진 것이라고는 돈밖에 없다.)
3 이것이 어제 그녀가 나에게 보낸 것이다.

Ready for Exams p. 99

1 ⑤ 2 ①
3 ②
4 We checked everything (that) we needed.
5 This is not what she wants.

해설

1 목적격의 관계대명사가 제한적 용법으로 사용되면 생략할 수 있다. ①부터 ④까지가 이에 해당된다. ⑤는 주격 관계대명사가 쓰였으므로 생략할 수 없다.

2 ⓐ ⓑ 주격으로 쓰인 관계대명사 ⓒ ⓓ 동사 다음에 목적절을 이끌어 주는 접속사 ⓔ '저것'이라고 해석되는 지시대명사

3 ②는 의문사이고 나머지는 관계대명사이다.

4 목적격 관계대명사는 생략할 수 있다.

5 선행사를 포함한 관계사 what을 넣어야 6단어로 쓸 수 있다.

UNIT 20 관계부사

Let's Check It Out p. 101

A 1 when 2 where
3 why 4 how

B 1 (1) which[that] (2) at which (3) where
2 (1) The way (2) How
3 (1) which[that] / on (2) on which (3) when
4 (1) for which (2) why

C 1 in which 2 how
3 when 4 why

Ready for Exams p. 102

1 ① ⑤ 2 ③
3 where / were held 4 how

해설

1 ② 관계부사 where가 있을 때는 문장 끝에 전치사 in을 쓸 수 없다. ③ 관계사 which로 연결되었을 때 문장 끝에 전치사 in이 필요하다. ④ 관계사 that은 전치사와 함께 쓰일 수 없다.

2 ⓒ the reason이 뒤 문장에서 for the reason인 부사 역할을 하므로 관계부사 how가 아니라 why가 알맞다.

3 전치사 in이 포함된 장소의 관계부사 where와 나머지 문장을 쓴다.

4 방법을 나타내는 관계부사 how가 적절하다.

Review Test p. 103

01 ③ 02 ④
03 ③ 04 ① ② ⑤
05 ① ② 06 ③
07 ④ 08 ② ④
09 ⑤ 10 ①
11 ① ③ ⑤ 12 ①
13 ④
14 ⓐ which → who[that]
15 the person who(m)[that] I work with
16 which 또는 that
17 (1) 내가 그곳에서 본 것은 나를 놀라게 했다.
(2) 동진이는 그녀의 직업이 무엇인지 알지도 모른다.
18 I bought a new computer whose monitor is big. 또는 I bought a new computer(,) the monitor of which is big.
19 She ate the curry and rice which[that] her son made.
20 that → which
21 (1) which[that] / at (2) at which (3) where
22 마지막 문장의 which → when 또는 in which

해설

01 첫 번째는 사람(someone)이 선행사인 주격 관계대명사이므로 who[that], 두 번째는 사물(church)이 선행사인 주격 관계대명사이므로 which[that]가 가능하다.

02 who는 선행사가 사람일 때 쓰이므로 사물인 sport에는 쓰일 수 없다.

03 첫 번째 문장은 선행사 a book이 뒤 문장에서 소유격으로 쓰였고, 두 번째는 선행사를 포함한 관계대명사 what이 필요하다.

04 ① 전치사 다음에 쓰인 관계대명사는 생략할 수 없다. ② ⑤

관계대명사 주격은 생략할 수 없다.

05 ⓐ와 ⓑ가 틀렸고 ⓒ는 틀린 곳이 없다.

06 camp 뒤에 전치사 at이 있으므로 관계부사 where는 쓸 수 없고 관계대명사 which가 알맞다. (that도 가능)

07 ⓐ 선행사 people이 복수이므로 동사는 know가 되어야 한다. ⓑ 선행사 the boy가 단수이므로 동사는 comes가 되어야 한다. ⓒ 선행사가 the books로 복수이므로 동사는 are가 되어야 한다. ⓔ 선행사가 anyone으로 단수이므로 동사는 speaks가 알맞다.

08 ② the way 와 how는 함께 쓸 수 없고 둘 중 하나만 써야 한다. ④ 관계대명사 that은 전치사와 나란히 함께 쓰일 수 없다.

09 이유를 나타내는 관계부사 why가 들어간 문장이다. Do you know the reason why she is so upset?으로 영작할 수 있다.

10 the way와 관계부사 how는 함께 쓰이지 않는다. 둘 중 하나만 써야 한다.

11 ② 선행사 the book과 관계사 다음에 명사 covers(표지)가 왔으므로 소유격 whose가 알맞다. ④ 주어로 선행사가 포함된 명사절이므로 That이 아니라 What이 와야 알맞다.

12 Mozzarella cheese pizza is what I want to eat[have] right now.로 영작할 수 있다. 선행사가 포함된 what(= the thing which[that])이 들어가야 빈칸 개수와 맞다.

13 ④ Tell me what you want to get. 문장에서 선행사가 포함된 관계사 what이 필요하다. ① This is the tallest building I have ever seen. ② That is the watch my best friend bought for me. ③ This is the movie she is fond of. ⑤ It is a pen I drew the picture with.

14 선행사가 the man으로 사람이므로 관계사는 who[that]가 되어야 한다.

15 사람이 선행사이며 뒤 문장의 목적격 대신 쓰는 관계대명사 who(m) 또는 that을 쓴다.

16 선행사 the mirror가 사물이므로 관계대명사는 which나 that이 사용되어야 한다.

17 (1) what은 선행사가 포함된 관계사로 '~한 것'이라고 해석한다.

(2) what은 '무엇'이라고 해석되는 의문사이다.

18 반복되는 명사가 Its인 소유격이므로 관계사 whose 또는 of which를 넣어 문장을 연결한다.

19 the curry and rice가 다음 문장에서 목적격으로 쓰였기 때문에 생략 가능한 관계대명사는 which[that]이다.

20 콤마 다음에 계속적 용법으로 관계사 that을 쓸 수 없다. 여기서는 선행사가 사물이므로 which로 고쳐 써야 한다.

21 사물(the hospital)이 선행사로 쓰였으므로 관계사 which를 쓴다. 뒤에 있는 전치사는 관계사 앞으로 올 수 있고, at which는 장소를 나타내므로 관계부사 where로 쓸 수 있다.

22 the future가 다음 문장에서 시간 부사(in the future) 역할을 하므로 관계사는 which가 아니라 when이 알맞다. (미래에, 우리는 작은 가방을 갖게 될 것이다. 그것은 안에 우리가 원하는 무엇이든 넣을 수 있는 가방이다. 나는 모든 것이 이루어지는 미래가 빨리 오기를 원한다.)

시험 직전에 챙겨 보는 비법노트 p. 106

한눈에 쏙!

1 1) who 2) who(m) 3) which 4) which
2 1) 소유격 2) 전치사 3) very 4) only 5) every

헷갈리지 말자!

1 who 또는 that
2 that 또는 which
3 the way 또는 how

해설

1 관계대명사 다음에 동사 can live가 왔으므로 주격 who 또는 that이 알맞다.

2 선행사가 있으므로 what이 아니라 목적격 관계대명사 that 또는 which를 써야 한다. 선행사로 -thing 상당 어구 everything이 왔으므로 관계사 that을 주로 쓴다.

3 the way 와 how는 함께 쓸 수 없고 둘 중 하나만 써야 한다.

CHAPTER 09 비교 구문

UNIT 21 비교 변화, 원급 이용 비교 구문

Let's Check It Out p. 109

A
1 earlier / earliest 2 greater / greatest
3 larger / largest 4 hotter / hottest
5 more expensive / most expensive

B
1 more careful 2 smallest
3 worst 4 stronger
5 better

C
1 worse than
2 better than
3 the last

D
1 (1) as shallow as (2) deeper than
2 (1) less (2) is not / as

Ready for Exams p. 110

1 ③ 2 ②⑤
3 ②③ 4 Daniel, Kevin, Sam, Jin

해설

1 ⓐ as ~ as는 원급 비교 ⓑ than 앞에 비교급을 쓴다.

2 ② as ~ as 동등 비교이므로 원급 large를 써야 한다. ⑤ worse는 bad의 비교급으로 more를 쓰지 않는다.

3 주어진 문장은 틀린 부분이 없으며, possible은 주어 my sister의 주격 she와 can의 과거형 could로 바꾸어 쓸 수 있다.

4 Sam이 Jin보다 크고, Kevin과 Daniel은 Sam보다 큰데, Kevin은 Daniel보다 작으므로 Daniel이 가장 크고 그 다음으로 Kevin, Sam, Jin 순이다.

UNIT 22 여러 가지 비교 구문

Let's Check It Out p. 112

A 1 the 2 in
3 Nothing 4 students

B 1 (1) more exciting than
(2) no other / than basketball
(3) no other / as / basketball
2 (1) No other
(2) larger than any
3 (1) larger than
(2) four times smaller than

C 1 the more 2 Which
3 taller 4 the strangest
5 longer and longer

Ready for Exams p. 113

1 ⑤ 2 ④
3 (1) twice as long
(2) four times longer
4 ⓐ building → buildings

해설

1 ⑤는 배가 다른 과일들만큼 맛있다는 뜻이므로 알맞지 않다. 나머지는 배가 가장 맛있다는 의미이다.

2 ⓐ 「one of the+최상급+복수 명사」이므로 actor → actors ⓑ 비교급+and+비교급: 점점 더 ~한 (→ shorter and shorter) ⓒ the+비교급, the+비교급: ~하면 할수록 더욱 ~한 (As higher → The higher)

3 (1) 그래프에서 바닷가재가 상어보다 2배 오래 살고 배수를 나타낼 때 as가 있는 것으로 보아 원급을 사용한다. 「A ~ 배수사+as+원급+as B」
(2) 사람은 상어보다 4배 오래 살고 than이 있으므로 「A ~ 배수사+비교급+than B」를 쓴다.

4 「one of the+최상급+복수 명사」이므로 building은 buildings가 되어야 알맞다.

Review Test p. 114

01 ② 02 ③
03 ③ 04 ③
05 ⑤ 06 ④
07 ① ⑤
08 I can play chess as well as my dad.
09 as long as possible
10 She is the smartest student in my class.
11 (1) No mountain is higher than Mt. Everest.
(2) No mountain is as high as Mt. Everest.
12 The more / the smarter
13 tool → tools
14 best[most] / favorite
15 (1) less than (2) more than
16 The higher / the lower

해설

01 • than 앞에 비교급 worse가 와야 한다. (bad – worse – worst)
• '가능한 한'이라는 의미가 되도록 possible 또는 he could(과거형)가 알맞다. (hit에 -s가 붙지 않았으므로 과거 시제임을 알 수 있다.)

02 ⓐ -ful로 끝나므로 more colorful이다. ⓒ 「one of the+최상급+복수 명사」이므로 animals이다. ⓓ high(높은, 높이)의 비교급은 higher, highly(매우)의 비교급은 more highly이다.

03 ③ frogs와 fish가 바뀌어야 한다. '사람들은 물고기만큼 개구리를 좋아하지 않는다.'가 알맞다.

04 최상급+of+복수 명사: … 중에 가장 ~하다

05 ⑤는 '목성은 태양계의 다른 행성들만큼 크다.'라는 의미이고, 나머지는 '목성이 태양계에서 가장 큰 행성이다.'라는 의미의 최상급 표현이다.

06 둘 다 비교급 강조 표현이 와야 한다. very는 원급 강조 표현이다.

07 ① 시제가 과거(answered)이므로 can 대신 could가 와야 한다. ⑤ 비교급 앞에는 quite가 아니라 much, even, still, far, a lot이 수식한다.

08 play chess well이 '체스를 잘 두다'는 의미로, good을 부사 well로 바꾸어야 한다.

09 as+원급+as+possible: 가능한 한 ~한/하게

10 smart의 최상급은 the smartest이고 my class는 단수 집단이므로 in을 쓴다.

11 부정 주어+비교급 = 부정 주어+원급 = 최상급

12 The+비교급+주어+동사 ~, the+비교급+주어+동사…: ~하면 할수록 더욱 …하다

13 「one of the+최상급+복수 명사」 구문이다. (컴퓨터는 가장 널리 사용되는 과학적 도구들 중 하나이다.)

14 부사의 최상급에는 the를 생략할 수 있다.

15 (1) 열등 비교 less than: ~보다 덜 …한/하게
(2) 우등 비교 more than: ~보다 더 …한/하게

16 The+비교급+주어+동사 ~, the+비교급+주어+동사…: ~하면 할수록 더욱 …하다 (산을 높이 올라가면 올라갈수록 기온이 낮아진다.)

시험 직전에 챙겨 보는 비법노트 p. 116

한눈에 쏙!

1 1) than 2) the 3) better 4) worse
5) worst 6) most

2 1) than any other 2) 비교급 3) than 4) 원급
3 1) the 2) the 3) of

헷갈리지 말자!

1 than
2 than any other jewel
3 the colder

해설

1 앞에 열등 비교급 less 가 있으므로 as는 than으로 써야 알맞다.
2 비교급 more expensive 다음에 than any other+단수 명사가 와야 한다.
3 the+비교급 ~, the+ 비교급 …: ~하면 할수록 더욱 …하다

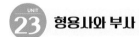

CHAPTER 10
형용사, 부사, 분사

UNIT 23
형용사와 부사

Let's Check It Out
p. 119

A
1 two thousand (and) forty-eight
2 three point five eight
3 seven-tenths 또는 seven over ten
4 four and three quarters 또는 four and three-fourths

B
1 something hot
2 for me
3 turn it off

C
1 어색한 곳 없음
2 look at me
3 try this on

D
1 something cold
2 Seven-eighths / nine-tenths
3 forty-two point one nine five
4 As a result

Ready for Exams
p. 120

1 ② ⑤
2 ⑤
3 ① three-fortieths (또는 three over forty)
② twenty-seven point two seven
4 She set up a school for the blind.

해설

1 여자친구가 착하고 귀엽다고 했고 뒤의 문장도 장점을 첨가하는 내용이 나오므로 '게다가'라는 의미의 연결사가 적절하다.
2 '타동사+부사'에서 대명사는 가운데 쓴다. (take off it → take it off)
3 ① 분수는 기수, 분모는 서수이며 분자가 복수이면 분모에 -s를 붙인다. ② 소수점 이하는 한 자리씩 읽는다.
4 어휘 설명에 '설립하다'라는 의미의 set up이 있고, '시각 장애인들'은 the blind로 표현할 수 있다.

UNIT 24
분사

Let's Check It Out
p. 122

A
1 dancing
2 stolen
3 broken
4 living
5 built
6 wearing

B
1 현재분사
2 동명사
3 현재분사
4 현재분사
5 동명사
6 동명사

C
1 어색한 곳 없음
2 singing
3 talking
4 imported
5 어색한 곳 없음
6 어색한 곳 없음

D
1 exciting
2 depressed
3 shocking
4 amazing
5 pleasing
6 touching

Ready for Exams
p. 123

1 ②
2 ④
3 ① ② ⑤
4 tied / tired

해설

1 • 소녀가 모자를 쓰고 있으므로 능동의 현재분사 wearing이 와야 한다.
• 남자가 실려갔으므로 수동의 과거분사 taken이 와야 한다.
2 직업이 지루하게 하는 것이므로 능동의 현재분사 boring이 되어야 한다.
3 [보기]와 ①, ②, ⑤는 현재분사이고 ③, ④는 동명사이다.
4 첫 번째 빈칸은 말이 나무에 묶여 있으므로 수동의 과거분사를 쓰고, 두 번째 빈칸은 말이 피곤해 보이므로 수동의 과거분사를 써야 한다.

Review Test
p. 124

01 ③ ⑤
02 ④
03 ③
04 ⑤
05 ④
06 ②
07 ②
08 ④
09 (1) (zero) point one two four
(2) three quarters 또는 three-fourths
10 was taking → were taken
11 Something wonderful has happened to her.

12 nine-tenths of my classmates have this smartphone
13 ⓐ has worked ⓓ something different
14 released / exciting
15 However
16 Did he say anything interesting?
17 ⓑ turn off it → turn it off
18 waiting in line look like

해설

01 ③ 분자가 복수이므로 분모는 fifths로 읽는다. ⑤ three-sevenths 또는 three over seven이라고 읽어야 한다.
02 The young은 '젊은 사람들'이라는 뜻으로 복수를 의미하므로 they로 써야 한다.
03 전기를 절약하는 예가 나와 있으므로 ③이 적절하다.
04 look for는 '자동사+전치사'로 바로 뒤에 명사가 오며, -one은 형용사가 뒤에서 꾸며준다. look into는 '~을 조사하다'의 뜻이다.
05 첫 번째 빈칸은 소년이 서 있었으므로 현재분사를 사용해 was standing을 쓴다. 두 번째 빈칸은 버스가 붐빈다는 수동의 의미라 과거분사가 와야 한다.
06 주체가 동작을 받으므로 과거분사로 써야 한다.
07 ②는 용도를 나타내는 동명사이고, 나머지는 상태를 나타내는 형용사(현재분사)이다.
08 ⓐ using → used ⓒ frustrating → frustrated
09 (1) 소수 읽기에서 0.에서 0은 생략해도 되며, 소수점 이하는 한 자리씩 읽는다.
(2) 분수에서 분자는 기수로, 분모는 서수로 읽고 분자가 복수일 경우 분모에 -s를 붙인다.
10 The wounded는 '부상을 당한 사람들'이란 뜻으로 복수 동사를 써야 하며, 주체가 동작을 받으므로 수동태로 써야 한다.
11 -thing은 형용사가 뒤에서 꾸며준다.
12 90%를 분수로 나타내면 9/10이다. 분자는 기수로, 분모는 서수로 읽되 분자가 복수이면 분모에 -s를 붙인다. 반 아이들 중 9/10이므로 복수 동사를 써야 한다.
13 ⓐ 과거의 동작이 현재까지 연결되므로 수동태가 아닌 능동태 현재완료로 써야 한다. ⓓ -thing으로 끝나는 단어는 형용사가 뒤에서 수식한다.
14 첫 번째는 게임이 release된(출시된) 것으로 과거분사가 알맞고, 두 번째는 게임이 흥미진진한 것이므로 현재분사가 들어간다.
15 그래픽 카드는 좋지만 램이 겨우 4기가라는 상반되는 내용으로 '반면에'의 의미를 갖는 접속부사가 적절하다.
16 anything은 형용사가 뒤에서 꾸며주며, anything과 interest의 관계가 능동이므로 현재분사로 써야 한다.
17 「타동사+대명사+부사」 순으로 쓴다.
18 wait in line은 주어를 꾸며주어야 하고 의미상 능동이므로 현재분사로 쓰며, look like는 주어가 복수이므로 그대로 쓰면 된다.

시험 직전에 챙겨 보는 비법노트 p. 126

한눈에 쏙!

1 1) -body 2) -thing
2 1) 형용사
3 1) 진행 2) 완료 3) 동작 4) 용도
4 1) 사물 2) ~하는 3) 사람 4) ~되는[지는]

헷갈리지 말자!

1 something new
2 found
3 touching

해설

1 something은 형용사가 뒤에서 수식한다.
2 본동사는 looked이고 the cat이 발견된 것이므로 found로 써야 한다.
3 순간(moment)이 감동을 주는 것이므로 touching으로 써야 한다.

CHAPTER 11 접속사

UNIT 25 명사절, 때의 부사절, 상관 접속사

Let's Check It Out p. 129

A 1 that 2 if
3 whether

B 1 When 2 Before
3 while 4 after
5 until 6 since

C 1 both / and 2 either / or
3 neither / nor 4 not only / but also
5 not / but

Ready for Exams p. 130

1 ③ 2 ⑤
3 ④ 4 will go → go
5 Not only children but also their mothers

해설

1 문맥상 you like your new teacher는 hope의 목적어 역할을 한다. 따라서 빈칸에는 명사절을 이끄는 접속사 that이 필요하다.
2 의미상 '비가 오기 전에'라고 하는 것이 자연스럽다. (After → Before)
3 ⓑ 「neither A nor B」는 B에 수를 일치시키므로 are는 am이 되어야 한다. ⓓ 「B as well as A」는 B에 수를 일치시키므로 don't는 doesn't가 되어야 한다.

4 시간의 부사절에서는 현재 시제가 미래를 나타낸다.
5 not only A but also B: A뿐만 아니라 B도

UNIT 26 조건, 양보, 이유, 결과의 부사절

Let's Check It Out
p. 132

A
1 If
2 though 또는 although, even though
3 Because 또는 As, Since
4 so

B
1 If
2 Even though
3 Because
4 that

C
1 so
2 As
3 Though
4 Unless
5 that

Ready for Exams
p. 133

1 ⑤
2 ②
3 will snow → snows
4 Unless I am busy this summer
5 It was so foggy that I could not see anything.

해설

1 • 비가 내려서 나는 내 방 창문을 닫고 있다.
 • 그는 짐 꾸리는 것을 끝낼 수 있도록 일찍 일어났다.
2 ② I want to drink water로 보아 접속사 Even if는 Because로 고치는 것이 알맞다. ③ Unless는 if ~ not의 의미로 부정어를 이미 포함하고 있으므로 조건절에서 부정어를 사용하지 않는다. 따라서 맞는 문장이다.
3 시간 및 조건의 부사절에서는 현재 시제가 미래를 대신한다.
4 if ~ not은 unless로 바꾸어 쓸 수 있다.
5 so ~ that...(너무 ~해서 …하다) 구문을 사용해서 영작하면 된다.

Review Test
p. 134

01 ⑤
02 ③
03 ④
04 ②
05 ②
06 ①
07 ③ ⑤
08 ③
09 ④
10 After I eat dinner, I'm going to do my homework in my room.
11 if 또는 whether
12 as well as
13 unless
14 ⓐ will rise → rises ⓑ will come → comes
15 Though[Although, Even though] it rained heavily, he climbed the mountain.
16 The tea is so hot that I can't[cannot] drink it.
17 I think that people drink too much coffee.
18 Neither he nor I am a climate scientist.
19 As[as]
20 Since he has a toothache

해설

01 you made the right choice는 think의 목적어 역할을 하므로 빈칸에는 목적어절을 이끄는 접속사 that이 필요하다.
02 문맥상 '그는 걷는 동안 나에게 노래를 불러주었다.'라고 해석하는 것이 가장 자연스러우므로 빈칸에 알맞은 것은 while이다.
03 ④ 관계대명사 ① ② ③ ⑤ 명사절을 이끄는 접속사
04 • 조건을 나타내는 접속사: '만약 ~라면'
 • 명사절을 이끄는 접속사: '~인지 (아닌지)'
05 ② 「either A or B」는 B에 수를 일치시킨다. (are → am)
06 if ~ not은 unless로 바꾸어 쓸 수 있다.
07 빈칸에는 '~할지라도'라는 의미를 지닌 양보의 접속사가 들어가는 것이 적절하다.
08 조건을 나타내는 부사절에서는 현재 시제가 미래를 대신한다.
09 문맥상 첫 번째 문장은 '~할 때', 두 번째 문장은 '~하기 때문에'라고 해석하는 것이 자연스러우므로 빈칸에 알맞은 것은 ④이다.
10 시간을 나타내는 부사절에서는 현재 시제가 미래를 대신한다. (will eat → eat) 나는 저녁을 먹은 후에 내 방에서 숙제를 할 것이다.
11 if[whether]: ~인지 (아닌지)
12 not only A but also B = B as well as A: A뿐만 아니라 B도
13 if ~ not = unless: ~하지 않는다면
14 시간과 조건의 부사절에서는 현재 시제가 미래를 대신한다.
15 '비가 많이 왔는데도 등반을 했다'라고 해석하는 것이 자연스러우므로 양보를 나타내는 접속사가 알맞다.
16 so ~ that...: 너무 ~해서 …하다
17 '~인지 (아닌지)'가 아니라 '~라고 생각한다'라는 해석이 자연스러우므로 if는 that으로 고쳐야 한다.
18 neither A nor B(A도 B도 아닌)에서 동사의 수는 B에 일치한다. 이 표현에 이미 부정의 의미가 들어 있으므로 not을 쓰면 안 되는 것에 주의하도록 한다.
19 접속사 as는 '~할 때' 또는 '~ 때문에'라는 의미로 사용된다.
20 '치통을 앓고 있기 때문에 그는 사탕이나 초콜릿을 먹을 수가 없다.'라고 해석하는 것이 자연스러우므로 알맞은 접속사는 Since이다.

시험 직전에 챙겨 보는 비법노트
p. 136

한눈에 쏙!

1 1) 명사 2) if
2 1) 현재 2) 미래
3 1) only 2) also 3) as well as

헷갈리지 말자!

1 that
2 if 또는 whether
3 go

해설

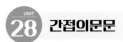

1 he is honest 문장을 명사로 만들어 줄 접속사 that이 알맞다.

2 wonder 동사 다음에 문장을 이끌어 줄 접속사는 if 또는 whether가 알맞다.

3 unless(만약 ~하지 않는다면)가 사용된 조건절에서는 현재 시제가 미래를 대신한다.

CHAPTER 12

의문문

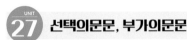

UNIT 27 선택의문문, 부가의문문

Let's Check It Out p. 139

A 1 or
2 or
3 Which

B 1 are you 2 can't he
3 didn't she 4 shall we
5 will you 6 haven't you

C 1 or
2 Which / or
3 or

D 1 aren't you 2 won't she
3 didn't he 4 has he
5 shall we 6 will you

Ready for Exams p. 140

1 ② 2 ③
3 ④ 4 didn't she
5 Let's go fishing / shall we

해설

1 '명성과 돈 중 어느 것이 더 중요하니?'라는 선택의문문이므로 빈칸에 알맞은 것은 Which이다.

2 ⓐ be동사 was를 써야 하므로 wasn't she?라고 해야 한다. ⓓ 주절에 완료 시제인 hasn't finished가 쓰였으므로 has he?라고 해야 한다.

3 선택의문문은 두 가지 중 하나를 선택하는 의문문이므로 Yes나 No로 대답하지 않는다. Yes를 빼고 대답해야 한다.

4 주절의 주어는 Yuna이고 동사는 went이므로 부가의문문은 didn't she?가 알맞다.

5 Let's ~로 시작하는 문장의 부가의문문은 shall we?이다.

UNIT 28 간접의문문

Let's Check It Out p. 142

A 1 if[whether] Emily is at her office
2 if[whether] they live here
3 if[whether] he has a car
4 if[whether] she is married

B 1 how old he is
2 what time it is now
3 why she went home early
4 who invented the computer
5 where Ted went yesterday

C 1 What do you think we should do?
2 Who do you guess can solve the problem?

Ready for Exams p. 143

1 ① ⑤ 2 ③
3 ②
4 I don't know what they are talking about.
5 Do you know if[whether] he likes to play sports?

해설

1 의문사가 없는 간접의문문을 이끌 때는 if나 whether를 쓴다.

2 의문사가 있는 의문문이 다른 문장의 일부가 될 때는 「의문사+주어+동사」의 어순을 취한다.

3 주절의 동사가 생각이나 추측을 나타내는 동사일 때 간접의문문의 의문사는 문장의 맨 앞으로 이동해야 하므로 ⓒ는 잘못된 문장이다. (→ Who do you think will go to the party?)

4 의문사가 있는 간접의문문이므로 know의 목적어 역할을 할 때 「의문사+주어+동사」의 어순을 취한다.

5 he likes to play sports는 의문사가 없는 간접의문문이므로 앞에 if나 whether를 붙여야 한다.

Review Test p. 144

01 ③ 02 ③
03 ① 04 ⑤
05 ⑤ 06 ②
07 ① 08 ①
09 by bus or on foot
10 Which / cookies or chocolate
11 Let's go to the concert together / shall we
12 how you swim so well
13 Sarah and her family moved to Toronto, didn't they?
14 (1) if the store is open today
(2) whether the store is open today
15 What do you think it is?
16 Close the window, will you?
17 Amy hasn't been to China, has she?

해설

01 'A와 B 중 어느 것을 ~하니?'라고 할 때는 「Which ~, A or B?」라고 한다.
02 주절이 긍정문이므로 부정의 부가의문문으로 바꿔야 한다. (does she → doesn't she)
03 • 주절이 부정문, 주어는 you, 동사는 haven't taken이므로 이에 알맞은 부가의문문은 have you이다.
• 명령문이므로 알맞은 부가의문문은 will you이다.
04 ⓑ can he → he can ⓓ → What do you think it means?
05 동사 likes는 일반동사이고, 주어가 3인칭 단수이고, 시제가 현재이므로 does가 부가의문문에 쓰여야 한다.
06 간접의문문에 쓰인 if는 '~인지 (아닌지)'의 뜻으로 whether와 바꾸어 쓸 수 있다.
07 의문사가 있는 간접의문문이고, how many plants가 간접의문문의 주어이므로 how many plants 다음에 there are가 나와야 한다.
08 주절에 think가 쓰였으므로 간접의문문에 쓰인 where는 문장의 맨 앞인 ①에 위치해야 한다.
09 선택의문문으로 두 가지 선택 대상을 or로 연결한다. (by bus: 버스로 / on foot: 걸어서)
10 여자아이는 식탁에 있는 쿠키와 초콜릿을 놓고 고민하고 있으므로 Which should I eat first, cookies or chocolate?이라고 한다.
11 Let's ~로 시작하는 문장의 부가의문문은 shall we를 쓴다.
12 의문사가 있는 의문문이 다른 문장의 일부가 될 때 「의문사+주어+동사」의 어순을 취한다.
13 주절이 긍정문이므로 부정의 부가의문문으로 고친다. 주절의 동사가 moved이므로 시제는 과거이며, 주어는 Sarah and her family (= they)이므로 부가의문문은 didn't they?라고 해야 한다.
14 의문사가 없는 의문문이 다른 문장의 일부가 될 때는 문장 앞에 if나 whether를 쓰고, 그 뒤에는 「주어+동사」의 어순을 취한다.
15 주절에 생각이나 추측을 나타내는 동사가 있을 때는 간접의문문의 의문사를 문장의 맨 앞으로 이동시킨다.
16 명령문의 부가의문문은 will you를 쓴다.
17 주절이 부정문이므로 긍정의 부가의문문을 쓴다. 주절에 완료 시제가 쓰였고 주어는 Amy이므로, 올바른 부가의문문은 has she이다.

시험 직전에 챙겨 보는 비법노트 p. 146

한눈에 쏙!

1 1) wasn't 2) can she
2 1) whether

헷갈리지 말자!

1 do you
2 if you know
3 who they are

해설

1 앞 문장에 don't가 쓰였으므로 부가의문문은 do you 가 알맞다.
2 의문사가 없는 간접의문문은 「if[whether]+주어+동사」의 순서로 do가 필요 없다.
3 의문사가 있는 의문문이 다른 문장의 일부가 될 때에는 if나 whether를 쓰지 않고 곧바로 「의문사+주어+동사」를 쓴다.

CHAPTER 13 가정법

UNIT 29 조건문과 가정법 과거

Let's Check It Out p. 149

A
1 came 2 hurried
3 gets 4 regret
5 Would

B
1 were 2 would
3 wouldn't 4 had
5 would

C
1 am / can't[cannot] take
2 weren't[wasn't] / could go
3 knew / would tell
4 had / could fix

D
1 snowed / would make
2 visit / go

Ready for Exams p. 150

1 ④ 2 ②
3 were (was도 가능) / would wear
4 you had a million dollars / how would you spend it

해설

1 가정법 과거의 조건절 형태는 「if+주어+과거 동사」이므로 studies를 studied로 써야 한다.
2 ⓒ are → were ⓔ needed → would need
3 현재 사실에 반대되는 가정이므로 가정법 과거로 완성하면 된다. would는 '소망'이나 '의도'를 나타낸다.
4 문장이 If로 시작하므로 뒤에 주어와 과거 동사를 쓰고, 의문문이므로 주절은 의문사부터 배열하면 된다.

UNIT 30 I wish 가정법 과거, as if 가정법 과거

Let's Check It Out

p. 152

A 1 were 2 could
3 wish 4 were

B 1 doesn't 2 is not
3 doesn't rule 4 knows

C 1 had 2 didn't have to
3 knew

D 1 could speak
2 as if[though] he knew
3 as if[though] she were[was]

Ready for Exams

p. 153

1 ② 2 ③
3 ② ③ ⑤ 4 it were[was]
5 she isn't[is not] angry

해설

1 I wish 가정법 과거에서는 조동사나 동사의 과거형을 쓴다.
2 as if 가정법 과거(긍정)는 In fact 직설법 현재(부정)로 바꿀 수 있다.
3 ② lives → lived ③ can → could ⑤ won't → wouldn't
4 현재의 실현될 수 없는 소망은 I wish 가정법 과거로 표현한다. 주어는 그림 속 문장에서 쓰인 비인칭 주어 it을 쓰면 된다.
5 as if 가정법 과거(긍정)는 In fact 직설법 현재(부정)로 바꾸어 쓸 수 있다.

Review Test

p. 154

01 ③ 02 ①
03 ② 04 ④
05 ③ ⑤ 06 ② ④
07 ③ 08 ① ③
09 don't tell / cannot[can't]
10 she weren't[wasn't] angry / would listen to
11 If she rode her bike more carefully
12 The game would be more exciting if Kate were[was] playing.
13 He walks as if he were[was] drunk.
14 wish / were
15 ⓔ is
16 wishes (that) she had confidence in herself
17 The lady is sitting on a tiger as if it were a chair.

해설

01 가정법 과거는 if절에 과거형 동사를 쓴다.
02 가정법 과거 문장으로 if절에는 동사의 과거형이, 주절에는 'would+동사원형'이 온다.
03 직설법 현재는 긍정 ↔ 부정으로 가정법 과거로 바꿀 수 있다.
04 가정법 과거의 주절에는 can이 아니라 could로 써야 한다.
05 ③ could → couldn't ⑤ was → is, didn't → won't
06 실현 불가능한 소원은 I wish로 표현하며, 주어진 문장은 I wish (that) everybody found me attractive.로 영작할 수 있다.
07 '그는 내가 귀가 안 들리는 것처럼 소리친다'라는 의미의 가정법 과거 문장으로 '나는 귀가 안 들리지 않는다'라는 의미이다.
08 ① I wish 가정법 과거이므로 has를 had로 써야 한다. ③ 현재 사실에 반대되는 가정을 하므로 I'm을 I were[was]로 써야 한다.
09 가정법 과거는 직설법 현재의 반대 문장으로 전환할 수 있다. (네가 나에게 사실을 말해준다면, 나는 너를 도울 수 있을 텐데. → 네가 나에게 사실을 말해주지 않아서 나는 너를 도울 수 없다.)
10 '그녀가 화나지 않았다면, 내 변명을 들어줄 텐데.'로 쓰면 되며, 빈칸 수를 맞추기 위해 첫 빈칸에는 줄임말 weren't 또는 wasn't를 쓰면 된다.
11 가정법 과거 문장으로 「if+주어+동사의 과거형」 순으로 쓰면 된다.
12 가정법 과거 문장인데 The game으로 시작하므로 if절을 뒤에 쓰면 되며, exciting의 비교급은 more exciting이다.
13 as if 또는 as though로 쓸 수 있는데, 3번째와 4번째 단어의 글자 수를 같게 해야 하므로 as if로 써야 하며, 보어로 사용되는 서술적 용법을 써야 하므로 drunk를 써야 한다.
14 실현 가능성이 희박한 내용을 소망하는 문장이므로 wish를 쓰고, 현재 사실의 반대이므로 가정법 과거 were를 써야 한다.
15 주절이 will인 조건문에서는 현재 시제를 쓴다. 나머지는 가정법 과거이므로 were 또는 was가 들어간다.
16 Sharon이 자신감이 있기를 바라고 있으므로 「주어+wish+가정법 과거」로 쓰면 된다.
17 '여자는 마치 호랑이가 의자인 것처럼 앉아 있다.'라는 의미의 문장으로 「주어+동사+as if+가정법 과거」 순으로 배열하면 된다.

시험 직전에 챙겨 보는 비법노트

p. 156

한눈에 쏙!

1 1) 현재 2) 과거 3) 과거 4) 현재
5) 현재
2 1) 불확실 2) 미래 3) 확실 4) 현재
3 1) 현재 2) 미래 3) 소망 4) 과거 5) 현재
4 1) 현재 2) 현재

헷갈리지 말자!

1 were 또는 was
2 had
3 isn't 또는 is not

해설

1 주절의 조동사의 과거형으로 보아 가정법 과거형 구문이므로 were[was]로 써야 한다.
2 I wish 가정법 과거 구문으로 had로 써야 한다.
3 as if 가정법 과거는 In fact, 현재형으로 바꿔 쓸 수 있으므로 isn't 또는 is not으로 써야 한다.

MEMO

MEMO

내공

신 략

중학영문법 2

개념이해책

문장을 쓰면서 머릿속에 담는

쓰담쓰담

내신영문법

실제 중학교 최신 내신 응용문제 수록

최신 기출 응용문제와 실전 예상문제로 서술형 문제 완벽 대비!

3

정답 및 해설

쓰담쓰담

내신영문법

3

정답 및 해설

Chapter 1
to부정사

UNIT 01
단순부정사와 완료부정사

PRACTICE p. 010

1 The children seem to have colds.
2 She seemed to be honest.
3 Minji seems to have passed the exam.
4 He seemed to be playing the guitar.
해설 '기타를 치고 있는'이라는 진행의 의미를 담고 있으므로 to be playing이 쓰였다.

NOW REAL TEST 1 p. 011

1 It seems that he is a good songwriter.
2 seem to be scared
3 seems to have got(ten) enough rest for his next role
해설 휴식을 취한 것이 주절(현재)보다 앞선 시제인 과거이므로 완료부정사를 사용해야 한다.
4 ③
해설 두 번째 문장의 동사가 seem으로 현재 시제이므로 It seems가 되어야 하고, 주절보다 that절의 시제(bought)가 앞서 있으므로 완료부정사를 사용해야 한다.
5 (1) seems that the boy is late for school
(2) seems to be late for school
해설 It seems that + 주어 + 동사 = 주어 + seem(s) to + 동사원형
6 ③
해설 주절과 that절 둘 다 과거 시제이므로 단순부정사를 써야 한다. ②도 어법상으로는 가능하지만 원래 문장에 진행형(was looking)이 사용되었으므로 be looking이 의미상 더 적절하다.
7 (1) seemed that she was upset
(2) seem to have known the truth at that time
해설 **(1)** 단순부정사이므로 주절과 that절의 시제를 일치시킨다. **(2)** 주절과 that절의 시제가 다르므로 완료부정사를 쓴다.
8 ①
해설 그가 좋은 선생님인 것이 현재의 사실인데 주절에 과거형 seemed가 사용되어 어색하다. is를 was로 바꾸거나 seemed를 seems로 바꾸어야 한다.
9 (1) It seems that JYP is a creative company.
(2) It seemed that Edison was a genius.
10 (1) Sujin seems to take good care of her younger brother.
(2) Jongguk seems to have driven very well in the dark.
해설 **(2)** 운전한 시점이 주절보다 앞선 시제인 과거이므로 완료부정사를 사용한다.

NOW REAL TEST 2 p. 014

1 ⓒ It seemed that she was a pianist. (또는 She seemed to be a pianist.)
2 to be real
해설 Ghosts를 주어로 하면 'seem + to부정사'로 표현해야 하는데, 주절과 that절의 시제가 같으므로 단순부정사인 'to + 동사원형'이 와야 한다.
3 to have made a mistake
해설 실수한 것이 더 과거이므로 완료부정사인 to have p.p.를 써야 한다.
4 (2)
해설 **(2)**는 맞는 문장이므로 고칠 필요가 없다.
5 (1) that she wasn't (= was not) there yesterday
(2) not to have been there yesterday
해설 **(2)** to부정사의 부정은 not을 앞에 쓴다.

UNIT 02
가주어, 가목적어 it

PRACTICE p. 016

1 It was brave of the reporter to reveal the truth.
2 It is very important for you to learn English.
3 It was kind of you to help me.
4 It is strange that he is still not back.

NOW REAL TEST 1 p. 017

1 (1) It is dangerous for me to swim in the deep river.
(2) It is kind of you to let me know this information.
해설 **(2)** 사람의 성품·성질을 나타내는 kind가 있으므로 의미상 주어에는 of를 써야 한다.
2 (1) for us to carry these boxes
(2) of you to break the cup
3 ①
해설 ② → for her ③ → for us ④ → for us ⑤ → of you
4 ③
해설 ③은 사람의 성질·성품을 나타내는 stupid가 쓰였으므로 of가 들어가고, 나머지는 for가 들어간다.
5 It is not good for Eric to watch TV until late at night.
6 (1) for me (2) of you
해설 **(1)** 일반적인 의미상 주어 **(2)** 사람의 성품을 나타내는 형용사가 있는 경우 의미상 주어
7 ①
해설 important는 일반적인 형용사이므로 의미상 주어는 for you가 맞다.
8 It was wise of Miran to refuse the offer.
9 (1) It's very nice of you to look after stray animals.
해설 사람의 성품을 나타내는 nice가 있으므로 of you가 맞고, 진주어로 to부정사를 써야 한다.
(2) 네가 길 잃은 동물들을 돌보는 것은 아주 착한 일이야.
10 (1) It is safe for Kevin to wear a helmet when inline skating.
(2) It was brave of Inpyo to catch a robber.
해설 **(1)** 일반적 형용사이므로 의미상 주어에 for를 사용한다.

(2) '용감한'이라는 사람의 성질을 나타내는 형용사가 있으므로 의미상 주어에 of를 사용한다.

NOW REAL TEST 2 p. 020

1 (1) for you to (2) that

해설 (1) 가주어 It, 의미상 주어 'for + 목적격', 진주어 to부정사 구문 **(2)** 가주어 It, 진주어 'that + 주어 + 동사'

2 ②

해설 첫 번째 문장과 세 번째 문장은 일반적 형용사여서 for가 적절하고, 두 번째 문장은 사람의 성질을 나타내는 형용사여서 of가 적절하다.

3 (1) It was exciting for Zidane to lead Real Madrid.

(2) It was generous of Enrique to encourage his players in spite of their faults.

해설 (1) 지단이 레알 마드리드를 이끄는 것은 exciting하다는 의미가 되어야 하므로 가주어 It, 의미상 주어 for ~, 진주어 to부정사를 사용한다. **(2)** 엔리케 감독이 선수들의 실수에도 불구하고 관대하게 그들에게 용기를 주었다는 엔리케 감독의 성품을 나타내는 문장이다. 따라서 가주어 It, 의미상 주어 of ~, 진주어 to부정사를 사용해야 한다.

4 It was much cheaper for us to stay there.

해설 가주어 It, 의미상 주어 for us, 진주어 to stay

5 it is important for you to be on time

해설 가주어 It, 의미상 주어 for you, 진주어 to be

선생님, 헷갈려요! p. 022

1 (1) too, to (2) so, that, couldn't

2 (1) so that (2) in order to (또는 so as to)

Chapter 2
관계사

UNIT 03
관계대명사

PRACTICE p. 024

1 I have a cousin, who went to Japan to study.

2 I have a brother, who is a lawyer.

3 I will ask you a question, which is difficult to answer. (또는 I will ask a question of you, which is difficult to answer.)

4 What the thief found in the house was a small ring.

6 (1) Here is some water, which is very cold.

(2) I know the woman who(m) Jason danced with last Saturday. (또는 I know the woman, with whom Jason danced last Saturday.)

해설 (1) 관계대명사의 계속적 용법은 '접속사 + 대명사'를 관계대명사로 바꾸는 것이므로 and it을 which로 변환하고 앞에 콤마를 쓴다. **(2)** the woman과 her가 동일 인물이므로 목적격 관계대명사를 써야 한다. 따라서 and를 who(m)으로 바꾸고 her는 삭제한다.

7 What I want to eat for dinner is pasta.

8 What my father cooked for us yesterday

해설 what이 the thing that[which]의 의미이므로 something을 what으로 받아서 표현한다.

NOW REAL TEST 1 p. 025

1 what they

해설 선행사를 포함한 관계대명사 what은 the thing(s) that [which]의 의미이다.

2 what Becky told us is a lie (또는 what she told us is a lie)

해설 what은 선행사를 포함한 관계대명사이다.

3 (1) He said nothing, which made me angry.

(2) Simon hates hot weather, which makes him tired.

해설 관계대명사의 계속적 용법이므로 콤마를 사용해야 한다. **(1)** It을 앞 문장 전체 내용을 받는 관계대명사 which로 바꾼다. **(2)**에서는 선행사인 hot weather가 사물이므로 which를 사용한 것이다.

4 what I want to have

해설 '내가 가지기를 원하는 것(= the thing that I want to have)'이라는 의미이다.

5 (1) This is not what I really wanted.

(2) What Joy wants is freedom.

해설 (1) 선행사를 포함한 관계대명사 what **(2)** what Joy wants = the thing that Joy wants의 의미이며, what절은 문장에서 주어 역할을 한다.

NOW REAL TEST 2 p. 027

1 what makes my family worried

해설 My sister's sickness is the thing that makes my family worried.라는 문장을 만들 수 있고, 여기서 the thing that을 what으로 바꾸면 된다.

2 what is special about him is that he invented Hangeul

해설 선행사를 포함한 관계대명사 what과 명사절을 이끄는 접속사 that을 사용한다.

3 ②

해설 〈보기〉와 ②의 what은 관계대명사이고, ①, ③, ⑤의 what은 간접의문문의 의문사이며, ④의 what은 감탄문에 쓰인 의문사이다.

4 ④

해설 관계대명사 that은 콤마(,)와 함께 쓰는 계속적 용법으로 쓸 수 없다.

5 (1) What I want to do

(2) What I want to get

(3) What I want to eat

해설 각 문장에서 what이 이끄는 관계대명사절은 주어 역할을 하며, what은 the thing that[which]의 의미이다.

UNIT 04
관계부사

PRACTICE p. 029

1 Amy goes to the school where her father teaches.

2 Do you know the reason why Suji is angry?

3 Tell me the reason why she put the plants in front of the window.

4 He buys a lot of bread whenever he stops by the bakery. (또는 Whenever he stops by the bakery, he buys a lot of bread.)

NOW REAL TEST 1 p. 030

1 where they grew up had

해설 The house가 장소를 나타내는 선행사이므로 관계부사 where를 사용한다.

2 ④

해설 선행사가 각각 이유인 the reason과 장소인 the place이므로 관계부사 why와 where를 사용한다.

3 the reason why I am scolding you

해설 이유에 해당하는 선행사와 관계부사인 the reason why를 쓰고, 그 뒤에 '주어 + 동사'인 I am scolding you가 나온다.

4 (1) why (2) where (3) when (4) where

해설 **(1)** 이유의 관계부사 **(2)** 장소의 관계부사 **(3)** 시간의 관계부사 **(4)** 장소의 관계부사

5 ①

해설 관계부사를 쓰거나 '전치사 + 관계대명사'를 써야 하는데 ①에는 전치사 on이 없다.

6 No matter how busy you are

해설 however = no matter how (아무리 ~하더라도)

7 (1) whichever bike you choose

(2) No matter how well you drive

해설 **(1)** no matter which ~ = whichever ~ (어느 쪽의 ~이라도) **(2)** however + 부사 = no matter how + 부사 (아무리 ~할지라도)

NOW REAL TEST 2 p. 032

1 in where → where 또는 in which

해설 관계부사 앞에는 전치사가 올 수 없고, 관계부사 단독으로 쓰거나 '전치사 + 관계대명사'를 써야 한다.

2 ④

해설 첫 번째 문장에서는 선행사가 시간을 나타내는 the day이므로 on which 또는 when을 써야 한다. 두 번째 문장에서는 선행사가 장소를 나타내므로 at/in which 또는 where를 써야 한다.

3 (1) However (2) No matter how

해설 however + 형용사 = no matter how + 형용사 (아무리 ~할지라도)

4 (1) when, bought

(2) where, bought

(3) why, bought

해설 **(1)** 선행사가 the day이므로 시간을 나타내는 관계부사 when을 쓰고, 과거의 일이므로 bought를 쓴다. **(2)** 선행사가 the store이므로 장소를 나타내는 관계부사 where를 쓰고, 과거의 일이므로 bought를 쓴다. **(3)** 선행사가 the reason이므로 이유를 나타내는 관계부사 why를 쓰고, 과거의 일이므로 bought를 쓴다.

5 ⓐ where ⓑ reason ⓒ why ⓓ day ⓔ when

해설 ⓐ 내용상 영국 프리미어 리그를 훌륭한 축구 선수들을 만나는 장소로 표현했으므로 관계부사 where가 적절하다. ⓑ, ⓒ 영어를 열심히 공부해 온 이유를 말하고 있으므로 the reason why를 써야 한다. ⓓ, ⓔ 어제가 입단 테스트가 시작된 날이었다는 표현이므로 the day when이 적절하다.

6 the day when

해설 달력을 보면 내일이 방학이 시작되는 날이므로 '시간을 나타내는 선행사(the day) + 관계부사(when)'를 써야 한다.

선생님, 헷갈려요! p. 034

(1) why (2) for which (3) which, for (4) that
(5) that, for

Chapter 3
완료형, 수동태, 비교 구문

UNIT 05
완료형

PRACTICE p. 036

1 She has been teaching us music for three years.

2 The Bible has been giving people lessons for a long time. (또는 The Bible has been giving lessons to people for a long time.)

3 She has been listening to the song for 30 minutes.

4 When we got to the theater, the movie had already begun. (또는 The movie had already begun when we got to the theater.)

NOW REAL TEST 1 p. 037

1 has been playing, for

해설 과거부터 현재까지 계속 진행 중인 일이므로 현재완료 진행형을 쓴다.

2 When I stopped by her house, she had gone out. (또는 She had gone out when I stopped by her house.)

3 have been learning for a year

해설 1년 동안 배워 오고 있다는 의미가 되어야 하므로 현재완료 진행형을 쓴다.

4 (1) had left, got (2) bought, had eaten

해설 (1) 내가 역에 도착한 게 과거이고, 기차는 그것보다 먼저 출발했으므로 과거완료를 쓴다. (2) 사촌이 모든 햄버거를 다 먹은 것이 먼저 일어난 일이므로 과거완료를 써야 하고, 새로 햄버거를 산 것은 그 다음에 일어난 일이므로 과거이다.

5 When I got to school, the class had already started

해설 학교에 도착한 것이 과거이고, 수업은 그보다 먼저 시작한 것이므로 과거완료로 표현한다.

6 has been playing *Overwatch* for an hour (또는 has been playing a game for an hour)

7 ③

해설 가방을 잃어버린 것이 새 가방을 산 것보다 먼저 일어난 일이므로 과거완료(had lost)로 나타낸다.

8 your grandfather had bought before your father was born

해설 할아버지가 우표를 산 60년 전에 아버지는 태어나지 않았으므로 우표를 산 것이 먼저 일어난 일이다. 따라서 과거완료로 표현한다.

NOW REAL TEST 2 p. 039

1 My father has been washing his car since this morning.

해설 오늘 아침에 세차를 시작하여 아직도 하고 있으므로 현재완료 진행형을 쓴다.

2 (1) been watching (2) been shopping

해설 (1) 세 시간 동안 TV를 계속 보고 있으므로 현재완료 진행형을 쓴다. (2) 아침부터 쇼핑을 계속 하고 있는 중이므로 현재완료 진행형을 쓴다.

3 came home, had, eaten

해설 Henry가 집에 온 시각인 5시는 현재(6시)를 기준으로 과거이고, Jack이 그 전(4시)에 치킨을 먹었으므로 과거완료로 나타낸다.

4 (1) has been studying (2) will have finished

해설 (1) 1시부터 영어 공부인데 지금이 2시이므로 한 시간 동안 공부를 해 온 것이다. 따라서 현재완료 진행형이 적절하다. (2) 4시는 현재 시점에서 미래이고, 그때 영어 공부가 완료될 것이므로 미래완료를 써야 한다.

5 (1) will have climbed (2) will have come

UNIT 06
수동태, 비교 구문

PRACTICE p. 041

1 The shoes are called *jipsin*.

2 The bag may be thrown away by Mark.

3 The baby has been taken care of by Sylvia for a year.

4 The older we get, the wiser we become.

NOW REAL TEST 1 p. 042

1 The harder you study, the higher score you will get.

2 have been memorized by Sam since Monday (또는 have been memorized by Sam for five days)

3 How long has she been taught by Silvia?

해설 현재완료 수동태이다.

4 the more detailed

해설 '~하면 할수록 더 …한'이므로 「the + 비교급 ~, the + 비교급 …」을 사용한다.

5 *Bulgogi* has been loved by Koreans for a long time.

해설 현재완료의 수동태는 have/has been p.p.이다.

6 The more heavily it snows, the more snowmen (the) children make.

7 should be rolled like a wheel

해설 조동사의 수동태는 「조동사 + be p.p.」이므로 should be rolled가 되어야 한다.

8 has been written

해설 2시부터 지금까지 계속 곡이 쓰여져 오고 있었으므로 현재완료 수동태가 적합하다.

9 The higher we go up, the colder it becomes.

10 hasn't (= has not) been exposed to Korean culture before

해설 '경험'을 나타내는 현재완료의 수동태이며 부정형이므로 have/has not been p.p.가 된다.

NOW REAL TEST 2 p. 045

1 taller and taller

해설 비교급 + and + 비교급: 점점 더 ~한

2 More slowly you eat, healthier you will be. → The more slowly you eat, the healthier you will be.

해설 the + 비교급 ~, the + 비교급 …: ~하면 할수록 더 …한

3 have been collected by

해설 현재완료의 수동태인 have/has been p.p.를 사용한다.

4 should be kept very carefully in your house

해설 빈칸 뒤에 나오는 부가의문문 shouldn't it?으로 보아 조동사 should를 사용해야 하고, 조동사의 수동태는 「조동사 + be p.p.」이다.

선생님, 헷갈려요! p. 046

(1) is, worried about

(2) is known to

(3) was, disappointed at/with/about/by

해설 (3) 수동태의 부정은 be동사 뒤에 not을 쓴다.

Chapter 4
조동사, 간접의문문

UNIT 07
조동사

PRACTICE p. 048

1 She must have forgotten me.
2 He should have written his name in the visitors' book.
3 You shouldn't (= should not) have bought the concert ticket.
4 He used to travel with his friends in summer.

NOW REAL TEST 1 p. 049

1 (1) There used to be (2) must have given
해설 (1) 지금은 없고 과거에 있었으므로 「used to + 동사원형」이 와야 한다. (2) must have p.p.: ~했음이 틀림없다
2 ④
해설 부정이므로 You should not have believed her.가 되어야 한다.
3 should have gone to bed early
4 might have skipped
해설 Ted가 평소에는 아침을 많이 먹어서 에너지가 넘치는데, 오늘은 지쳐 보이는 것으로 보아 아침을 안 먹었을지도 모른다는 의미의 표현이 적절하다.
5 used to wear glasses before
해설 예전의 상태이므로 「used to + 동사원형」으로 표현한다.
6 should have thought
해설 Charles는 롤러코스터 때문에 심장 박동이 빨라진 것을 자기가 Jasmine을 좋아하는 것으로 착각해서 그녀에게 좋아한다고 말한 것을 후회하고 있다. 이런 상황에서 Charles에게 해 줄 수 있는 조언으로는 "너는 두 번 생각했어야 했는데."라는 의미가 적절하므로 should have p.p.를 사용한다.
7 shouldn't have left
해설 열쇠를 탁자 위에 올려 놓지 말았어야 했다는 과거에 대한 후회이므로 should not have p.p.를 쓴다.
8 (1) can't (= cannot) have made
(2) shouldn't (= should not) have bought
해설 (1) 그가 고의로 실수했을 리가 없다. (2) 그녀는 그렇게 비싼 가방을 사지 말았어야 했다.
9 used to have long hair
해설 엄마가 15년 동안 머리가 길었다가 어제 머리를 잘랐으므로, '(예전에) 머리가 길었다'는 표현의 used to have long hair가 적절하다.

NOW REAL TEST 2 p. 052

1 You should have seen it.
해설 영화가 환상적이었으므로 '네가 그것을 봤어야 했다.'라는 의미의 should have p.p.가 적절하다. You must have seen it.은 '너는 그것을 봤음이 틀림없어.'라는 의미이다.
2 There used to be a big well here
3 ③
해설 ③은 '~하는 데 익숙하다'라는 의미의 be used to -ing 표현이다. 나머지는 과거의 습관이나 상태를 나타내는 「used to + 동사원형」이다.
4 would rather not have[eat]
해설 '차라리 ~하지 않겠다'의 의미이므로 「would rather not + 동사원형」을 쓴다.
5 I shouldn't have asked him → I should have asked him
해설 형에게 물어보지 않고 싶었으므로, '물어봤어야 했는데'의 의미가 되어야 한다.

UNIT 08
간접의문문

PRACTICE p. 053

1 I wonder whether[if] a tiger is faster than a rabbit. (또는 I wonder whether[if] the tiger is faster than the rabbit.)
2 You should ask yourself what you really want.
3 They wondered how fast he drove the car.
4 Why do you think she was late for the conference yesterday?

NOW REAL TEST 1 p. 054

1 (1) where the zoo is
(2) how much time he has
해설 간접의문문이므로 「의문사 + 주어 + 동사」의 순서로 쓴다.
2 (1) what will you do
(2) what you will do
(3) 간접의문문이므로 「의문사 + 주어 + 동사」의 어순이 되어야 한다.
3 Tell me why you watched TV until late last night.
해설 Tell me가 문두에 있으므로 「의문사 + 주어 + 동사」의 간접의문문이 와야 한다.
4 I wonder how many kinds of paper flowers you can make with a piece of paper.
해설 I wonder 뒤에 간접의문문이 와야 하고, how many kinds of paper flowers가 한 덩어리로 묶여 의문사구의 역할을 한다.
5 how much they are
해설 간접의문문이므로 「의문사 + 주어 + 동사」의 순서로 쓴다.
6 she is good at playing tennis (또는 she is good at it)
해설 간접의문문이므로 「의문사 + 주어 + 동사」의 순서로 쓴다.
7 how much money we have
해설 how much money는 한 덩어리로 묶어 생각한다.
8 what her parents are like
해설 What are her parents like? (그녀의 부모님은 어떠시니?)를 간접의문문으로 만든 것이다.
9 where your new math teacher lives
10 ④
해설 think는 간접의문문을 만들 때 의문사를 문두로 보내야 하는 동사이다.

NOW REAL TEST 2 p. 057

1 if they bought it

해설 의문사가 없으므로 「if[whether] + 주어 + 동사」로 쓴다.

2 ③

해설 간접의문문은 「의문사 + 주어 + 동사」의 어순이므로 when we can start가 맞다.

3 if[whether] he has an extra book

4 One day, a farmer saw a big egg in the field. He wondered why the egg was in his field. He wanted to know who put the egg there. He asked his wife if she had put it there, but she said she hadn't done that. He asked his wife again, "Who do you think put it in my field?"

해설 He wondered 다음에 간접의문문이 오기 때문에 「의문사 + 주어 + 동사」의 어순이 되어야 한다. He asked 다음에 의문사 없는 간접의문문이 오므로 「if + 주어 + 동사」의 어순으로 쓴다. think가 주절의 동사일 때는 간접의문문의 의문사가 문장 맨 앞으로 나온다.

선생님, 헷갈려요! p. 058

1 You had better not water the cactus too often.

2 ④

해설 would는 과거의 상태를 나타낼 수 없으므로 used to가 되어야 한다.

Chapter 5
접속사

UNIT 09
접속사 that, 등위 접속사

PRACTICE p. 060

1 I think that the Internet speed in Korea is very fast.

2 The fire is so strong that it can burn (down) the whole building.

3 That he ate all of the ice cream is true. (또는 It is true that he ate all of the ice cream.)

4 Break your promises easily, and you will lose your friends.

NOW REAL TEST 1 p. 061

1 so, that

해설 so ~ that ...: 너무 ~해서 …하다

2 (1) Study English hard, or you will not be a global leader.

(2) Forgive others, and you will be forgiven someday.

해설 (1) 명령문, or ~: …해라, 그렇지 않으면 ~할 것이다 **(2)** 명령문, and ~: …해라, 그러면 ~할 것이다

3 more machines so that it would produce more products

해설 so that + 주어 + 동사: ~하기 위해

4 or more trees will be cut down

해설 명령문, or ~: …해라, 그렇지 않으면 ~할 것이다 (종이를 낭비하지 마라, 그렇지 않으면 더 많은 나무들이 베일 것이다.)

5 He took the subway so that he wouldn't be late.

해설 so that + 주어 + 동사: ~하기 위해

6 The table was so messy that she decided to clean it up first.

7 learn sign language so that he can communicate

해설 '~하기 위해'라는 의미의 so that 뒤에는 '주어 + 동사'가 와야 한다.

8 so that you (can) understand him better

해설 so that + 주어 + 동사: ~하기 위해 (네가 그를 더 잘 이해하기 위해서 그의 말에 귀를 기울이는 게 좋아.)

9 (1) Work hard, and you will succeed in the future.

(2) Work hard, or you won't (= will not) succeed in the future.

10 make any noise, or

해설 명령문, or ~: …해라, 그렇지 않으면 ~할 것이다 (시끄럽게 하지 마, 그렇지 않으면 잠자는 아기를 깨울 거야.)

NOW REAL TEST 2 p. 064

1 ②

해설 주어 역할을 하는 명사절을 이끄는 접속사 that

2 ⑤

해설 so that + 주어 + 동사: ~하기 위해 / that: 목적어 역할을 하는 명사절을 이끄는 접속사 / 명령문, and ~: …해라, 그러면 ~할 것이다

3 (1) Don't stop donating, or many poor children won't be able to go to school.

(2) Don't leave this city, or you will regret it.

4 ③

해설 ③의 that은 지시형용사이고, 나머지는 명사절을 이끄는 접속사이다.

5 so that they

UNIT 10
부사절을 이끄는 접속사

PRACTICE p. 066

1 Because this T-shirt is too big, I want to exchange it. (또는 I want to exchange this T-shirt because it is too big.)

2 Although Maggie is blind, she can feel his love. (또는 Maggie can feel his love although she is blind.)

3 I will borrow the book after he finishes reading it. (또는 After he finishes reading the book, I will borrow it.)

4 Many people like Siyeong since she is very kind. (또는 Since Siyeong is very kind, many people like her.)

NOW REAL TEST 1 p. 067

1 Though[Although / Even though] their house was old and small, they were happy there. (또는 They were happy there though[although / even though] their house was old and small.)

2 Even though[if], is, can't decide

3 Though[Although] there were many good books in my uncle's house

4 Because[Since / As] he didn't get enough sleep last night, he needs to take a nap now. (또는 He needs to take a nap now because[since / as] he didn't get enough sleep last night.)

5 ③, ⑤

해설 내용상 최선을 다하지 않았기 때문에 결과를 걱정하는 것이 자연스러우므로 '이유'를 나타내는 접속사가 들어가야 한다.

6 (1) like Jinyeong's acting in the drama though [although / even though] he is a rookie

(2) thinks badly of him because[since / as] he helps many poor people

7 though (또는 although)

8 Since they were forced to use a foreign language at that time

9 As soon as the girls saw the singer, they burst into tears. (또는 The girls burst into tears as soon as they saw the singer.)

10 (1) Although Ken had dinner, he is still hungry.

(2) Although Jane is disappointed, she is smiling.

NOW REAL TEST 2 p. 070

1 Though (또는 Although)

2 ②

해설 ⓐ '가까이 볼 때' ⓑ '무명의 화가에 의해 그려졌음에도 불구하고'

3 ②

해설 ②는 '~하는 반면에'의 의미이고, 나머지는 '~하는 동안에'의 의미이다.

4 ①

해설 ①은 '~ 이후로'라는 의미의 전치사이고, 나머지는 '~하기 때문에'라는 의미의 접속사이다.

5 ③

해설 ⓐ는 양보의 의미가 되어야 하므로 as 대신 though나 although가 적절하다. ⓓ는 '~하기 때문에'라는 의미가 되어야 하므로 as soon as 대신 because, since, as 등이 적절하다.

선생님, 헷갈려요! p. 072

1 (1) Because[Since / As] she was sick

(2) Because of, sickness

2 (1) Although he failed, he never gave up.

(2) Despite his failure[failing], he never gave up.

Chapter 6
분사구문

UNIT 11
분사구문의 의미

PRACTICE p. 074

1 Getting up late, I couldn't take the school bus.

2 Crying sadly, Susan was singing a song.

3 Carrying balloons, Jinhun played with a ball.

4 Being very young, he can't take the subway by himself.

NOW REAL TEST 1 p. 075

1 Wearing

해설 Because[Since / As] she was wearing의 의미이다.

2 Not being rich

해설 분사구문의 부정은 Not + -ing를 쓰면 된다. (그는 부자가 아니었기 때문에 소박한 삶을 살았다.)

3 (1) Having (2) Because[Since / As] I was

4 ③

해설 접속사와 주어를 없애고 동사를 -ing로 바꾸는 분사구문을 만든다. (길을 잃었기 때문에 Robert는 전화로 지도를 보았다.)

5 Listening to, is reading

6 Having a lot of knowledge, she could win the quiz contest.

해설 Because [Since / As] + 주어 + 동사 → -ing로 변환

7 (1) Not being hungry, he skipped his meal.

(2) Doing his homework, he usually sits on the sofa.

8 ⑤

해설 그는 돈이 하나도 없어서: As he didn't have any money → Not having any money

9 Working together on the farm

10 ⓐ Having sad → Being sad

ⓑ If → Though[Although / Even though]

ⓒ we → they

해설 ⓐ 동사가 was이므로 분사구문으로 만들 때 being이 되어야 한다. ⓑ 내용상 '바닷가에 사는데도 불구하고'라는 양보의 의미가 적절하다. ⓒ 분사구문의 주어는 주절의 주어와 동일하므로 we가 아니라 they가 되어야 한다.

NOW REAL TEST 2 p. 078

1 Being stuck in a bad traffic jam

2 (1) Hearing the news
(2) Finishing washing the dishes

3 (1) Studying for an exam
(2) Because[Since / As] he doesn't exercise at all

4 (1) Thinking about his mistake
(2) Not knowing how to operate the washing machine
(3) Taking pictures at the zoo

UNIT 12
주의해야 할 분사구문

PRACTICE p. 079

1 She cleaned the house with the windows closed.
2 Lie down with your legs lifted.
3 Having lost his memory, he doesn't even remember his name.
4 Judging from your voice, you are nervous now.

NOW REAL TEST 1 p. 080

1 Frankly speaking, what, mean
해설 '솔직히 말하면'은 Frankly speaking이다. / 선행사를 포함하는 관계대명사 what을 사용한다.

2 My (younger) brother came home with his hair cut.

3 (1) (being) broken (또는 having been broken)
(2) Having finished (doing) your homework
해설 **(1)** 주절과 종속절의 주어가 다르므로 주어 The window를 앞에 써 주었고, Because[Since / As] the window was[had been] broken을 수동 분사구문으로 변경한다. **(2)** Because[Since / As] you finished (doing) your homework를 분사구문으로 바꾼 문장이다.

4 His computer having been fixed
해설 주절과 부사절의 주어가 서로 다르므로 부사절의 주어를 분사구문 앞에 써야 하고, 부사절의 시제가 더 앞서 있고 수동태이므로 완료 수동형 분사구문인 having been p.p.가 와야 한다.

5 with his boots covered with mud

6 Strictly speaking, your report should be revised more.

7 Written in easy Chinese, the book is easy to read.
해설 책이 중국어로 쓰여진 것이므로 수동의 의미를 갖는 p.p.를 사용한다.

8 Sarah was standing with her arms folded.
해설 '팔이 접혀 있는'이라는 수동의 의미이므로 p.p.를 사용해야 한다. (with her arms folded는 '팔짱을 끼고 있는'이라는 뜻이다.)

9 calling her friend with the door closed
해설 문이 닫혀진 것이므로 수동의 의미를 갖는 p.p.를 사용한다.

10 with your seatbelt fastened

NOW REAL TEST 2 p. 083

1 Having failed the bar exam several times
해설 부사절의 시제가 주절보다 앞서므로 having p.p.를 써야 한다.

2 Having been there many times before

3 ⑤
해설 '그의 제복으로 판단해 볼 때'

4 ③
해설 수동형 분사구문 Having been p.p.에서 Having been은 생략 가능하다.

5 Ms. Page having given us a lot of homework
해설 주절과 부사절의 주어가 다르므로 부사절의 주어를 분사구문 앞에 써 주어야 하고, 부사절의 시제가 주절보다 앞서므로 having p.p.를 써야 한다.

선생님, 헷갈려요! p. 084

1 (1) what to buy (2) what he should buy
2 (1) where to wait (2) where they should wait

Chapter 7
가정법

UNIT 13
가정법 과거

PRACTICE p. 086

1 If he knew how to play the piano, he would play for her. (또는 He would play for her if he knew how to play the piano.)

2 If I were taller, I would join the volleyball team. (또는 I would join the volleyball team if I were taller.)

3 If I were Iron Man, I would defeat bad guys. (또는 I would defeat bad guys if I were Iron Man.)

4 I wish (that) I knew the answers on the upcoming exam.

NOW REAL TEST 1 p. 087

1 I wish (that) I had some siblings.
해설 I wish 가정법 과거(I wish + 주어 + 동사의 과거형)는 '유감'을 나타낸다. 부정문의 any는 긍정문에서 some으로 바뀐다.

2 were you, I would let her wear your hat

3 as if he were a millionaire

해설 as if 가정법 과거(as if + 주어 + 동사의 과거형)는 '마치 ~인 것처럼'의 의미이다.

4 (1) I were a good cook, I could make delicious food for you

(2) wish (that) I could drive fast

5 (1) had some money, could

(2) were careful, would not, fall

해설 (2) 현재 사실의 반대이므로 가정법 과거이고, 이 경우 be동사는 were만 사용한다.

6 (1) I wish I could speak French well.

(2) If he weren't (= were not) sick, he could play soccer today.

7 If I were a doctor, I would[could] cure poor people.

8 saw SHINee in the street, we would ask them to take a picture with us

9 ⓐ would waste ⓑ had ⓒ won ⓓ wouldn't (= would not) buy

해설 가정법 과거의 형태는 「If + 주어 + 동사의 과거형 ~, 주어 + 조동사의 과거형 + 동사원형 …」이다.

10 (1) would reduce prices

(2) would cancel all exams

NOW REAL TEST 2 p. 090

1 ③

해설 가정법 과거이므로 If절의 be동사는 주어에 관계 없이 were를 사용한다.

2 ④

해설 「as if + 주어 + 동사의 과거형(마치 ~인 것처럼)」에서도 be동사는 were를 사용한다.

3 (1) Without (2) But for (3) If it were not for

4 (1) weren't, would[could]

(2) didn't have, would[could]

UNIT 14
가정법 과거완료

PRACTICE p. 091

1 I wish (that) she had bought a ticket for BTS's concert.

2 If I had remembered her name, she wouldn't have been disappointed. (또는 She wouldn't have been disappointed if I had remembered her name.)

3 She talks as if she had spoken with Eric in person.

4 If he hadn't (= had not) had a hard time, he couldn't have succeeded. (또는 He couldn't have succeeded if he hadn't (= had not) had a hard time.)

NOW REAL TEST 1 p. 092

1 had exercised, could have lost

해설 과거 사실에 대한 반대이므로 가정법 과거완료로 나타낸다.

2 had had a car, we could have driven to the beach

3 (1) as if, had known

(2) had found

4 If I had been Steve, I couldn't have solved the problem.

해설 과거 사실에 대한 반대이므로 가정법 과거완료로 나타낸다.

5 (1) I had known his email address, I could have sent him an email

(2) it hadn't (= had not) been windy enough, they couldn't have flown the kites in the park

해설 과거 사실에 대한 반대이므로 가정법 과거완료로 나타낸다.

6 ⓐ hadn't (= had not) lent

ⓑ couldn't (= could not) have bought

7 had studied (English), would have got(ten)

8 If Lincoln had given up after losing elections, he wouldn't have won the election in 1860.

9 hadn't (= had not) thought differently, I couldn't (= could not) have invented useful products (또는 I wouldn't (= would not) have invented useful products)

NOW REAL TEST 2 p. 095

1 ⑤

해설 가정법 과거완료 표현

2 ⑤

해설 ①~④는 '~이 없었다면'이라는 동일한 의미의 표현이다. ⑤는 '~이 없다면'이라는 의미의 가정법 과거 표현이므로 주절과 시제가 맞지 않는다.

3 ④

해설 가정법 과거완료 표현

4 (1) I had worked harder

(2) I had been friendlier to others

선생님, 헷갈려요! p. 096

(1) help (2) to give (3) delayed (4) sent
(5) (to) carry

Chapter 8
화법과 일치

UNIT 15
화법(1)

PRACTICE p. 098

1 Mr. Kim said (that) he didn't want to give me[us] a lot of homework.

2 She told him (that) he looked pale that day.

3 The doctor asked me if[whether] I was feeling sick then.

4 Tommy asked me what I liked to do on weekends.

NOW REAL TEST 1 p. 099

1 told, I had to, my, that night

2 he could help her make a choice

3 if[whether] she (had) sent him an email the previous week

4 ②, ④
해설 의문사 없는 의문문의 간접화법에는 if나 whether를 사용한다.

5 where he could buy fruit

6 ③
해설 주절의 시제가 현재이므로 그대로 현재로 쓴다.

7 ④
해설 의문사가 있는 의문문의 간접화법이므로 간접의문문(의문사 + 주어 + 동사)을 사용해야 하며, 주절과 같은 과거형으로 써야 한다.

8 (1) told her (that) she was afraid of speaking in public
(2) said to him, I want to speak clearly in public

9 ②, ③, ⑤
해설 ② have → had ③ are → were ⑤ was the museum → the museum was

10 (1) why he had waited for her for 90 days
(2) if[whether] he could wait for ten more days
해설 **(1)** 주절의 시제가 과거이므로 현재완료를 과거완료로 바꾼다. **(2)** 의문사가 없는 의문문이므로 if나 whether를 사용한다.

NOW REAL TEST 2 p. 102

1 where he wanted to go then

2 ②
해설 간접화법으로 전환 시 평서문은 that을 사용하고, 의문사 없는 의문문은 if나 whether를 사용한다.

3 (1) I said to my dad, "Can I go abroad to study more?"
(2) My aunt asked me where I had bought that shampoo.

4 (1) why she was late for school so often
(2) if[whether] she wanted him to give her a wakeup call every morning

UNIT 16
화법(2), 일치

PRACTICE p. 103

1 He told me to do my best.

2 The teacher ordered us not to make any noise.

3 Every worker wants to eat pork for lunch.
해설 every + 단수명사 + 단수동사

4 The number of the tigers is thirty.
해설 the number of ~ 뒤에는 단수동사가 온다.

NOW REAL TEST 1 p. 104

1 to be happy forever from then on
해설 명령문의 간접화법이므로 to부정사로 바꾼다.

2 not to take pictures there
해설 명령문의 간접화법은 to부정사를 쓴다. 부정형은 'not + to부정사'이다.

3 ②
해설 the poor = poor people이므로 복수 취급한다. (is → are)

4 ③
해설 a number of ~ 뒤에는 복수동사, the number of ~ 뒤에는 단수동사가 온다. deer는 단수형과 복수형이 동일하다.

5 have increased → has increased
해설 the number of ~ 뒤에는 단수동사가 온다.

6 ④
해설 명령문의 간접화법 전환 시에는 to부정사를 사용한다.

7 He told[advised] me not to eat too much for dinner.

8 ③
해설 'every + 단수명사'이므로 people wait은 person waits가 되어야 한다.

9 One of the most popular singers in Korea are Gummy. → One of the most popular singers in Korea is Gummy. / A number of my friends at school thinks → A number of my friends at school think / Every students in my class → Every student in my class
해설 one of + 복수명사 + 단수동사 / a number of ~가 주어이므로 복수동사 / every + 단수명사 + 단수동사

10 ⓐ Mathematics is ⓑ were going to
ⓒ is not enough
해설 ⓐ -s로 끝나는 과목명은 단수 취급한다. ⓑ 주절의 동사(said)가 과거이므로 종속절의 동사(are)도 과거가 되어야 한다. ⓒ '이틀'이라는 시간을 하나의 단위로 보아 단수 취급한다.

NOW REAL TEST 2 p. 107

1 (1) Tommy told his sister not to use his computer.
(2) Mrs. Jin told her husband to turn on the TV.

2 (1) The children asked the old man to give them some chocolate.
(2) He said to her, "Don't give my son anything."

3 The number of children is 30.
해설 the number of ~(~의 수)는 단수 취급한다.

4 (1) I told my brother that the capital of Canada is Ottawa.
(2) I believed that Jessie had already finished her homework.
해설 (1) 불변의 진리이므로 현재형을 쓴다. **(2)** 주절보다 먼저 일어난 일이므로 had p.p.를 쓴다. (주절이 과거이면 that절에 현재완료를 쓸 수 없다.)

선생님, 헷갈려요! p. 108
1 (1) said, he is (2) said to be
2 (1) said, he was (2) said to have been

Chapter 9
강조, 도치, 동격

UNIT 17
강조

PRACTICE p. 110

1 I did hear many students talk[talking] loudly on the bus.
2 I did make her a sandwich yesterday. (또는 I did make a sandwich for her yesterday.)
3 It was bread that she ate for breakfast today.
4 It was last night that the accident happened in front of the building.

NOW REAL TEST 1 p. 111

1 was the bathroom that Sally cleaned yesterday
2 It was yesterday that Alice made a strong mailbox.
3 It was the hunter that[who] showed us a rabbit.
4 It is his cell phone[smartphone] that he is looking for.
5 It was yesterday that I visited my uncle.
6 (1) It was Emily that[who] bought some food at AW Market this afternoon.
(2) It was this afternoon that Emily bought some food at AW Market.
해설 (1) 누가 샀는지 물었으므로 주어인 Emily를 강조한다. **(2)** 언제인지 물었으므로 때를 나타내는 부사구인 this afternoon을 강조한다.
7 (가) It was Ms. Jin that[who] paid for the new glasses.
(나) did
8 (1) was Jackson that[who] broke the window yesterday
(2) was at a department store that she bought this computer
9 is Daejeon that
10 I did send you a pretty bag.
해설 '보냈다'를 강조하기 위해 did send를 쓴다.

NOW REAL TEST 2 p. 114

1 (1) does take (2) did call
2 That was spaghetti that I ate for lunch yesterday.
→ It was spaghetti that I ate for lunch yesterday.
해설 강조하고자 하는 것이 스파게티이므로 It ~ that 강조 구문을 사용한다.
3 was Steve, stole the car
4 (1) that[who] sent me the gift box
(2) a watch that was
(3) in my house that

UNIT 18
도치와 동격

PRACTICE p. 115

1 are standing many people
2 was she at home when I visited her
3 does he play computer games
4 comes the school bus

NOW REAL TEST 1 p. 116

1 ④
해설 the fact와 동격인 절을 이끄는 that이 쓰여야 한다.
2 the hill stands a castle
3 (1) the idea of
(2) that, made me
4 ②
해설 be동사와 일반동사의 도치
5 ④
해설 부정어구 + did + 주어 + 동사원형
6 ④
해설 ④의 that은 관계대명사이고, 나머지는 동격의 that이다.
7 they seen such a dirty restaurant
해설 부정어구 현재완료 도치: 부정어구 + have/has + 주어 + p.p.

8 (1) did she know that Jake didn't like her
(2) does my pet cat go out without me

9 ①, ②, ③
해설 조동사의 도치: 부정어구 + 조동사 + 주어 + 동사원형

10 (1) that (2) has she tried
해설 **(1)** 동격의 that **(2)** 부정어구 현재완료의 도치: 부정어구 + have/has + 주어 + p.p.

NOW REAL TEST 2 p. 119

1 (1) stands an old tree
(2) came the rain
(3) does my boss sit down when he is working

2 (1) comes a big bus
(2) she comes finally
해설 **(2)** 주어가 대명사일 경우에는 도치가 일어나지 않는다.

3 ③
해설 〈보기〉와 ③은 동격의 that이고, ①은 명사절을 이끄는 접속사 that, ②는 It ~ that 강조 구문, ④는 지시대명사(저것), ⑤는 주격 관계대명사이다.

선생님, 헷갈려요! p. 120

1 Not all basketball players are
2 gave, did, stop

memo

memo

memo

쓰담쓰담
내신영문법 3